IRELAND BEFORE THE FAMINE

1798–1848

GEARÓID Ó TUATHAIGH

Gill & Macmillan

Gill & Macmillan Ltd
Hume Avenue, Park West, Dublin 12
with associated companies throughout the world
www.gillmacmillan.ie
© Gearóid Ó Tuathaigh 1972, 1990, 2007
978 07171 4217 0
Typography design by Make Communication
Print origination by TypeIT, Dublin
Printed in Malaysia

This book is typeset in 11 on 13.5 pt Minion.

The paper used in this book comes from the wood pulp of
managed forests. For every tree felled, at least one tree is
planted, thereby renewing natural resources.

A CIP catalogue record for this book is available from the
British Library.

5 4 3

IRELAND BEFORE THE FAMINE

1798–1848

Do
Síle Ní Chinnéide,
ollamh, múinteoir, agus cara

CONTENTS

PREFACE TO THE FIRST EDITION

I have been helped by many people in writing this book, and wish to express my gratitude. Firstly I would like to record my deep sense of obligation to those who have helped me involuntarily — namely, the authors of the many excellent contributions to modern Irish history whose work I have consulted in preparing this volume. I have indicated in my bibliography those to whom I owe a special debt. Most of the credit for whatever merit this volume possesses is due to the researches of these writers.

To my general editor, Dr M. MacCurtain O.P., I express my gratitude for her helpful suggestions, her unfailing kindness, and her limitless patience.

Mr Pádraig de Brún drew my attention to some useful material in Irish. The English translations of Irish material quoted in the text are my own.

I have profited from conversations with Mr Joseph Lee on various aspects of Irish history.

To Mr Seán Ó Briain my thanks for compiling the Index.

My greatest debt is expressed in the Dedication.

I need hardly add that I alone am responsible for any errors of fact or heresies in interpretation that may remain.

Finally, I would like to thank the Master and Fellows of Peterhouse, Cambridge, for financing my stay in surroundings which encourage the writing of history.

Gearóid Ó Tuathaigh

01 REFORM, REBELLION AND UNION

THE SOCIAL CONTEXT

'The Irish', Frank O'Connor once remarked, 'are like Orpheus, forever looking back at the Eurydice they are attempting to bring home from the Shades.' Certainly throughout the first half of the nineteenth century there was scarcely a section of Irish society which did not, at one time or other, cast a nostalgic look over its shoulder at some cherished image of a happier past. As successive waves of O'Connellite agitations swept the countryside in the second quarter of the century, many of the gentry sighed for the departed days when life was calm and the peasantry knew their place; before the insolent Dan had begun to excite them. On the other hand, as the hard times of the pre-famine era filled their cup of misery, many of the peasantry sought refuge in an idealised conception of a vanished age, in which they were not the dispossessed; an age free from the burdens of tithes, taxes or rents. In 1834 Inglis noted among the poorer peasants '. . . a hankering after what they deem their rightful possessions; and an indistinct notion that, one day or other, they will have their rights.'

As economic and social problems multiplied in the pre-famine decades it became a theme of Repeal propagandists to contrast the current economic crises with the halcyon days of the late eighteenth century. For Repealers the year of the Union became the *annus horribilis* in the fortunes of the Irish people, and they drew the appropriate conclusions. Those who dwelt on the contrasts between the acute problems of Irish society in the pre-famine decades and the relative prosperity of the late eighteenth century did appear to have, *prima facie*, a good case. Certainly the second half of the eighteenth century may fairly be described as an expanding era for Ireland. Throughout the period there was a continuing increase (allowing for short-term slumps) in output from both industry and agriculture. Population expansion in Britain, as well as at home, made for an expanding market for both foodstuffs and manufactured goods, and trade (overseas and internal) enjoyed a lengthy period of buoyancy. From the mid-century a steady rise in agricultural prices encouraged increased production, and in the closing decades of the century the rapid expansion of tillage was reflected in a sharp rise in grain exports. In 1778 the total value of grain, flour and oatmeal exports to Britain was put at £72,211; by 1798 the total value of such exports to England alone was some £291,010. Pork exports also increased. Butter and beef exports remained high throughout the period, though by the close of the century salt beef exports were beginning to decline in response to changes in the market.

A significant feature of this economic expansion was the fact that in almost every area of increased production the British market became the dominant focus for the Irish export effort. For example, in 1720 exports to Britain accounted for some 44.4 per cent of all Irish exports, but by 1800 this figure had jumped to 85.4 per cent. These changes in the structure of Irish overseas trade were in response to the market situation. As the eighteenth century progressed, it gradually became apparent that British agricultural produce alone would be insufficient to meet the rising demand for food from an ever-expanding population. During 1758–9 Britain suspended her Cattle Acts against Irish imports, thus allowing entry to the British market to Irish cattle, beef, butter and pork. This gave Irish exporters access to a convenient and expanding market, and rendered the effort to vault continental tariff barriers unattractive and ultimately unnecessary. Britain thus became the main customer for all Irish agricultural exports.

Industrial activity also expanded during this period. Here the staple was linen. The eclipse of the Irish woollen industry in the early eighteenth century had been accompanied by a corresponding expansion in linen production. Irish linens enjoyed a duty-free access to the British market and accordingly they shared the expanding market with British domestic linens. In 1720 Irish linen exports amounted to 2,637,984 yards, by the mid-century the figure was 11,200,460 yards, and in 1790 it had reached 37,322,126 yards. The advent of cotton caused a temporary contraction in the linen industry in the early decades of the nineteenth century, yet it is important to realize how crucial the industry was in the pre-Union decades; in 1788 linen accounted for over 70 per cent of all Irish exports, and even as late as 1798 it still accounted for some 582 per cent of all exports. The industry was mainly centred on the north-east. The relatively backward state of small-farming in Ulster had, it seems, contributed to the industry's growth in that area, since small-farmers were willing to undertake part-time spinning and weaving in order to supplement inadequate farm income. However, there was also widespread spinning of coarse and fine yarn not only throughout the rest of Ulster but also in north Leinster and over wide areas of Connaught. Dublin drapers and merchants provided much of the early credit for the expansion of the industry and for most of the eighteenth century Dublin was the port through which shippers and drapers exported their linens. However, by the end of the century an increasing number of Northern bleachers had begun to by-pass Dublin and to deal directly with buyers in Britain.

There was also industrial activity in areas other than linen. Woollen textile production was substantially for home consumption. In the last quarter of the century both glass-manufacture and brewing experienced changes in organisation and production, leading to improved compatibility in both cases. Other industries, though heavily dependent on imported raw materials — sugar refining in the port towns, silk in Dublin — were able, with the help of protective tariffs in the last decades of the century, to maintain considerable activity until the early post-Union decades. The basic raw material for much of this industrial activity — coal — had to be imported; imports of coal from Britain increased from about 150,000 tons in 1760 to about 400,000 tons in 1800.

The effects of this expansion in trade were apparent in the appearance of the countryside and of the towns. The remaining tracts of open land were gradually closed, divided, and bounded by hedges, ditches or stone walls. Increasing tillage brought a considerable amount of virgin soil into cultivation. The complex network of fairs and markets was linked by an ever-improving road system. Along many of the rivers flour-mills and distilleries provided further evidence of the expansion in trade.

The signs of expansion were no less evident in the towns. Many of the inland towns prospered from the expansion in markets and fairs, and as trade expanded the increasing use of money was a stimulus to the activities of traders. Cork was the centre of the provision export trade for the south and much of the west, and in the 1770s Arthur Young described it as 'the busiest, most animated scene of shipping in all Ireland.' Towards the end of the century Belfast began a long period of expansion, resulting from the growing industrial activity in the north-east. But it was Dublin, the confident capital, which constituted the most outstanding monument to the age of expansion. Already by 1750 its population was about 130,000 and by the end of the century this had increased by a further fifty per cent. Dublin was the hub of the Irish universe, the port which handled the greatest volume of trade, the site for a wide spectrum of industries, the centre of a complex system of credit and exchange. It was also the seat of Parliament. In the closing decades of the century an ambitious surge in public and private building made Dublin one of the most impressive capitals in Europe. Sackville Street was joined by the Carlisle Bridge with the elegant streets linking Parliament House, Trinity College and St Stephen's Green. Further east, stately Georgian residences for the gentry were under construction. The confident surge of commercial activity was symbolised by Gandon's masterpiece, the Customs House, proudly surveying a bustling port.

Yet there was another side to these latter decades, and as the century reached its close the storm-clouds of distress were already casting a lengthening shadow over sections of Irish society. From the 1780s tariffs and bounties gave many Irish industries a warm coat of protection against the icy winds of competition, enabling some of them to survive, largely on domestic markets, without having to seek either new techniques of production or increased efficiency in existing methods. The progress of the industrial revolution in Britain was soon to change these conditions drastically.

However, the factor which gave greatest cause for concern was the rapid rise in population from the mid-century. From about 2.5 million in 1767 the population of Ireland had risen to over 4 million by 1781, and twenty years later it was close on 5 million. Demographers are still not agreed on the *primum mobile* of this rapid acceleration in growth. A falling death-rate (resulting from improvements in the quantity, quality, and distribution of food supplies from the 1740s); a rising birth-rate (caused by earlier and more frequent marriages, and by higher fertility resulting from diet improvements); the gradual exhaustion of some of the killer diseases — each of these explanations (or various combinations of them) has found supporters. Furthermore, common to many advocates both of the falling death-rate and of the rising birth-rate theories, is the view that Irish population growth was in some unique way a consequence of the increased cultivation of the potato crop. The high nutritional content of the root is seen on the one hand as a key factor in reducing mortality, while on the other hand, as a crop capable of supporting a family on a tiny holding, the potato is cited as a crucial factor in encouraging earlier marriages and hence a rising birth rate. However, rapid population increase was a phenomenon throughout much of Europe in the second half of the eighteenth century; in England the population rose by 50 per cent between 1750 and 1800 and in Finland by 100 per cent in the same period. This suggests that perhaps the root causes of the accelerated population growth are to be found in factors common to all of these countries. At any rate we are not called upon to give judgement here. What is incontestable is that the population did increase dramatically from the 1750s. And what is equally certain is that as Dr Cullen has put it, '. . . as population continued to grow in the late eighteenth and early nineteenth centuries, the proportion of the population relying on a potato diet increased.'

The effects of these developments on the condition and structure of rural society were profound. Throughout the century the tenant-farmer had been the backbone of the rural community. However, increased potato cultivation caused a rapid increase in subdivision, particularly on poorer land, leading to an accelerating increase in the numbers of cottiers and labourers. During the closing quarter of the century the disproportionate growth of the cottier relative to the tenant-farmer element was already causing a growing imbalance within the agricultural community. While prices continued to rise this trend was not, in some respects, unwelcome to many landlords and farmers. Increased output required an expanding labour force; and the sharp competition among the growing cottier and labourer classes for minute holdings virtually ensured that most of the profits of this increased output would be absorbed by rising rents. But the social consequences of this imbalance were alarming. As the century reached its close a condition of continuous and deep poverty was becoming more widespread among an ever-increasing section of the rural community.

A further alarming consequence of the desperate competition for land which accompanied population increase in the late eighteenth century was the spread of outbreaks of agrarian violence throughout parts of the countryside. Already in the 1760s secret societies like the Whiteboys in Munster and the Hearts of Oak and Hearts of Steel in the North, were active in seeking summary redress for a wide spectrum of grievances — enclosure of commonages, rent increases, tithes and the unreasonable demands of some priests for excessive dues. In the North, however, the agrarian violence soon settled in a sectarian mould, especially in the border counties where Catholics and Protestants were most evenly balanced in numbers. Catholic tenants, desperate to regain some hold on the lands which had been confiscated from their forefathers, were generally prepared to offer higher rents and accept lower living-standards than Protestant tenants, whose tradition encompassed a different concept of landlord-tenant relations. During the 1770s groups of Protestant 'Peep o' Day Boys' and Catholic 'Defenders' engaged in intermittent rural warfare in a series of attacks and reprisals. Armagh was the seat of particularly bitter sectarian feeling. Clashes between large forces of these societies became common, and it was after one such 'battle' in Co. Armagh in September 1795 that the victorious Protestants founded a society destined to play a significant role in the subsequent history of Ireland — the Orange Society. By this time, however, the role of these sectarian societies was undergoing important changes; from a relatively straightforward conflict of interest between competing economic groups, the function which the societies fulfilled was beginning to assume wider political dimensions. The original oath of the Orange Order illustrates this change very clearly; it declared:

> I, do solemnly swear that I will, to the utmost of my power, support and defend the king and his heirs as long as he or they support the protestant ascendancy.

Clearly this gradual sharpening of sectarian hostility in the late eighteenth century was part of the course of events occurring in the wider context of political life during this period.

THE COLONIAL PARLIAMENT
Inspired by the American revolution of 1776, the 'patriot' element in the Irish colonial Parliament had demanded an end to the direct control which the Westminster Parliament exercised over Irish legislation. The patriots were backed by a 40,000 strong Volunteer force, and in 1782 the British Government gave way to their demands. But the offspring of the 1782 settlement, Grattan's Parliament, though in form an independent legislature sharing a

common monarch with its British counterpart, was in reality considerably less 'free' in its activities. The Irish Executive was not answerable to the Irish Parliament; its members were appointed by, and answerable to, the British Ministry of the day. In ensuring majority support in the Irish Parliament, the Irish Executive relied on the power and patronage controlled by a clique of pro-Government office-holders, among whom John Fitzgibbon, the Lord Chancellor, and the Beresford family were most prominent. Likewise, the Opposition group in the Irish Parliament gradually moved into alignment with the Whig opposition in the British Parliament. In short, the political cleavages in the 'independent' Irish Parliament mirrored the cleavages among parliamentary groups in Britain with remarkable fidelity.

Along with its deceptive 'independence', Grattan's Parliament was distinguished by its unrepresentative and corrupt nature. It was an entirely Protestant Parliament; Catholics, who comprised over two-thirds of the population, formed no part of the elected or the electorate. Nor indeed was it more than marginally representative of Irish Protestant opinion. Over two-thirds of the 300 MPs sat for 'borough' constituencies, many of which had few or no electors and were simply seats in the gift of a patron. Seats were frequently bought and sold, and the Government's own supply of patronage was bloated with sinecures and pensions.

Not surprisingly, this corrupt apparatus came in for heavy criticism. But there were strong differences of opinion among would-be reformers. Some would have been satisfied with a mere 'purification' of Parliament, i.e. a pruning of sinecures and pension-lists. Others demanded fundamental reforms in the entire electoral system. Opinions were sharply divided on the question of whether or not Catholics should be included in any proposed reform. Only the more advanced radicals of Ulster and Dublin (where James Napper Tandy, the son of an ironmonger, came to prominence) were enthusiastic for the inclusion of Catholics in sweeping franchise reforms. As a crowning complication, among the recognised Catholic spokesmen there was an influential element (including the gentry and the hierarchy) which was totally out of sympathy with political radicalism. All these dissensions vitiated the efforts of reformers throughout the 1780s, and as the decade came to its close the prospects for reform were not over-encouraging. Then revolution erupted in France, and the winds blew the message of *liberté, égalité, fraternité*, across the face of Ireland.

THE REBELLION

For Irish radicals, as for radicals throughout most of Europe, the enunciation of the principles of liberty and equality, the abolition of privileges, the reshaping of the institutions of the state in accordance with the rights and wishes of 'the people' — all these seemed to herald the dawn of a new era. The Dissenters of Belfast, a politically-conscious middle-class who resented the landed Episcopalian control of the levers of power in the corrupt Parliament, found the events in France particularly encouraging. Numerous radical debating societies flourished in Dublin and in Belfast. A young Dublin-born barrister, Theobald Wolfe Tone, soon began to attract attention. In 1790 a pamphlet of his reviewing critically the affairs of the session earned him the recognition of the Irish Whigs. A further essay into controversy soon won him the admiration of the advanced northern radicals. England and Spain seemed on the verge of war, and Grattan's declaration of support for England implied that the interests of Ireland and England were identical; Tone challenged this assertion, arguing that Ireland had no quarrel with Spain and going on to deplore the control of Irish affairs by England. His views continued to develop along these lines and by late 1791 he had reached the conclusion, expressed in a powerfully written pamphlet entitled 'An Argument on behalf of the Catholics of Ireland', that only by a thorough reform of Parliament could England's stranglehold on Irish affairs be broken. This reform depended on the combined efforts of the Catholics and the Protestant Dissenters — old prejudices should be laid aside, the interests of both groups demanded co-operation. These views won wide acceptance among the advanced radicals of Belfast and Dublin, and in late 1791 Tone was invited to a meeting in the 'Athens of the North'. This meeting led to the founding, in

October 1791, of the Belfast Society of United Irishmen. On his return to Dublin Tone made contact with Napper Tandy and in November the Dublin Society of United Irishmen came into existence.

The original aims of the Society were clearly set out in the pledge taken by members:

> *I, in the presence of God, do pledge myself to my country that I will use all my abilities and influence in the attainment of an impartial and adequate representation of the Irish nation in Parliament; and as a means of absolute and immediate necessity in the establishment of this chief good to Ireland, I will endeavour, as much as lies in my ability, to forward a brotherhood of affection, an identity of interests, a communion of rights and a union of power among Irishmen of all religious persuasions, without which every reform in Parliament must be partial, not national, inadequate to the happiness of this country.*

This explicit declaration of objective needs little elaboration; parliamentary reform and interdenominational harmony, these were the aims, and from late 1791 Paine's *Rights of Man* usually provided the verbal dressing for their exposition.

The methods of the Society at the outset were directed mainly towards educating public opinion, and involved, *inter alia*, presenting petitions, publishing pamphlets and drawing up schemes of reform. In Belfast the movement soon had its own newspaper, *The Northern Star*. It was all legal and above board in these early days, and when we consider the membership of the Societies it is hardly surprising that it should have been so. For the leaders of the United Irishmen were, in the main, middle-class radicals who enjoyed the exhilaration of political debate. In the North there was Robert Simms, merchant and part-owner of a newspaper; Thomas Russell, the genial officer home on half-pay; Samuel Nielson, draper and printer; Henry Joy McCracken, a Presbyterian cotton manufacturer; the ubiquitous ideologue, Dr William Drennan. Besides Tandy, the Dublin leaders included

Thomas Addis Emmet, son of a State physician, a lawyer; Dr Rowan Hamilton; Oliver Bond, woollen merchant; John and Henry Sheares, lawyers; William McNevin and John Lawless, doctors; John Sweetman, brewer; and Arthur O'Connor, Trinity-educated son of a merchant family. There were, of course, exceptions to this middle-class predominance. Lord Edward Fitzgerald, brother of the Duke of Leinster, Ireland's premier peer, immediately comes to mind. At the other end of the social ladder we encounter Jemmy Hope, a northern weaver, whose views envisaged more sweeping changes in the social order. Hope's influence was negligible at leadership level, but among his own northern fellow-weavers he was well respected.

In 1791–2 the Society was busy proclaiming (in debates, manifestos, newspapers, etc.) its gospel of radical reform and the brotherhood of Irishmen, irrespective of religion. Volunteer corps, now under radical control, showed renewed activity. Radical opinions tended to move to the left in step with the march of events in France and strictly republican views (hitherto virtually the exclusive property of the Belfast elements) began to find wider acceptance. Nevertheless, a major assembly of Ulster reformers at Dungannon in early 1793, is evidence of the continued strength of the simple demand for parliamentary reform. However, the execution of Louis XVI in January and the declaration of war between England and France on 1 February 1793 changed drastically the context of political activity. The ferment of excitement now paid dividends for the group who were the most successful pressure group in Ireland in the period 1791–3 — the Catholics. Encouraged by the early days of *liberty* in Catholic France, and sharing the impatience of the times, the Catholic middle-class radicals (e.g. John Keogh, Richard McCormick and Edward Byrne) had, by the end of 1791, succeeded in wresting control of the Catholic Committee from the old cautious aristocrats. A meagre relief measure passed in Parliament in 1792 merely spurred them to greater activity. They hired Tone as assistant secretary and resolved to hold a national Catholic convention to petition for relief. The convention met in late '92 (despite the opposition of the Catholic gentry and the timidity of some of the bishops), drew up its petition and, deciding to by-pass the unsympathetic 'Castle regime', brought its case straight to London. The delegates charged with presenting the petition in London were fêted en route by the Belfast Dissenters, and were cordially received by the King and some of the leading ministers. The Government was anxious to conciliate the Catholic leaders; it was vital to prevent the French from capitalising on Irish Catholic discontent. Moreover, the Catholic leadership in France and throughout Europe was playing a powerful counter-revolutionary role. It was now hoped that it would do likewise in Ireland and in 1793 the Government put through the Irish Parliament a measure granting Catholics the franchise on a 40/– freehold, as well as removing restrictions of access to all political goals other than Parliament and the highest offices in the land. It was a major concession and was gratefully received by the Catholic leaders.

The placation of the Catholic establishment was but one aspect of the direction which the onset of war had imposed on Government policy. The other face of this policy involved a crack-down on all subversive elements on the home front, the habitual reaction of Governments in time of war. This policy applied in Britain as well as in Ireland. In the Irish context, a series of measures were passed in 1793 to meet the internal threat; a Convention Act outlawed the meeting of assemblies purporting to represent any large section of Irish opinion; the Volunteers were suppressed, and the Government set up, under its own control, a paid militia (composed largely of Catholics) as an auxiliary force for the preservation of internal security. A series of minor reforms were enacted in an attempt to isolate as far as possible the more implacable radicals.

In fact the position of Francophile radicals became extremely difficult after the outbreak of war, and some of the United men, through a mixture of impatience and indiscretion, fell foul of the law. In late '93 carelessness left Tandy and Hamilton open to sedition charges; Tandy took flight, Rowan Hamilton was jailed. In the Spring of 1794 a French emissary named Jackson came to Dublin, where Tone foolishly presented him with documentary evidence on the state of the country and on the favourable reception which would be accorded a French 'army of liberation'. Jackson revealed all this to an old confidante of his. This confidante was in fact a Government agent; Jackson was arrested and committed suicide in the dock in April 1795. Tone, compromised as he was, could not remain in the country, and accordingly he fled, first to America and thence to France where he arrived on 1 February 1796.

Meanwhile conditions in Ireland became even more disturbed. Agrarian outrages, directed chiefly against tithes but including a wide spectrum of objectives, were common throughout wide areas of the south and midlands. Tithes were also a source of discontent in the north, but here the disturbances continued to take the form of sectarian warfare despite the *fraternité* plank in the United Irishmen's platform. Antipathies seemed to be hardening. Many Presbyterians were alarmed at the events of 1793; Catholics now had the vote; even more alarmingly, they were now coming into possession of arms as members of the militia. Events seemed to be moving too fast; the spectre of Catholic engulfment began to haunt many moderate Presbyterians. Their fears were not allayed by the knowledge that many Catholic Defenders were infiltrating the militia; accordingly, many Presbyterian Volunteers held on to their arms and began to join various local Protestant societies. It was in this atmosphere, crackling with violence, that the Orange Society was born. It was against this background that the famous 'Fitzwilliam incident' now took place.

In 1795, the Earl Fitzwilliam, friend of Grattan and the Irish Whigs, was appointed Lord Lieutenant. At once he dismissed John Beresford and pledged himself to granting full Catholic emancipation and parliamentary reform. In so doing he went further than his Government was prepared to concede. Fitzgibbon hastened to London to point out the dangers of Catholic emancipation. The Government refused to support Fitzwilliam; he was recalled, and before long Beresford was back in business again. The disappointment felt by the radicals was intense, and for the advanced Catholics the foundation of

Maynooth was poor consolation for the shattered hopes of emancipation.

Many of the United Irishmen had by this time reached the end of their patience and in 1795 the Society was reconstituted as a secret oath-bound society pledged to the establishment of an Irish republic. Tone was empowered to seek French aid. A complex hierarchy of local, baronial, county and provincial committees was set up, with an Executive Directory in Dublin. By May 1795 the new organisation was well advanced in Ulster, and Leinster soon followed suit. An elaborate system of signs and codes was devised for the purpose of recognition and communication. During 1796 and early 1797 a military organisation was gradually constructed on the base of the new secret society, and in anticipation of French aid preparations were made for a rising. Throughout 1796 Tone had been pressing the French Directory to send an army to Ireland; the strategic advantages to the French of such a move were obvious, and Tone guaranteed a friendly reception from the Irish populace. Eventually Carnot, one of the two most influential Directors, agreed, and in December 1796 an expedition force of 14,000 men under General Hoche set out for Ireland. Hoche's expedition was scattered by gale winds and the commander's own ship blown far out in the Atlantic. The remnants of the fleet, including Tone's ship, arrived off Bantry Bay but, owing to bad weather and the indecisiveness of the French second-in-command, Grouchy, they returned directly to France.

The near-success of the Bantry Bay invasion alarmed the Government and lent a new urgency to their efforts to stamp out the discontented elements. These efforts were already quite extensive and quite brutal. An Insurrection Act of unprecedented severity was passed in early 1796 empowering the Lord Lieutenant to proclaim any district and place it under martial law; the death penalty was prescribed for administering unlawful oaths, transportation for life for taking such oaths; suspects were liable to be seized and sent off in the fleet on the order of magistrates. By the end of 1796 the Habeas Corpus Act was suspended throughout all of Ireland. A Protestant Yeomanry corps was now established, officered by the gentry, to defend the constitution. The United Irishmen had by this stage linked up with the Catholic secret societies and thousands of Defenders were taking the oath and preparing to rise in rebellion upon the arrival of French aid. In the North the political polarisation along sectarian lines was working itself out in brutal rural warfare. From late 1795 the Orange Society conducted a systematic campaign of terrorism in Armagh to drive Catholics from their homes and into Connaught. It had considerable success. The Protestant gentry were now not only encouraging but gradually joining the Orange Society, seeing it as a bastion for upholding the Protestant ascendancy. This was a struggle about suppression and survival, and the radical Presbyterian who remained faithful to the United Irish concept of the brotherhood of Irishmen was indeed a man of firm faith and not a little courage. As for the Catholic Defenders who were now being sworn in as United men, they, like the Catholic peasantry of Leinster and Munster, saw the Society as an agent for the removal of the burden of tithes, rents and taxes from their backs. In the southern provinces fear bred fear; the increasing strength of the 'rebels' caused the Protestant gentry to demand that the army be allowed to crush the seditious movement, and they themselves, as leaders of the Yeomanry, were more than willing to assist in this operation. In the campaigns of terrorism which continued throughout 1796 to 1798 the paid militia joined with the Yeomanry and the regular army in an attempt to stamp out every spark of sedition.

The role of the Government in this rural warfare was not very creditable. The chief objective of the Castle clique was to preserve the Protestant ascendancy, and this meant crushing the United Irishmen. To achieve this objective they were prepared to accept help from any source. They were willing to use the sectarian wedge as a device to abort the plans of the United Irishmen. This was clearly shown in 1797 when General Lake was instructed to 'disarm' Ulster. The framers of the policy made no secret of the fact that the 'disarming' and 'pacification' of Ulster was to be conducted on a selective basis — i.e. it was designed to terrorise the United Irishmen. The Presbyterian radicals of Antrim and

Down (the most steadfast republicans), and the United Irishmen (heavily Catholic) throughout the rest of the province were its victims. The attitude towards the Orange Society was very different. The commander at Dungannon, announcing that he was starting a search for unregistered arms, stated:

> *And this I do, not so much with a hope to succeed to any extent, as to increase the animosity between the Orangemen and the United Irishmen, . . . Upon that animosity depends the safety of the centre counties of the North. Were the Orangemen disarmed or put down, or were they coalesced with the other party, the whole of Ulster would be as bad as Down and Antrim.*

Orangemen were enrolled into the Yeomanry corps and were also allowed to act as magistrates. This policy provoked a deep bitterness and accepted indiscipline and brutality among sections of the army and the Yeomanry as a means to its end. At the end of 1797 General Abercromby, a distinguished soldier, was appointed commander-in-chief of the forces in Ireland and after a tour of inspection he gave his famous verdict that the army was

> *. . . in a state of licentiousness which must render it formidable to everyone but the enemy.*

Flogging, half-hanging and the use of the pitch-cap were but some of the refinements which the soldiers and the yeomanry indulged in. Abercromby proposed imposing strict discipline on the troops; however, his views were not liked by the officers 'in the field', nor by the Government, and he resigned. To the indiscipline of the army was added the abuse of the Courts, in a system of judicial terror.

By late '97 the situation in Ulster, due largely to Lake's campaign, was under firm control. It was otherwise in parts of Leinster and Munster, where rumours of Orange pogroms and of impending French aid combined to drive not only many poor peasants but also some of the more prosperous Catholics into the United ranks. The peasantry looked forward to a social revolution; fear and calculation accounted for the attachment of many of the more prosperous elements to the Society. There was sporadic intimidation and terrorisation of Protestants in certain areas. The leaders of the United Irishmen, fearing that the Government's campaign would soon sap the strength of the movement, and encouraged by reports promising aid from France, now determined on a rebellion and fixed 23 May 1798 as the day for the rising. Lord Edward Fitzgerald, the military commander, estimated that he could call on a fighting force of about 100,000 men, and it was hoped that, due to the late influx of prosperous Catholics into the Society, funds would not be lacking. All of these plans were soon thrown into confusion. As its membership increased the Society's security system became as perforated as a sieve. It was riddled with informers, some of them the close intimates of the United leaders themselves. Consequently, when the Government decided to move in on the Society's leaders, it was soon able to lay hands on them. A swoop on a meeting of provincial delegates on 12 March in Bond's house was followed by the arrest of Bond, Emmet, McNevin, Sweetman and other leaders. O'Connor was arrested in Margate, Kent, while on his way to seek French aid. Lord Edward went into hiding and for a time, all the while co-ordinating plans for the insurrection, remained free. But he too was betrayed, wounded during arrest, and died in a state of delirium in Newgate prison in early June. The Sheares brothers were likewise betrayed and captured, leaving only the alcoholic Nielson of the main leaders still at large in Dublin. The circumstances of his capture provide a somewhat absurd dénouement to the collapse of the metropolitan organisation — he was recognised and arrested by the military outside Newgate while shouting abuse at the jailer. It seems he was *personally measuring the height of the walls* of the jail in preparation for an attack thereon!

Meanwhile the Government had accompanied the seizure of the leaders with a determined drive to disarm the rank and file. At the end of March martial law was declared. The military, yeomanry and militia were given free rein in the methods used to disarm the United Irishmen — the firing of homesteads, 'salutary' executions, flogging and the pitch-cap became the order of the day. Rumours circulated among Catholics of an Orange oath to wipe them out. It was at this stage that the long-delayed insurrection of 1798 finally erupted.

With the collapse of the Dublin leadership the initiative now rested with local leaders. In the last week in May the United Irishmen in Kildare, Meath and Carlow rose in rebellion. After some initial successes they were soon crushed by the military. By this stage, however, Wexford was ablaze. The United movement had never been strongly established in the south-east — the priests had warned Catholics against joining secret societies and in any case farming was more prosperous and rural social relationships more satisfactory there than in most parts of the country. However, the reign of terror against 'croppies' which the yeomanry and militia had prosecuted in the Wexford-Wicklow area in early 1798, had driven the peasantry to a desperate pitch of fear. On 25 May this pent-up flood broke loose with savage fury. An army of some 500 peasants, led by local priests, decimated a force of infantry at Oulart Hill and the rebellion quickly spread throughout the county. At first the makeshift army of pikemen carried all before them — Enniscorthy and Wexford were captured by the insurgents who, showing a frightening disregard for cannon or cavalry, seemed to the demoralised militia and yeomanry like men possessed. Gradually, however, the tide turned as the vast undisciplined rebel army were faced with a regular army better equipped in leadership and arms, and rapidly increasing in numbers as reinforcements poured into the country. On 5 June, after a bloody battle, the insurgents were defeated at Ross; a rebel army attempting to push into Wicklow was defeated at Arklow. The net tightened, and by 21 June the core of the rebel forces, some 20,000 in all, were massed on Vinegar Hill, surrounded by General Lake's army of 10,000 troops with heavy artillery. In the ensuing battle the insurgents were routed. By early July, Lord Cornwallis, the new Lord Lieutenant and commander-in-chief, was quickly gaining control of the situation; with the golden fields of Wexford promising a good harvest, he offered a general amnesty to the rebels provided they surrendered their arms and took an oath of allegiance. Gradually calm returned to Wexford.

While Wexford blazed throughout early June the remnants of Ulster's army of United Irishmen had at last risen in rebellion. A force of about 6,000, led by Henry Joy McCracken, attacked Antrim town. The garrison was prepared for them and the insurgents were defeated. To the south the United men of Down, a straggling force of some 7,000 men led by Henry Munro, a Lisburn draper, rose up and for a time were in command of the north-east of the county. But they were soon defeated by superior forces at Ballinahinch. McCracken, Munro and the other leaders were executed and in some areas 'an example' was made of suspected sympathisers. The revolt had lasted less than a week and by mid-June Ulster was firmly under Government control.

The hope which had done much to sustain the spirits of the United Irishmen in '97 and early '98 was that French aid would be forthcoming in the hour of decision. This did not happen. Government fears in May, that Napoleon Bonaparte was ready to lead an invasion fleet bound for Ireland, were unfounded; his objective was Egypt. As news of the rebellion reached France, Tone redoubled his efforts to secure aid. Eventually, on 23 August a French force of 1,100 men under the command of General Humbert landed at Killala Bay in north Connaught. They were to be the advance force of a larger expedition which was ready to set sail from Brest. Connaught was the province where the United Irishmen had made little headway and the French 'liberators' were seen by the Mayo peasantry as something of a curiosity. However, they were 'curiosities' who seemed ready to supply uniforms and food and accordingly they were joined by many of the poorer peasants. The French, for their part, viewed their Irish peasant allies with a mixture of sympathy, exasperation and contempt. Humbert, anxious to consolidate his position in Mayo, determined on capturing the strategic centre of the county and on 27 August his army of about 1,400 (half of whom were Irish) stood outside the town of Castlebar, where Generals Hutchinson and Lake had taken up a defensive position. What followed has since become immortalised as 'the races of Castlebar'. As the

French force attacked, the garrison dropped their arms, turned and ran all the way to Tuam. The French entered the town and a local Catholic gentleman, John Moore, was appointed President of the Provisional Government of Connaught.

The French joy, however, was short-lived. Cornwallis, with a huge army, was closing in on Humbert. Bewildered at the non-arrival of the rest of the French invasion force, and despairing of inspiring the Connaughtmen to rise 'en masse' against the English, Humbert decided to link up with a small insurrection force which had shown signs of activity in Longford. It was a hopeless gamble, and on 8 September at Ballinamuck in Co. Longford Humbert's little force of 850, after a token show of resistance to satisfy honour, surrendered to the combined forces (about 10,000) of Cornwallis and Lake. Within a fortnight General Trench had scattered the remnants of the rebel army in Mayo. The final curtain for 'bliain na bhFrancach' was rung down on 12 October in an engagement off the north coast. The long-delayed Brest expedition, amounting to some 3,000 troops, having finally set sail for Ireland, was now intercepted by a superior British fleet off the north coast. Virtually the entire French force was captured. Tone, who was on board the flag-ship, was brought to Dublin, tried and sentenced to be hanged. On 12 November his gaolers found him with his throat cut. On 19 November he died.

The year of insurrection was now drawing to its exhausted end. It had cost the country dearly. Thomas Pakenham estimates that:

> In the space of a few weeks, 30,000 people . . . were cut down or shot or blown like chaff as they charged up to the mouth of the cannon.

Over a million pounds was subsequently claimed by the loyalists for damage to property. The losses suffered by the disloyal peasants were not calculated. The cost in psychological terms which the year's slaughter had inflicted was incalculable.

Any analysis of the events of the 1790s must begin by reflecting on the almost total failure of the United Irish movement to bring to fruition any of its lofty aims. The fratricidal slaughter of the 1798 insurrection was a complete negation of the cherished aim of the movement — a brotherhood of Irishmen irrespective of religious persuasion. Part of the blame for this failure can be laid at the doorstep of the movement's leaders. Courageous as many of them were, they were yet deficient in many of the attributes most necessary for the direction of a secret revolutionary movement. Some of these defects are obvious — the woefully lax security system; weakness of liaison between the central directory and the local committees; disagreements on tactics among the leaders. Again, even allowing for the heavy reliance placed on the arrival of French aid, the military preparations made by the leaders on the home front were totally inadequate. Furthermore, the belief of the leaders that, once the revolution had started, officers and men from the yeomanry and particularly from the militia would defect to their side, turned out to be ill-founded. There was little military talent among the leading committee of the Society; even Lord Edward Fitzgerald had more of the dash of a gallant soldier than the directing genius of a revolutionary leader.

On the other hand it hardly seems fair to blame the leaders for factors over which they could exercise little or no control. They had little real influence on the process of decision-making which dictated when, if at all, the French might be willing to spare an expedition for Ireland. They can hardly be held responsible for the inclement weather which caused the Bantry Bay fiasco. Likewise, they were merely spectators of the developments in the main theatres of war between England and France, vital though these developments were in determining the English Government's policy towards Ireland.

However, the failure of the United Irish movement was due, in the last resort, to the fact than in Ireland the forces operating against it proved too strong in the end. The Government, with its effective spy network and huge garrison, was relentless in its determination to crush the movement. The Catholic hierarchy, viewing with horror the progress of events in France, was unlikely to show sympathy with the 'Irish Jacobins', and condemned the

Society from the outset. Most serious of all, however, was the failure of the movement to find a solution to the crucial problem of how to overcome the deep religious and class divisions of Irish society. In mid and south Ulster the struggle between rival sectarian agrarian secret societies was deeply rooted. When the official mood of concession began to include *political* rights, a 'Catholic peril' bogey quickly developed, giving a more explicitly political framework to agrarian violence; Protestants of high degree, in seeking to maintain the Protestant ascendancy, found it to be in their interests to combine with the secretly organised Protestant peasantry. The Orange Society exemplified this trend in its first decade. Simultaneously the United movement, as it moved from political radicalism to social revolution proclaiming a union of the have-nots of all creeds, seemed to be headed for uncharted territory. Many of even the most liberal Protestants feared that this territory would be Catholic-dominated; accordingly they either avoided or actively opposed the United movement. There were exceptions to this trend, Presbyterian republicans whose conviction even Lake's campaign could not suppress, but in general the counties of mid and south Ulster proved barren ground for the gospel of the United Irishmen.

In Belfast and the north-east counties of Down and Antrim, the erosion of the United support during the 1790s was a more complex process. Belfast was the hotbed of Irish political radicalism, the natural birth-place of Irish republicanism. During the 1790s, however, subtle changes were taking place in the nature and direction of radical opinion in the north-east. French continental ambitions and the growing disagreements between France and America, diminished Belfast's admiration for the young republic; the prospect of the arrival of a French 'army of liberation' became less attractive. Even more disturbing to Belfast radicals was the unbridled violence which had set in after the 'dawn of liberty' in Paris. As the United Irish movement lurched leftwards, many prosperous Presbyterians declined to move with it; a thorough reform of the corrupt, puppet-Parliament at Dublin was one thing, a social upheaval, where property, and even life itself, would be in danger, was quite another matter.

They decided that they could wait a little longer for their political reforms.

Tone had foreseen this development when he stated:

> *If the men of property will not help us they must fall; we will free ourselves by the aid of that large and respectable class of the community — the men of no property.*

But by 1798 the United Irishmen in the Belfast area could not count on the support of more than a minority of this latter class. Lake's campaign of 1797 had frightened many into submission. Moreover the accounts of events in Wexford confirmed widely-held suspicions about the dangers of alliance with a Catholic jacquerie. The Orange balladeer recounted the story:

> *Hundreds they've burned of each sex, young and old,*
> *From heaven the order; — by priests they were told;*
> *No longer we'll trust them, no more to betray,*
> *But chase from our bosoms these vipers away.*
> *Derry down, down, croppies lie down.*

Still, the shrunken ranks of the United Irishmen who rallied to Henry Joy and Munro in '98 were largely Presbyterian 'men of no property'. (The Catholic Defenders, due to the advice of the priests, fear of the military, and suspicion towards their Protestant neighbours, were only thinly represented in the insurrection in the north-east.) Die-hard republicans of unshakeable conviction, they rose in rebellion to achieve social justice and political equality. Disciplined in combat, they were not disgraced in defeat. But defeated they most certainly were, and 'advanced' political opinion in Belfast, though it did not die, gradually changed its character. Although no less democratic, many Presbyterian radicals now decided that the best hopes lay in reform rather than in revolution. The character of the region's economic development was soon to lead many Presbyterians to question Tone's advice to 'break the connection with England'. In short, there was a congealing of that peculiarly north-east brand of non-revolutionary and anti-separatist nonconformist radicalism which Gladstone was later to find so baffling.

Finally, let us consider briefly the failure of the United Irish movement in Leinster and Munster. When the United leaders (mostly urban radicals, as we have seen) advocated social revolution among the Catholic peasantry it was almost inevitable, due to the nature of the power structure, that the peasantry should have translated it into religious terms. The precise meaning of what this social revolution would involve varied in detail from place to place, as local leaders added local glosses to the main text, but the abolition of tithes and taxes was everywhere a main objective. The political tradition to which the Catholic peasantry belonged induced in them a consciousness that they were the dispossessed, and that this state of affairs had come about simply because they had refused to change their religion.

On the other hand, the growing fear of social revolution during the 1790s drove even the most moderate Protestants over to the side of the Government with its hard-line policy of law and order, leaving but a tiny minority of Protestant United Irishmen high and dry in a sea of Catholic peasant discontent. Accordingly, the reprisals which followed the Bantry Bay scare, the conduct of the garrison throughout 1797, and above all the campaign of terror conducted by the Government troops throughout the south and midlands in the spring of 1798, were all classified by the peasantry as aspects of an overall Protestant plan for persecuting Catholics (though in fact some of the *instruments* of the terror, e.g. the militia, included many Catholics). In these circumstances it was hardly surprising, when the peasantry of the south-east eventually came out in rebellion, that the *dies irae* was marked by the wholesale execution of Protestants, all of whom were now bracketed as 'Orange oppressors'. The burning of over 100 Protestants in a barn at Scullabogue by a group of rebels retreating in panic from the defeat at New Ross is one of the most gruesome episodes of that grim year of slaughter.

Yet to describe the insurrection of '98 in the south and midlands simply as 'a religious crusade' is to indulge in over-simplification. Such an explanation ignores two important points; firstly, the class divisions within the Catholic community; and secondly, the curious mixture of political cultures which attended the efforts of some United Irishmen to graft the language of continental republicanism to the elemental antipathy of the Catholic peasantry towards 'alien authority'. The majority of the more prosperous Catholics were no less appalled than their Protestant counterparts at events in France. Nor were they enthusiastic for a social upheaval in Ireland. Furthermore, the Catholic bishops consistently opposed the United Irishmen's 'conspiracy'. There was, it is true, an influx of Catholic middle-class radicals into the movement in the period of disillusion which followed Fitzwilliam's recall, and during the terror of '97–'98 many well-off Catholics showed sympathy with the United Irishmen. But when the call for insurrection came, many of the Catholic middle-classes whose station in life gave them leading positions in the underground army shrank from the conflict. The lament of the peasant-poet captures the bewilderment of the peasants when they found themselves without leaders:

Níor tháinig ár Major i dtús an lae chugainn,
Is ní rabhamar féin ann i gcóir ná i gceart,
Ach mar sheolfaí tréada de bha gan aoire,
Ar thaobh na gréine de Shliabh na mBan.[1]

Where involvement was unavoidable, as in Wexford, they found themselves carried along by the flood of peasant fury. Elsewhere the Catholic bourgeoisie in '98 were generally content to lie low until the storm had blown itself out.

Lastly, let us say a few words about the political content of the '98 rebellion in the south-east. Many historians have contrasted the politico-ideological basis of the United Irishmen movement in the north-east, with the socio-religious antagonisms which lay at the root of the '98 explosion in the south-east. There are good grounds, as we have seen, for such a contrast; and yet a caveat seems necessary. Many of the local United leaders in Leinster and

Munster had a political consciousness no less acute than their northern fellow-citizens, though with certain distinctions — France was the ideological well for southern republicans, while the older example of America still remained a focus of northern admiration. But the interesting point is that the southern United leaders *did try* to fuse the ideas of continental republicanism with the older roots of Catholic peasant alienation. If to Castlereagh's description of the Wexford rising as 'a Jacobin conspiracy with popish instruments' we add the separatist intentions of the United leaders, we have all the elements which, as evidenced in a bizarre collage of symbols and slogans, gave motive force to the Wexford pikemen — the liberty tree and the harp without a crown, pikes and crucifixes, liberty caps and blessed scapulars, the Carmagnole and the Hail Mary. The symbols of political confusion, some may say; but then popular attitudes to politics rarely conform to the models of the political ideologist.

The legacy of '98, then, is a dual legacy; a story of incredible bravery and indescribable brutality. Yet, despite its failure, the United Irishmen movement profoundly influenced the thinking of later generations of Irishmen. The concept of a *republic* as the quintessential constitutional expression of Irish separatism originated with the United Irishmen. Moreover, the republic was something for which men had fought and died. For many nationalists of later days the 'purest' form of Irish nationalism was that which asserted itself in arms. This, and the essentially egalitarian nature of the rising, cemented a political tradition which has persisted right up to our own day.

THE UNION AND AFTERMATH

The *immediate* consequence of the rising produced one of those cruel ironies so common in history. The rising which was to 'break the connection with England' precipitated the passing of an Act of Union between Ireland and Britain. A legislative union between the two kingdoms had been suggested at various times throughout the eighteenth century. The divergence of views between the two Parliaments over Pitt's commercial proposals in 1785 and, more seriously, during the regency crisis of 1789, both highlighted the dangers inherent in the constitution of 1782. Embroilment in war increased Britain's anxiety to effect a Union, though in fact the Irish Parliament fully supported the war policy. Yet prior to 1798 the predictable storm of opposition which the proposal of a Union would provoke in the Irish Parliament inhibited English ministers from making any direct overtures on the matter. The '98 rebellion, however, gave Pitt both the incentive and the opportunity to act decisively. He was influenced by the ever-present danger that an effective French force might capitalise on Irish disaffection, and also by the sheer physical drain on British resources involved in maintaining order in Ireland. Furthermore, Pitt, realising the full extent of Catholic alienation from the ascendancy ruling in Dublin, calculated that only a 'new deal', with London holding the initiative, could offer any real hope of achieving social harmony in Ireland.

Accordingly, within weeks of the insurrection's beginning, Pitt set to work in the task of winning Irish support for the Union. The omens were promising. The Lord Lieutenant, Cornwallis, the young acting Chief Secretary, Lord Castlereagh, and the powerful Fitzgibbon now Earl of Clare, all favoured the idea. On one aspect of the proposed terms, however, Clare was adamant — Catholic emancipation must not form part of the deal. Pitt himself had hoped to couple emancipation with the Union in a bid to secure the widest possible good-will for the new policy. But the anti-emancipation influences in London and Dublin proved too strong even for Pitt and he reluctantly agreed to proceed with the Union on the existing parliamentary base, leaving the Catholic question to be settled as soon as the Union was passed.

The first attempt by the Government, in January 1799, to have the principle of the Union accepted in the Irish Parliament was defeated by 111 votes to 106, and Castlereagh immediately set to work to ensure that when next the matter came before Parliament the result would be different. His task was by no means an easy one; the opposition was quite strong, even if it was composed of an assortment of groups with little else in common save their opposition to the idea of a Union. Predictably, the place-men and office-holders were quick to jump to the defence of 'Ireland's

constitutional independence'. Many of these 'outraged con-
sciences' were, however, open to appeasement — provided the
price was right. The virulent opposition offered by the
Orangemen to the Union derived from different sources.
Orangemen of high and low degree, rightly suspecting Pitt and
Castlereagh of being pro-Catholic emancipation, now saw the
Union proposals as something of a constitutional Trojan horse
which would lead to the overthrow of the Protestant ascendancy
in Ireland. A Protestant Parliament sitting in Dublin might be
trusted with the protection of this ascendancy against Catholic
incursions; a Parliament in London, differently composed and
with different preoccupations, was by no means as reliable a
guardian.

A further element in the opposition to the Union came from
members who felt the pressure of extra-parliamentary opinion.
This 'public' opposition to the Union centred chiefly in Dublin,
whose inhabitants rightly judged that the importance of the
capital would seriously suffer from an abolition of its Parliament.
Elsewhere in the country opposition came from commercial
interests who feared for their survival in the face of competition,
while feelings of reluctance to change the *status quo* strengthened
the resolve of some of the county members. Finally, opposition to
the Union proposals came from a group, richer in talent than in
numbers, whose historical sense of Ireland's constitutional rights
was outraged at the suggestion of a Union; who felt that Ireland
needed an independent Parliament to express her political
identity, and who claimed that the Irish Parliament had no right
to vote itself out of existence. Grattan, the architect of the 1782
Constitution, was the most illustrious exponent of this argument,
while out of Parliament a small group of Catholic lawyers, led by
a young barrister named Daniel O'Connell, pledged their support
to the Protestant party opposing the Union.

The first round in the Union battle had been won narrowly by
the Opposition in 1799. Castlereagh, however, called on all his
resources to secure a different result in 1800. Pensions, places, and
peerages were handed out to those whose votes were up for
auction. Patrons and borough-owners whose seats were due for

abolition were compensated for their earlier investments. Direct cash payments were necessary in some few cases. The total outlay of the Government was quite substantial; it is estimated that the total 'compensation for disturbance' paid to patrons amounted to over one and a quarter million pounds. If all this smacks of corruption it must be remembered that such transactions were an accepted part of eighteenth-century political life. The Commons, in England as well as Ireland, had to be carefully 'managed' by the Executive, and patronage was an invaluable, indeed essential, instrument of effective management. The methods employed by the Government in securing a majority for the Union represented nothing novel in political tactics, even if they were on a scale of expense enormous even by contemporary standards.

Moreover, many borough-owners and office-holders considered the acceptance of rewards simply as a legitimate form of compensation for a species of property (in this case political power) which they were being asked to surrender. Many of them had no aversion to the idea of a Union; they simply did not want it to cost themselves too dearly. In fact the majority of those who in early 1800 gave their support to the Union proposals were probably swayed more by fear than by the promise of favour. The country had been brought to the edge of the abyss of social as well as political revolution. Even now, after the rebellion had been contained, there was still widespread agrarian disorder. The sole security which the Irish ascendancy possessed against the dual dangers of invasion from without and anarchy within the country, was the security provided by the massive British garrison in Ireland. The Government, it is true, showed some flexibility in modifying some of the commercial and administrative details of the Union proposals in order to remove the misgivings of waverers. This showed a shrewd tactical sense. But ultimately the strongest card in the Government's hand was the dilemma in which the Irish ascendancy found themselves — they wished to remain an ascendancy, and yet to hold their position of power they were forced to rely on the British garrison. However much the anti-Union forces might stress their constitutional rights their vulnerability on the security issue was inescapable. In the absence of the 40,000 or so British troops who protected them, the Irish ascendancy had no way of guaranteeing their continued control of the country. Fitzgibbon, in his telling speech for the Union, fixed on this Achilles heel of dependency with unerring skill:

> . . . *Next, if we become one people with England, the army of the Empire will be employed where it is most wanted for general service; and so long as it is found necessary to garrison every district in Ireland, for the internal safety of the country, force may be stationed here, without incurring additional expense in either country.* . . .

Against the force of this argument even the passionate eloquence of Grattan was to prove unavailing. By the end of March the fate of the Irish Parliament was sealed, and although the death rattles continued for some time longer the ultimate end was inevitable. On 1 August 1800 the Act of Union received the royal signature. The Irish Parliament, after 500 years of political life, had committed suicide.

The main terms of the Union can be easily summarised. The Irish Parliament being abolished, Ireland was henceforth to be represented in the Parliament of the United Kingdom in London by (a) twenty-eight Irish peers and four bishops in the House of Lords, and (b) one hundred MPs in the House of Commons. The financial clauses provided for the temporary retention by Ireland of a separate exchequer with an accompanying responsibility for her own national debt. At the same time Ireland's contribution to the joint United Kingdom expenditure was fixed at two-seventeenths of the total. Further clauses provided for a regular review of these terms and also for a full merging of the two financial systems as soon as conditions should prove favourable. The Established Churches of the two countries were united as the Established Church of England and Ireland. In trade and commerce the Union provided for the creation of a free trade area between the two countries. However, it was recognised that a period of adjustment would be necessary and it was decided to allow customs duties to remain on a specified range of manufactured goods for a period of twenty years. In addition, provision was made for adjusting differences between the two countries in certain tariffs so as to ensure the objective conditions of 'fair competition'. The legal clauses decreed that all existing statutes in both countries should continue in force. The power to change such laws, as indeed the power to amend any of the Union's clauses, was henceforth to reside within the United Kingdom Parliament.

Any estimate of the significance of the Act must begin by making some distinctions between its short-term and its long-term consequences. The immediate impact of the Union on Irish life, political or economic, was negligible. The Irish parliamentarians, both pro- and anti-Unionists, generally found little difficulty in accommodating themselves to their new political habitat, and within a few years most of them had become fully integrated into the political life at Westminster. This process should cause little surprise. The agenda of political issues with which the Irish Parliament had been concerned in its closing decades — Catholic emancipation, parliamentary representation, elimination of corrupt practices, etc. — was no different in substance from the agenda under discussion at Westminster. The Union debate itself was a debate in which all the participants shared certain common assumptions. The objective shared by all was finding the constitutional formula which would, with the least friction, harness Ireland and England together under a common monarch. The separatist voice was conspicuous by its absence; republicanism was a non-starter.

At the popular level, political life was equally uneventful in the immediate post-Union years. The one exception was Emmet's abortive rising in Dublin in 1803. This, the last fling of the remnants of the United Irishmen, was the epilogue rather than the prologue to a phase of Irish political activity. Emmet's revolt, a brief skirmish on the streets of Dublin, had no immediate effect on political life at any level; its importance lay in the legacy its leader left to later generations of republicans — a stirring oration, and the inspiring, romantic image of a young hero.

But throughout most of the country the mass of the people were scarcely aware of the passing of the Act of Union. In life Grattan's Parliament had never formed part of their political consciousness, its death left them unmoved. The Parliament was gone, but the entire power-structure remained as it was. The English Government had allowed the Irish ascendancy, in return for the surrender of its Parliament, to retain undisturbed and exclusive control of the sources of power within Ireland. Consequently, the Union did not in its early days represent any new initiative in removing the causes of domestic strife in Ireland.

If the immediate impact of the Union on Irish political life was slight, its long-term significance was enormous. The long list of grievances which had preceded the Union, and which its enactment left untouched, became even longer in the early nineteenth century, as social and economic difficulties became more acute. The very complexity of these difficulties ensured a large audience for those who, in *political* terms, seemed to be offering a simple solution. And what could be more simple than to claim that *the fons et origo* of all Ireland's problems could be traced to a single root cause, the Union with England. The undoing of that Union, whether through simple Repeal or, as later, through schemes of devolutionary Home Rule, came to be accepted by many as the panacea for all Ireland's problems. Republican separatists might draw water from their own ideological well, but for constitutional nationalists, the Union terms were inevitably the point of departure in any attempted redefinition of Ireland's constitutional requirements. The settlement which came into effect on 1 January 1801 defined the context of Irish parliamentary politics for over a hundred years.

If critics of the existing order of Irish society tended, sooner or later, to light on the Union in their search for political solutions, to the vested interests of that society the same Union represented the rock of security on whose permanence depended their continued control of power. In concrete terms this meant that the Protestant ascendancy class, considering their interests to be entirely bound up with the maintenance of the Union, were from the outset its staunchest supporters. There were, of course, exceptions; one has but to think of the Young Irelanders and Parnell to realise the Protestant contribution in leadership to nineteenth-century Irish nationalism. Furthermore, there were times, such as in the wake of the Disestablishment crisis of 1869, when a section of Protestants wavered for a time in their support of the Union. But these Protestant leaders were a minority within their own church and the interludes of serious Protestant 'Home Rule' feeling proved transient; Unionism was the political faith of the majority of Irish Protestants throughout the nineteenth century.

As regards the Catholic majority, it has often been said that the exclusion of Catholic emancipation from the settlement of 1800 ruined whatever hope there may have been of having the Union accepted as a real union between two nations. This may or may not be true. Yet one may be permitted to doubt whether in fact even the most timely concession of full *political* rights could have ensured the allegiance of the Catholic masses to the Union. True, the Catholic bishops were generally prepared, throughout the nineteenth century, to accept the Union framework in the pursuit of their political objectives (this is not to say that they all considered it to be the *optimum* framework for such exercises). Again, as the Catholic bourgeoisie gradually came into prominence in politics, trade and commerce and the professions — as they became, in effect, vested interests — many of them came to accept, if not exactly to acclaim, the Union settlement. But there were two main factors working against general acceptance of the Union by the Catholic body. In the first place, those who suffered deepest and longest from the social and economic crises of the nineteenth century were the Catholic masses; accordingly, they were always likely to prove an attentive audience for the political leader who would articulate their grievances in the most effective way. As we have suggested, the 'most effective way' came to be equated by many with the most simple remedy on offer — the undoing of the Union. The second major factor working against Catholic acceptance of the Union (a factor which induced even the most prosperous Catholics to listen favourably to schemes for its modification or repeal) was a question of simple denominational arithmetic. The Catholics knew they were in the *majority*, and as the extension of the franchise in the nineteenth century gave meaning, in terms of political power, to the concept of a majority, it became clear that the more 'home rule' Ireland could gain the greater would be the likelihood of a predominant Catholic influence in the administration of the country's affairs. This consciousness of numerical strength is a constant factor (leaving aside the emotional, non-rational elements of nationalist feeling) in explaining why campaigns such as O'Connell's for Repeal or the later Home Rule agitation were always assured of support from even the most prosperous of the Catholic community.

One further phenomenon requires notice in the context of the development of denominational/political correlation ships on the Union issue. This relates to the fact that the Union was to find its most coherent and lasting support among the Presbyterians of the north-east, a development which only the most perceptive of observers could have forecast at the time of its enactment. Here again the numerical factor was of some importance. The fact that the vast majority of Irish Presbyterians were concentrated in one area did much to strengthen their consciousness of the distinctive elements of their own cultural tradition. We have already noted how the transformation of north-east radicalism contributed to pro-Unionist sentiment among Ulster Presbyterians. In the first half of the nineteenth century events in the political context — reaction against O'Connell-style politics and against the increasing prominence of Catholic priests in the nationalist movements of the period — further strengthened Presbyterian attachment to the Union. However, important though these political factors undoubtedly were, it was the economic imperative which above all else dictated the response of the Presbyterians of the north-east to the Union. Belfast and its hinterland enjoyed industrial expansion and general economic prosperity under the Union (the only significant area in the country to do so). This very prosperity seemed to depend on the maintenance of the Union; it was the demand of the British market which kept the Belfast linen mills busy; after the mid-century it was to service the expanding trade of the Victorian empire that Belfast's ship-building industry came to world prominence. The expansion of the ancillary metal industries, indeed the health of the entire economy of the region, depended on access to the British market itself and a share in the expanding overseas markets of the empire. Any advocate of constitutional changes in the relationship between Ireland and Britain who sought to enlist the support of the Presbyterians of the north-east would have to satisfy them that such changes would not threaten (through a revision of tariff policy, etc.) the regional economy of the area. No nationalist politician of the nineteenth or indeed of the twentieth century was able to so convince them. Fear of absorption into an ailing economy joined fear of subjection to the influence of the Church of Rome as the twin pillars of the Unionism of the north-east.

Finally, let us comment briefly on the overall impact of the Union on the Irish economy. The clauses which produced the most immediate effects were those relating to Ireland's financial obligations. During Britain's struggle with Napoleon the war effort consumed a large proportion of national expenditure. Accordingly, the Irish exchequer's contribution represented an ever-increasing financial burden on the country. The result was a succession of loans and a continuous increase in the Irish national debt. The servicing of this debt was a serious drain on Irish capital (potential investment-capital) at a time when the Irish economy could least afford such a drain.

In the wider context, the impact of the Union on the performance of the nineteenth-century Irish economy is a more vexed subject of debate. Here it is of little use taking a short-term view, if only because many of the commercial and financial terms of the Union took over a quarter of a century to come into operation. The consequences for the Irish economy of its integration into the wider free-trade area created by the Union is left for a later chapter. However, two general points ought to be borne in mind in any assessment of the long-term economic consequences of the Union. Firstly, in the matter of overseas trade the Irish economy was already tied hand and foot to the British economy *before* the Union came into operation. In the year 1800 itself over 85 per cent of all Irish exports went to Britain, while 78.6 per cent of Irish imports came from Britain. The key, therefore, to the condition of the Irish economy lay in the way in which the interaction between the Irish and the British economies was regulated. This brings us to the second point under consideration; namely, the role of Government policy in the regulation of the performance of the economy. The Union changed the venue for the discussion and formation of economic policy from Dublin to London. After 1800 official policy regarding the Irish economy was decided by an assembly only a sixth of whose membership was Irish, an assembly in which Ireland's needs were seldom the main and never the sole considerations in the process through which major decisions on economic policy were reached. This is not to suggest that a native Irish Parliament would necessarily have been more successful in dealing with the main problems which beset the Irish economy throughout the nineteenth century. What can be said, however, is that the Irish economy was seriously affected by the fact that policy decisions vital to its performance were taken by an imperial Parliament sitting in London.

02 | THE CATHOLIC QUESTION

THE EIGHTEENTH-CENTURY BACKGROUND

During the course of the eighteenth century many of the more severe Penal laws against Catholics had been allowed to lapse. In fact, many of these statutes had never been fully enforced, and as the threat to the security of the State from a Stuart invasion became increasingly remote, it was felt safe to begin dismantling this penal code. The growth of the concept of religious toleration no doubt contributed its share towards the creation of this new attitude, although the outbursts of 'no popery' excitement during the 1756–63 war, or, more violently, the Gordon riots of 1780, served to testify to the widespread fear and suspicion of the machinations of Rome shared by all levels of British society. However, the continued expression of unswerving loyalty by the Catholic 'leaders' in Ireland ought to have gone some way towards allaying these fears. This is not to say that Catholic attitudes were entirely supine. Already between 1759 and 1763 there had been in existence a Catholic Committee dedicated to petitioning for relief measures. However, the tensions between the Catholic landed aristocrats and the increasingly assertive middle-class elements on this Committee soon proved its undoing. Nevertheless the tide of legislation was on the turn. By

1750 the lower levels of the army were thrown open to Catholics, and the 'Bogland Act' of 1771 (legalising leases, up to 61 years, of holdings under 50 acres of unprofitable land) at last restored to the Irish Catholic peasant some legal right to his native soil.

It was hardly surprising that from the 1770s the British Government, faced with the problem of containing the rising tide of Irish Protestant colonial nationalism, should have favoured a generous response to the demands for remedial measures from the unquestionably loyal Irish Catholic leaders. Moreover, when the reform cry gathered momentum in the 1780s it was only to be expected that the glaring picture of injustice which the position of Catholics in Ireland represented should stand out in stark and unpleasant relief. Despite this mood of concession on the part of the British Government, and despite the fact that a talented minority of the 'patriot' party in the Irish Parliament likewise favoured some concession, it needed the stimulus of external pressure to translate this good-will into remedial legislation. The French declaration of war on Britain in 1778, raising the old scare of invasion, convinced British statesmen of the need to meet in some way Irish Catholic demands, in the interests of imperial security. The result was Gardiner's First Catholic Relief Act of 1778, forced through the Irish Parliament in the teeth of bitter resistance. This Act permitted Catholics to take land on 999 year leases, though not as freeholds, and to inherit land on the same terms as Protestants, on condition of their taking an oath of allegiance. The abolition of the Tests Acts in 1780, making Dissenters eligible for office, is further evidence of this mood of concession, which found even fuller expression in Gardiner's Second Relief Act of 1782. Under the terms of this Act Catholics who had taken the oath of 1778 were permitted to purchase and bequeath freehold land on the same terms as Protestants, while other laws bearing on the registration of priests, the bearing of arms, and on education were also repealed. These concessions were viewed with deep misgivings by many of the Protestant establishment. Predictably, they were particularly worried lest the increasing Catholic presence within the law should lead to a questioning of the land settlements on which their own titles to property rested. To allay such fears an Act was passed in 1782 confirming all previous legislation on Irish land settlements.

In fact the 1782 Act was followed by a temporary halt in the flow of concessions. The Protestant Parliament was busy consolidating its newly-gained legislative and economic freedom and the divided counsels of the reformers in Parliament ensured the temporary eclipse of the Catholic cause. Then the French revolution burst upon the world, and the debate on Catholic disabilities assumed a new urgency. In the first place, the programme of the United Irishmen, together with Tone's appointment as Secretary of the Catholic Committee, indicated the real possibility that the demands for Catholic emancipation and for radical parliamentary reform might soon coalesce in an irresistible demand for a fundamental reconstruction of the Constitution. Simultaneously the initiative in championing the Catholic cause was passing from its old custodians, the Catholic gentry, such as Lords Kenmare, Fingall and Gormanstown, to the middle-class merchants and lawyers, led by John Keogh. The friction between these two groups had been a constant feature of the earlier Catholic Committees. With the landlords, the obedience born of fear for the security of their titles compounded with the elemental conservatism of a favoured minority in producing an ultra-loyal political outlook. Like their co-religionists in Britain, the Irish Catholic gentry lost no opportunity for professing their reverence for all aspects of the Constitution, other than the aspect which discommoded themselves. Already in 1782 the landlord-dominated Catholic Committee had informed the Government that they would not press their claims too insistently in the various proposals for reform then under discussion.

The Catholic middle-classes were in a somewhat different position. The enterprising lawyers felt quite acutely the limits set by penal laws to their prospects within the profession. Their exclusion from those offices of the State which recruited heavily from the Bar was a grievance deeply resented. As for the merchant-class, their self-assurance had grown throughout the eighteenth century as their own prosperity and their awareness of their importance to the economy had gradually increased. One of the unintended results of the anti-Catholic laws on land-holding and education had been the growing involvement of the ambitious Catholic middle-class in business and commerce. Here they found that profit makes no distinction of creed. The Catholic merchant, English-speaking, law-abiding, and growing daily in respectability, showed all the impatience of the self-made man at unwelcome restrictions on his social mobility. In political terms he saw no reason why he should be excluded from full participation in the working of the Constitution. By 1790 the initiative within the Catholic Committee lay with the middle-class men, and the excitement of the early stages of the French Revolution produced among some of them an impatience with the pace at which they were advancing towards political rights. It was in this mood that they invited Tone to become assistant secretary to the Catholic Committee.

The stiffening of purpose which Tone's appointment signified was even more evident later in the year 1792 during the proceedings of the Catholic Convention. At all events the pressure of 1792 was crowned with success in the following year by the passing of Hobart's Catholic Relief Act. This Act conceded to Catholics the right to vote as 40/– freeholders in the counties and in the open boroughs, to act as Grand Jurors, to bear arms, take degrees in Trinity College, become members of corporations, take commissions in the army below the rank of General, and to advance to certain minor offices in the service of the State. The higher posts in the Government remained outside their reach and, above all, Catholics were still excluded from Parliament.

The 1793 concession was, as we have seen, part of the general strategy of the Government as it entered the long period of war with France. Francophile radicals were to be isolated, discredited, and, if they represented a serious threat to security, crushed. On the other hand every effort was to be made to conciliate all the potentially loyal elements in the community. Viewed in these terms the immediate results of the 1793 Act must have pleased the Government. The Catholic Committee, immediately the Act was passed, voted a gift of £1,500 as a mark of gratitude to Tone, and then promptly dissolved itself. The reaction against the French blood-bath had already set in, and caution was the watchword for loyal Catholics.

In 1795 yet a further instalment in this conciliation policy was delivered, when the Government founded and endowed a national seminary at Maynooth for the education of Catholic priests. The anti-French stand taken by the bishops, their social conservatism, and their proven political malleability, were all factors influencing the Government's decision in making this significant gesture. The need to remove the sour taste left by the 'Fitzwilliam episode' was, no doubt, a further relevant factor. A more interesting consideration behind the Government decision was the deeply-held conviction that Irish candidates for the priesthood should be educated within the safe confines of the King's realms, thus avoiding ideological contamination through contact with the political and social heresies then sweeping continental Europe. How necessary was this precaution, or how satisfactory its results, are matters for conjecture. Certainly orthodox Catholic clergy on the Continent were unlikely to become disseminators of the revolutionary gospel. Nor indeed had previous generations of Irish emigré priests shown any marked proclivity for preaching social or political revolution when they returned to minister in Ireland. On the other hand the founding of Maynooth, while it may have given the Government some claims on the political loyalty of the hierarchy, and while it certainly played a part in the spreading of the English language and ideas in Ireland, nevertheless contained within its conception the roots of much discontent. For, after 1795, Irish priests received an education which was an exclusively Irish experience, and could not but reflect and be attuned to the tensions and problems present in Irish society. The provision, within Ireland, of theological education for Catholic priests had already started (for example, at Carlow and Waterford) before the founding of Maynooth, and the social origins and educational experience of the students at these seminaries is a key factor in any understanding of the role of the priests in politics in nineteenth-century Ireland.

This marked increase in the pace of concession to the Catholic grievances which characterised the closing decades of the eighteenth century gave grounds for the belief that it was only a matter of time before the final disabilities on Catholics would be removed. For a brief few months in early 1795 it seemed as if Fitzwilliam was about to grant the final measure of Catholic rights. But the strength of the opposition and the shifting power-balance in the British House of Commons combined to frustrate his plans and to secure his recall. There were very powerful forces working against the full concession of Catholic emancipation.

In the first place the English monarch, George III, bolstered by a strong anti-Catholic lobby among the aristocracy, and by a powerful current of anti-Popery running through the various strata of British society, was an implacable opponent of full Catholic emancipation. Secondly, the English Catholics, conscious of their position as an untrusted minority and anxious to give every evidence of their loyalty, were hardly likely to force the pace in demanding full emancipation. In Ireland itself the die-hard elements among the Protestant ascendancy were prepared to fight all concessions to Catholics to the last. Their main argument against emancipation rested on their claim that it would merely open the flood-gates to a Catholic takeover of power. But much of the vulnerability of the Catholic claim lay within the Catholic body itself. The Catholic Committee, even after the middle-class leaders took over from the Kenmare-Fingall interest, still represented only the narrow, if influential, interests of the Catholic professions and property owners. They had virtually no contact, in social status, political objective, or in organisation, with the great mass of Catholic peasants who, if numbers mean anything, constituted the Roman Catholic Church in Ireland. These peasants were uninterested in the complaints of lawyers that they were excluded from high office, while they themselves were in many cases on the treadmill of rackrent and agrarian violence in a struggle for survival. So long as the Irish Catholic leaders neglected to make contact with the potentially powerful grass-roots support of tenant-farmers and labourers, theirs remained just another pressure group, subject to all the vicissitudes of political pressure groups of the late eighteenth and early nineteenth century. Royal favour, patronage and the opportunities offered by the temporary coalition of political groups and interests in Government — this was the context of politics in which the pre-Union Catholic committees operated.

They had, nevertheless, gained substantial concessions, and when the Union settlement was being worked out there were strong indications that Catholic emancipation would form part of the settlement. This was Pitt's intention, and the sanction which the Catholic hierarchy gave to the Union idea derived in large degree from their belief, which Government soundings had confirmed, that emancipation with certain safeguards was to form an integral part of the scheme. The arguments in favour of including emancipation in the Union settlement were quite persuasive. By wiping clean the slate of Catholic grievances it would secure the good-will of the respectable classes of Catholics and thus send the new political experiment off on the right road. As for hesitant Protestants, they were reminded that in the new political unit the Catholics would be in a permanent minority and consequently would be unable to indulge in any invasion of the hereditary rights of the Protestants in Ireland. Persuasive though these arguments were they were not sufficient. The terrifying events of 1798 did not induce a mood of concession among Protestants, and together with the strong anti-concession lobby in England, and with the unmistakeable hostility of the King, the combined opposition proved too much for Pitt's proposal and the Union was passed without reference to Catholic emancipation. Many commentators have argued that the refusal to grant emancipation at the time of the Union ruined whatever chances there may have been for making of that settlement a meaningful union between the peoples of Britain and Ireland. This proposition is debatable. What is certain, however, is that by the time the Catholic question finally reached its solution the entire context of Anglo-Irish politics had been transformed.

SAFEGUARDS AND STAGNATION, 1800–1823

The Act of Union meant the removal of the forum of debate on Irish politics from Dublin to London. One important result of this was its effect on the dynamics behind the two major strands of political controversy in late eighteenth-century Ireland, namely, the demands for parliamentary reform and for Catholic emancipation. In the case of the agitation for parliamentary reform, the initiative henceforth remained very definitely with the British reformers. In the case of the Catholic question, however, the numerical strength of the various denominations virtually ensured that in the political conflict on emancipation the crucial theatre of struggle would be Ireland. What may cause some surprise is the apparently long gestation period which the Catholic question required before assuming political urgency in post-Union Ireland. This was due to many factors; but ultimately it hinged on the divisions among the Catholic leaders on a number of key problems which attached to all proposals for a settlement. These problems arose from the series of 'safeguards' (or 'wings' as they were called) which the Government deemed necessary as accompaniments to emancipation. The proposed safeguards centred on two main conditions:

1. that the State should have some form of control over the appointment of Catholic bishops and possibly of parish priests;
2. that some State provision should be made for the payment of the Catholic clergy.

The reasons underlying both these conditions are easily appreciated — they indicate a desire (already manifested in the foundation of Maynooth) to institutionalise in some way the State's claims on the loyalty of the Catholic clergy. When the views of the hierarchy were being canvassed on the eve of the Union they were informed of the proposed safeguards. The bishops indicated their willingness to accept some State provision for the payment of the priests, together with some Government control of the appointment of bishops and parish priests.

Emancipation was not on this occasion part of the package deal, but the incident illustrates that any difficulty in formulating satisfactory safeguards at this time was not owing to a lack of rapport between the hierarchy and the Government. These particular overtures, however, came to nothing, and for the next two decades the problem of the 'wings' was to frustrate every effort to solve the question. As with any political issue, the problem was aggravated through its confusion with, or subsumption under, other issues to which it had little apparent relevance. Yet the decisive paralysing factor can probably be traced to the differences of opinion among various sections of the Catholic body on this question of safeguards.

Firstly, the English Catholic Board had no objections to the proposed 'wings', and saw the Government's desire to retain certain levers of control as perfectly reasonable. Likewise, many of the Irish bishops saw no real objections to the principal safeguards. Indeed in some respects there seemed potentially much virtue in the proposals. For example, the remuneration of the Catholic clergy had been a problem throughout most of the eighteenth century and was to remain one for much of the nineteenth. The fact that ultimately the preference of the vast majority of priests and people was for the voluntary support system should not blind us to the possibility that there was some merit in the alternative proposal for State payment. Throughout the long period of church reconstruction which had occupied the attention of the Catholic bishops from the early decades of the eighteenth century, the imposition of some standards of uniformity in both the mode of collection and the actual amounts of sacerdotal offerings was a constant source of irritation. Nor was the problem confined to a simple issue of discipline and authority between bishops and the lower clergy. At times of economic depression the demands of the clergy for what were considered, under the circumstances, excessive sacerdotal offerings, were a cause of much popular ill-will. These incidents of friction, however, scattered as they were over time and territory, were not of sufficient moment to pose a serious threat to the general preference of priests and people for the voluntary system. On this aspect of the 'wings' there were important differences of opinion between the bishops and the priests in Ireland. Furthermore, the diplomatic consequences of the Pope's embroilment with Napoleon predisposed Rome to listen with favour to British counsels. Finally, among the politically aware Catholic laity in Ireland there was an increasing volume of opinion which was hostile to the 'wings' as part of the Catholic settlement. The principal spokesman for this body of opinion was a young barrister named Daniel O'Connell.

Daniel O'Connell was born on 6 August 1775 near Cahirciveen, Co. Kerry. His father was a small landowner-cum-shopkeeper, but the most important person in the early life of Daniel was his wealthy uncle Maurice ('Muiris an Chaipín'), the patriarchal head of the family. The O'Connells were an old Catholic gentry family, typical in many ways of the character of their class in eighteenth-century Ireland. Having survived the great upheavals of the seventeenth century, the O'Connells had settled down to increasing their wealth and maintaining their position, while at the same time withdrawing entirely from political participation in the affairs of the country. European in outlook, this class sent their sons to be educated in the Catholic colleges of Europe of the *ancien régime*. Many of these sons subsequently found careers in the armies of the Continent; many became priests and bishops. One of Daniel O'Connell's uncles became a General in the French army. Despite the penal laws, the family had contrived to retain their lands in Uí Rathach, with the family house at Derrynane. Maurice O'Connell, by combining in himself the talents of a hard-headed landlord, an extensive grazier and a successful smuggler, had amassed a considerable fortune.

The O'Connells represented not only the capacity for endurance shown by their class but also its changing character. They spoke the English language, since it was essential to social mobility and economic profit; and their relationship with the Irish-speaking peasantry, who still lacked the will or the capacity to accept the new political and social reality, was gradually changing from the patriarchal mode of the old Irish *taoiseach* with his followers to that of landlord with his tenant, each pursuing his own interest in a relationship based on the cash nexus of rent.

This change, however, was gradual, and residual elements of old ways continued to surface right up to the famine. Daniel O'Connell's own background is a good illustration of this process. With his uncle Maurice and with his other relations he communicated in English; and the political attitudes which he received from these relations were deeply conservative. However, he was also heir to the Gaelic tradition of his aunt Eibhlín Dubh Ní Laoghaire and her mother Máire Ní Dhuibh; this tradition with its strong note of alienation and defiance. O'Connell himself spoke Irish fluently. The popular culture of South Kerry, rich in Ossianic lore and Gaelic verse, was all about him in his youth and his subsequent life-style when at Derrynane shows that he possessed a knowledge of, and a genuine affection for, this part of his heritage.

Between 1791 and 1793 O'Connell studied at the colleges of St Omer and Douai. First-hand experience of the progress of the French revolutionary armies confirmed his Catholic conservatism and left him with an abiding horror of violence as a political weapon. In 1794 he began to read for the Bar at Lincoln's Inns, and embarked on a wide course of reading which was to change his political outlook from that of a Catholic conservative to that of a radical utilitarian, and which ultimately led to his becoming one of the most influential figures in the development of modern European Catholic liberalism. While in London he read Paine's *Age of Reason* and became for a while a convert to Deism. A more lasting influence was William Godwin, whose libertarian ideas greatly impressed O'Connell. Plentiful helpings of Voltaire, Rousseau, Smith's *laissez faire* doctrines and Bentham's utilitarianism — these formed the intellectual diet of the young radical-in-the-making. He emerged a firm believer in toleration and full civil and religious liberty, and in the economic canons of *laissez faire*.

O'Connell was called to the Irish Bar in 1798, and though he sympathised with much of the United Irishmen's programme of parliamentary reform he was horrified by the bloodshed of 1798.

This hatred of violence as an agent of political change was again
evident in 1803 when he joined a yeomanry corps of lawyers to
uphold law and order during Emmet's rebellion. Immediately
after the Union he became involved in the Catholic Committee,
and he soon emerged as the leader of the radical group, chiefly
lawyers, who were opposed to the Government's proposed
'safeguards'. After the passing of the 1793 Relief Act the energy of
Keogh and his middle-class colleagues seems to have been largely
exhausted and by the early nineteenth century the conservative
Catholic aristocrats were as entrenched as ever on the Catholic
Committee. These noblemen were in favour of safeguards. So
also were some of the respectable Catholic middle-classes
including some highly talented professional men, like Sheil, who
were anxious to reach agreement with their English co-
religionists. In Parliament, the old protagonist of the Catholic
claims — Grattan — together with other pro-emancipationists,
such as Plunkett — were also satisfied to accept conditions; and,
of course, so also were the English Catholics. Against all these the
O'Connellite group retained a united front of opposition. When
in 1808 Grattan spoke in the Commons in favour of accepting
some safeguards his suggestions were rejected, at O'Connell's
persuasion, by the Catholic Committee, and the bishops,
significantly, supported O'Connell's stand on this issue. In
1813–14 however there came a far more serious explosion of these
internal divisions in the Catholic ranks.

The trouble arose when Grattan proposed a Catholic Relief Bill
in the Commons in 1813. In its final form this Bill conceded the
right to the Government to exercise some form of control on
Catholic appointments. Accepted by the English Catholic Board
and by the Irish Catholic aristocrats, Grattan's Bill was rejected by
O'Connell and his followers. In 1814 the matter was referred to
Monsignor Quarantotti, who, with his Pontiff held captive by
Napoleon, was indeed walking a diplomatic tight-rope.
Quarantotti urged acceptance of the veto proposals, but
O'Connell persuaded the Catholic Committee to reject the
Monsignor's advice, and again he carried the hierarchy with him.
This was too much for the Irish Catholic nobility and they

withdrew from the Catholic Committee. In fact, when the Pope was eventually released he upheld the right of the Irish bishops to reach their own decision on the matter. To Grattan these events must have been a cruel disappointment; yet he persisted in championing the Catholic cause in Parliament until his death in 1820. Indeed the year after his death a Catholic Relief Bill, complete with veto proposals, did manage to pass in the Commons, only to be thrown out by the House of Lords.

However, after the shattering divisions of the veto controversy, the Catholic cause had, by the early 1820s, reached the nadir of its fortunes. The tactical bankruptcy of the Catholic advocates was well illustrated during George iv's visit to Ireland in 1821, when the almost hysterical manifestations of Catholic loyalty were unable to evoke more than the most general expressions of royal good-will. O'Connell at least seems to have realised that even with a pro-emancipation majority in the Commons (itself an uncertain basis for hope), the opposition of the King and of a solid majority in the Lords would always prevail until the Catholic leaders devised some new way of breaking the deadlock. A new conceptual approach and a fresh political initiative were necessary. And as he surveyed the political and social landscape of contemporary Ireland, O'Connell began to identify and select certain groups and strategies which were to provide him with the materials for victory.

STRUGGLE AND SUCCESS, 1823-29

One key factor of the new strategy was the organisation and manpower of the Catholic Church in Ireland. The Church had emerged from the penal period with its congregation for the most part intact, and with its organisation scarred but not destroyed. The process of reorganisation which had been going on throughout the late eighteenth century had by the early nineteenth already completed an impressive amount of church reform, in diocesan organisation, episcopal jurisdiction, sacerdotal discipline and in the establishment of meaningful lines of communication with Rome. Much remained to be accomplished, but the story of the Catholic Church in Ireland in the first half of the nineteenth century is one of increased efficiency and unrelenting expansion. A massive programme of church building, most of it post-1830, was undertaken; the opening of the first school of the Christian Brothers in 1802 signified a new expansion of the Catholic teaching orders to provide the peasantry with a formal Catholic education. The seminaries at Maynooth, Carlow and elsewhere spared no effort in ensuring that the expansion of the Catholic church establishment would keep pace with the increasing demands on manpower consequent on the population explosion. Of course, much of this church reconstruction took a long time to complete. Irregularities in discipline and sacerdotal practice continued to present serious problems throughout the period. Then, as now, the funding of this nationwide organisation was a constant challenge. The pace of reform often varied from diocese to diocese in response to the enterprise of particular bishops or the wide differences in the material condition of the people in different areas. However, even allowing for these differences there is little doubt that by the 1820s the machinery of the Catholic Church was adapting itself to meet the requirements of its increasing responsibility.

The political dimensions of this Catholic church establishment are worth noticing. In the first place there was at times a distinction between the political views of the hierarchy and those of the lower clergy. In some respects this might be seen as a reflection of the different social origins. It had long been a tradition in many dioceses for the bishops to be appointed from a definite pool of old established Catholic families. On the other hand the social base for the recruitment of priests widened as the Irish seminaries expanded; and those who might have found it beyond their means to educate their sons in a continental seminary, very often found Maynooth or Carlow well within their compass. Of the priests educated at home in the half-century before the famine, the sons of shopkeepers and tenant-farmers formed a sizeable percentage.

The differences in political outlook between the hierarchy and the priests did not apply to all areas of political debate. Nor can all questions be answered through reference to social origins. The kinds of political role in which the priest and the prelate were cast were often very different. The bishops were, after all, the ruling body of a nationwide organisation representing some eighty per cent of the population, and at the same time they were involved, as a hierarchy, in the complex world of international diplomacy, which formed the context for the political activity of the Church of Rome. Predictably, their world-view of politics was qualitatively different from that of the priest, whose political universe was peopled by proctors, parsons and police, magistrates, bailiffs and landlords.

A further distinction in the political attitudes of the Catholic priests was noted by many observant visitors to Ireland, such as Gustave de Beaumont. These commentators suggested that the younger (i.e. the home-educated) priests were far more politically involved than the older men (many of whom would have been educated abroad). Part of the explanation for this may lie in the simple changes of mood which often occur between two generations. More specifically it may have been due to the fact that whereas earlier continental-educated priests had returned to minister in a Church which was still obliged to earn official tolerance through good behaviour, the post-Union clergy were virtually certain, in view of their family background and their Irish seminarian education, to feel more involved in the social and political affairs of the country. With thirty years of concessions already behind them it is not surprising that they should also address themselves to the existing power-structure with greater confidence than their predecessors.

There was one further problem which, in its own peculiar way, contributed towards strengthening the Church's organisation. This problem was simply how best could the Church set about combating the loss of members (leakage, as this phenomenon is usually called); or, as the problem generally presented itself, how best could the priests combat proselytism. Defections had always been deemed a matter of deep regret among the Catholic community (even during the penal phase when the rewards for defection were substantial). But as the eighteenth century reached its close the increasing force of sectarian hostility was reflected in a more bitter and unforgiving treatment. However, it was in the decades immediately after the Union that the struggle between the priests and the missionary bible societies reached its full intensity. This proliferation of missionary bible societies was a by-product of the intense evangelical influences which came to dominate all branches of Irish Protestantism in the first half of the nineteenth century. The Protestant mission to redeem the Irish poor from the errors of Popery entailed the supply of itinerant preachers and scripture readers, and the distribution of religious tracts, spelling books, and chiefly the Bible, through which means the Catholic poor would come to see the error of their ways. A staggering mass of literature was distributed by such societies as the Hibernian Bible Society (1806), and the Religious Tract and Book Society (1810) which in 10 years distributed 4,400,000 tracts. The interdenominational Irish Evangelical Society, together with special societies run independently by Baptists and Presbyterians, all combined to constitute a quite impressive Protestant mission in the decades before the famine. Nor were their activities fruitless. The flood of theological literature caused some Catholics to doubt, and there were even some priests who changed religion during this period. The activities of Protestant missionaries among the poorer, Irish-speaking communities (such as Achill and Corca Dhuibhne) were a source of particular worry to the Catholic authorities.

In an obviously unintended way all this activity was a stimulus to Catholic expansion in the provision of elementary education and to renewed Catholic endeavours in the recruitment of candidates for the priesthood. Predictably, however, the proselytisers also provoked from the Catholic clergy a bitterly hostile opposition, of which MacHale's philippics are an outstanding example. Each side questioned the motives of the other, and in the bitter struggle between priest and proselytiser for the eternal souls of the Irish poor the canvas of Irish life was coloured an even deeper sectarian hue.

The Catholic church organisation was a key factor in O'Connell's new departure for the winning of emancipation. His strategy of action can now be stated. It was, simply, to change the agitation for emancipation from being merely the argument of an ineffective pressure group to the crusade of an irresistible mass movement. Over 80 per cent of the population of Ireland were Catholics; in Connaught it was as high as 96 per cent and even in Ulster, where the Protestant churches were strongest, over 60 per cent of the population were Catholics. If the Catholic masses could be mobilised politically so as to impress upon the legislature the unanimity of their support for emancipation, then, thought O'Connell (showing his deep liberal faith in the compelling power of opinion), the cause was bound to succeed. The successful transformation of the movement depended on the actions of two key elements, the Catholic masses and the politically-conscious Catholic leaders.

It was highly desirable to give a framework of political action to the Catholic masses in the early 1820s. The post-war price slump had produced severe hardship throughout parts of the countryside and fierce competition for land and the means of subsistence led to widespread popular unrest. There was a noticeable increase in rural disorder and the agrarian secret societies were active over an ever-extending area of the countryside. Given these increasing tensions, it is not inconceivable that a political agitation might have developed centred on some aspect or other of the causes of popular discontent; tithes, rents, church dues, or some more fundamental critique of the land system itself might have provided the focus for such an agitation. That they did not, and that the great political mobilisation of the masses in the 1820s centred on Catholic emancipation was due, in large measure, to the nature of the Catholic leadership.

On a personal level it is hardly surprising that O'Connell, Sheil and the Catholic lawyers, journalists, merchants and professional men should feel strongly on this issue. For lawyers and journalists and others who might be described as falling within a broad category of 'political careerists', the inability to enter Parliament or to enjoy high office was a very real source of dissatisfaction. Many of the provision-merchants and Catholic businessmen likewise could see no reason why they should be debarred from full participation in political life. The same was true for many of the Catholic tenant farmers of substance, for whom emancipation was, at the least, a political objective which they could unreservedly support (a consideration which might not be true were the agitation based on a social or economic issue). All these groups, then, might reasonably have been expected to support a campaign aimed at canalising popular discontent into a mass movement of constitutional agitation, which had as its objective the old demand for Catholic emancipation. With the institution of the Catholic Church providing an effective organisational framework for the agitation — as well as a disciplined officer corps in the field — the omens were encouraging.

The new departure began in the spring of 1823 with the founding in Dublin of the Catholic Association, with the object of using all constitutional means to gain emancipation. The new Association renounced any claims to being a representative assembly, decided to allow the press to attend at its meetings, and declared its accounts and minute books open for inspection. The yearly subscription for members was set at £1 1s od and there was to be a weekly meeting on Saturdays, for which 10 members would constitute a quorum. Although the number of subscribers soon passed 100 the first year of the Association's history was not spectacularly successful, and there was difficulty at some meetings in reaching a quorum. Nevertheless, the Association had already shown some novel tendencies, of which the most important was its readiness to discuss issues, such as membership of commercial concerns, nepotism and the petty tyranny of officialdom, which went somewhat beyond the simple question of emancipation. However, the fortunes of the Association really took flight in 1824 with O'Connell's programme for the involvement of the Catholic masses. It was decided to enrol associate members at a subscription of 1d a month. This would not only provide a sizeable fighting fund but would also create an unique bond between the subscribing peasantry and the Association. The idea of involvement through subscription was not new; it was also shared by the Methodists and by some of the reform clubs of the early nineteenth century. Even the various Catholic associations of the late eighteenth and early nineteenth century had all devoted some attention to devising schemes for raising subscriptions. But O'Connell's plan for the Catholic rent (as it was known) dwarfed in size and significance any previous attempt.

In each county a treasurer, secretary and committee were appointed to manage the collection; by June 1824 some 200,000 copies of the rent plan and 4,000 collector's books were in circulation. Voluntary committees of collectors divided up the entire country into areas of operation; subscriptions were forwarded to Dublin, in due course the Dublin newspapers arrived with due acknowledgement, and were promptly posted up in a public place. By the autumn of 1824 the rent was averaging £300 per week, and in March of the following year £1,840 was received in one week. Indeed, by March 1825 over £19,000 had been collected in subscriptions since the start of the Association. The rent was a useful reflection of both the uneven strength of the movement throughout the country, and of the fortunes of the agitation at various times throughout the period. The main strength of the movement was in Leinster and Munster and, to a lesser extent, Connaught; the Ulster receipts were never very high. In the same way the rent slumped during the political quietus of early 1827 but reached an all-time high during the excitement of the Clare election in 1829.

The local committees also held meetings to draw up a litany of their grievances, to be forwarded to Dublin, as well as petitions in favour of emancipation. The lawyers on their circuits encouraged the formation of committees and the small-shopkeepers, traders and farmers, under the priests' supervision, set about creating the local apparatus of collection and agitation. Reynolds describes the process as follows:

The largest chapel in the town was the setting; a peer or the local pastor, sometimes the bishop, presided; petitions were adopted setting forth specific instances of oppression; committees appointed to manage the rent collection, resolutions passed

> *expressing the confidence in and thanks to the Catholic
> Association, the chief agitators and the local clergy; and for a
> climax O'Connell or Sheil or some other of the grand orators
> denounced for an hour or two England's perfidy.*

The machinery also proved a valuable method for waging the
battle against proctor and proselytiser in many areas. When the
fortunes of the Dublin headquarters committee were temporarily
at a low ebb in late 1825 the continued increase in the number of
meetings held outside of Dublin testified to the vigour of the
movement throughout the country.

The Association's headquarters in Dublin expanded as the
movement spread, and the increasing attendance at the weekly
meetings soon necessitated a move to the more spacious rooms
of the Corn Exchange, which was to function as the nerve-centre
for O'Connellite agitation for almost twenty years. The affairs of
this 'popish parliament' were much the same as those of the local
committees, writ large. Statements of account, petitions, reports
of special committees investigating a wide spectrum of
grievances, a long litany of instances of official corruption;
arrangements for legal aid for victims of petty tyranny,
concluding with lengthy declamatory speeches from O'Connell,
Sheil, Lawless or Conway — these were the ingredients at the
Corn Exchange. The attendance was representative of most
shades of Catholic opinion, but from the very outset lawyers
predominated. The list of original members of the Association
gives some indication of the position; it included 31 lawyers
amongst its 62 members as against 11 merchants, 10 landed
gentlemen, 3 newspaper editors, 4 members of the aristocracy
and a Carmelite friar. The priests did not usually attend the Corn
Exchange meetings, their work being elsewhere. The Catholic
aristocracy were unable, with few exceptions, to accommodate
themselves to the new machinery to the extent of actually
participating in its operations. Many of them signified their
approval by contributing to funds or by occasionally chairing a
meeting. Nevertheless they were not without indirect influence;
O'Connell's anxiety to secure the maximum support from the

widest spectrum of opinion led him to use all his influence in
excluding from the deliberations of the Association issues, like
parliamentary reform, which might alienate support from the
basic plank in his programme. This wasn't always possible and it
is hardly surprising that prominent speakers like Sheil, or F. W.
Conway and Michael Staunton (the editors of two of Dublin's
newspapers), or Jack Lawless, should occasionally differ in their
views of political tactics within the Association. However,
O'Connell's was from the outset the dominating personality in
the affairs of the Association. A tall, broad-shouldered man, with
an air of defiance and an eloquence at once rich and violent,
O'Connell was at this time at the height of his powers. Without
equal at the Irish Bar in all-round ability, his political speeches
were a fascinating combination of passionate eloquence mixed
with humorous anecdotes; of repetitive digressions balanced by
impressive marshalling of evidence. Flattering or bullying his
audience as the occasion demanded, in his treatment of opponents O'Connell often resorted to bitter invective and occasionally
to downright abuse. During his long reign at the Corn Exchange,
his was at all times the commanding presence.

We have been discussing how the Catholic Association used its
resources to bring into the Irish political arena in 1824 a well co-
ordinated mass agitation for Catholic emancipation. It now
seems reasonable to ask why did the masses respond to the call;
what caused the rank and file of Irish Catholic peasants to enrol
in the great crusade? One factor often cited by O'Connell's
opponents, and which had some validity, was the element of
social pressure involved in the methods of the Association. This
did not necessarily mean intimidation or victimisation. In the
case of the Catholic rent it merely meant that in a community
where all were subscribing, pride or the desire to conform often
made abstention difficult. As Raifteirí so engagingly puts it:

> Goirm sibh a dhaoine 's ná bígí faoi tharcuisne,
> Molfaidh mé a choíche sibh, íocaidh an cíos Catoilceach,
> Is beagán sa mhí orainn feoirling san tseachtain,
> 'S ná tuilligí scannail ná náire.[2]

However, such a mass agitation could not have prospered without striking that genuine response which predisposes people to invest a great deal of voluntary effort in its progress, a great deal of faith in its ultimate success. That Catholic emancipation should evoke such a response among the Irish peasantry is usually attributed to O'Connell's charismatic leadership. O'Connell's leadership was indeed crucial. He stood in a relationship to the Catholic masses that was quite unique. In this respect, at least, there was no Irish leader before or since quite like O'Connell. He shared their historic sense, their hopes and aspirations. He had no need to imagine what the experience of being a Catholic in Ireland might be. He was one of them, and he articulated in ringing phrases their deep resentment at past wrongs and their firm resolve to make their presence felt. Balzac's comment that he (O'Connell) 'incarnated a whole people' captures in a phrase that subtle matrix of loyalties and resentments, old memories and shared pieties, which bound the Catholic peasantry to O'Connell.

Yet O'Connell's influence, enormous though it was, is not sufficient as a total explanation of the support given by the masses to the agitation for emancipation. For this we must look again at the workings of the Catholic Association. We have noted the wide spectrum of grievances which formed part of the deliberations of the Association at all levels. This illustrates shrewd political tactics on O'Connell's part, but it also reminds us how high were popular expectations of the benefits which would follow emancipation. We have already seen how the response of the peasantry to the 1798 rebellion revolved, in many instances, on the expectation of far-reaching changes in the very structure of society. This theme was to endure.

The mass of the peasantry in pre-famine Ireland may indeed have been technically illiterate but they had a rich and vital oral tradition, in song and story, which encompassed a peculiar politico-social and religious millenarianism. In the aisling (dream poem) genre of the eighteenth century it was forecast that when the hero (the Stuart pretender) returned to free the maid

(Ireland) from bondage, on that day the Gaill (usually cited as English-speaking, Calvinist usurpers) would be put down and the Gaeil (Irish-speaking and Catholic) restored to their ancient glory. Much of this, of course, represents literary convention; all of it became, as the century progressed, irreconcilable with any awareness of political reality. Yet the basic theme of deliverance endured and it lies at the root of much of the popular attitudes to politics in the half-century before the famine. A Meath poet in 1809 saw Bonaparte as the deliverer:

> *Cé go gcreideann go leor nach eagal dóibh cóir*
> *Nach bhfuil furtacht nó fóirthin le fáil dóibh;*
> *Ach tiocfaidh sé ón bhFrainc, an taoiseach gan mhoill,*
> *A bhainfeas sodar as na Gaill — sé sin Bónaigh.*[3]

And belief in Bony, and in the general theme of deliverance, carried over into the broadsheet ballads in English:

> *As Gráinne was wandering along the sea shore,*
> *For seventy weary long years and more,*
> *She saw Bonaparte coming far-off at sea,*
> *Saying rowl away, my boys, we'll clear the way*
> *So pleasantly.*

In due course O'Connell inherited the mantle of deliverer and the winning of emancipation became for many of the peasantry the pursuit of the millennium. By this time religion had become the prime element in the conceptualisation of role-reversal, and its implications for a reversal of social and economic status were often explicitly stated. Raifteirí, recommending payment of the Catholic rent, remarked:

> *Is beag ins an gcíos é, is saoróchaidh sé talamh*
> *An deachmhadh ní ghlaofar mar déantaí oraibh cheana,*
> *Beidh ceart agus dlí díobh i dtír is i dtalamh*
> *Ní baolach dúinn coíche faid is mhairfeas Ó Conaill.*[4]

In the early nineteenth century many believed Pastorini's prophecy (first published in 1771) that Protestantism would be extinguished for ever in the year 1825. The consequences of this day of retribution were often stated explicitly:

Now the day of ransom, thank God, is dated,
When tithes no more will oppress the land.
It's now those foreigners and proud invaders
Shall feel the weight of each Irish hand;
No vestry-cess of tithes we'll pay them,
We'll banish Brunswickers out of our land,
We'll free old Ireland from Orange traitors
Or die like heroes on Slieve na Mon.

It is not suggested that the peasantry believed in literally every word of this stuff. But when taken in conjunction with the proceedings of the Catholic Association, the millennial strand in the folk tradition goes some way towards explaining why the peasantry rallied with such enthusiasm to the flag of emancipation. O'Connell himself responded to these attitudes and in his own speeches the imminent dawn of a new era forms a constant theme.

The peasants weren't alone in believing that the agitation for emancipation was the prelude to a great change in society. Many of the ruling class were equally convinced that a revolution was at hand and a sizeable volume of correspondence reached the Castle with information about the impending rebellion. It was at one time believed that Christmas Day 1824 was to be the day of fulfilment for Pastorini's prophecy — the annihilation of Protestants — and strict precautionary measures were taken. However, 1825 dawned on an Irish Protestant establishment still very much alive and angrily calling on the Government to suppress the agitation. At Government level there were serious divisions on the entire question. Within the Liverpool Ministry there was a majority, including Lord Liverpool himself and Peel, who were against emancipation. As for the Irish Administration, the Viceroys, Lord Wellesley (1821–28) and after him Lord

Anglesey, were supporters of emancipation and they were supported by Plunkett, the Attorney General.

On the other hand, Chief Secretary Goulburn, Undersecretary Gregory, the Lord Chancellor and most of the other arms of government were strongly opposed to the idea. On one issue, however, official opinion was unanimous, namely, that the *modus operandi* of the Catholic Association could not be tolerated indefinitely. Accordingly, in early 1825 the Government introduced a Bill outlawing political associations of longer than 14 days duration. The Association anticipated the passing of this measure by dissolving itself and set about finding a way round the Act's restrictions by reconstituting itself the New Catholic Association. But the Association did not recover at once. In fact early 1825 brought a further set-back.

This set-back centred on the visit to London in early 1825 of O'Connell, Sheil and others, canvassing support for a stand against Goulburn's Bill. While in London they had talks with Sir Francis Burdett, who was about to introduce a Catholic Relief Bill in the Commons. O'Connell gave his support to Burdett's Bill which included two highly important 'conditions' to accompany emancipation:

1. State payment of the clergy
2. Disfranchisement of the 40/– freeholders.

A storm of protest followed O'Connell's acceptance of these clauses. The English radicals, like Cobbett, who had supported the Catholic Association as evidence of the advance of democratic tendencies, were particularly annoyed at the proposed abandonment of the 40/– freeholders. In Dublin, Lawless was not alone in strenuously opposing the agreement. O'Connell's reasons for this partial surrender are interesting. He claimed that State payment of priests need not mean any loss of independence. As for the 40/– freeholders, O'Connell held that under the existing electoral system they had no independence, being totally under the control of the county landed gentry. O'Connell's anxiety for a settlement may not have been unconnected with the difficulty of keeping a mass agitation at full stretch and yet within the law.

In any case, in this particular instance O'Connell's proclivity for pragmatic compromise produced a blank. Burdett's Bill although passing the Commons was thrown out by the Lords and a deflated O'Connell returned to face disgruntled faces in Dublin. Nevertheless he resolved to press on with the agitation, and with Dublin temporarily in eclipse the agitation throughout 1825 and into 1826 functioned chiefly through a series of impressive meetings in the countryside. Provincial meetings were held in Leinster, Munster and Connaught. But the excitement of 1824 was slow in returning. Then in 1826 came a general election, and in several constituencies it was decided to attempt a mobilisation of the 40/– vote to support the election only of candidates who pledged their support for emancipation. Using electoral pressure to secure parliamentary support for emancipation was not an entirely new idea; already in 1818 and 1823 there had been attempts to use these tactics. Electoral pressure however was far higher in 1826 than on any previous occasion. The initiative in the manoeuvre did not come from Dublin; in fact the central body of the Association, including O'Connell, remained either indifferent or opposed to these tactics until their prospects of success became virtually certain.

The chief tactician in 1826 was Thomas Wyse, a Waterford landlord of substance, who held strong views on the desirability of educating the electorate. In 1826 Wyse and a local committee in Waterford decided to back the pro-emancipation candidate, Villiers Stuart, against the powerful Beresford interest. The committee had been at work since the previous year and had spent a great deal of money in the campaign. There was no official backing from Dublin and only when victory seemed assured did O'Connell jump on the band-wagon, arriving in the constituency for a bout of speech-making a week before the elections. Great excitement prevailed, and though sectarian feelings ran high the campaign was kept free of disorder, and ultimately Beresford conceded defeat. The Waterford success was repeated in Louth, Monaghan and Westmeath, in all of which local organisations mobilised to secure the return of a pro-emancipationist.

This use of pressure at elections was viewed with alarm by the establishment. Hitherto the votes of the tenantry had, for the most part, been an integral part of the landlord's property. This does not automatically imply intimidation; the indifference of the tenants to electoral politics, the legitimate influence of the landlord and the deferential habits of the tenantry, must all be taken into account. But in 1826 the 40/– freeholders in many places had disobeyed their landlords and had voted for the candidate favoured by the local Catholic agitators. This break with the tradition of electoral influence caused ripples of despair to run through ascendancy circles. By the 1820s there were about 85,000 registered 40/– freehold voters in Ireland, and their potential electoral influence in the county constituencies was of major importance. The landlords had reason for concern. Not only had this latest development reduced still further the bonds between landlord and tenant, it also gave clear evidence of the arrival of a new force in the electoral system — the Catholic priests. Now the clergy, since the expansion of the electorate in 1793, were always, because of their position in the local communities, possessed of some measure of electoral influence. But in the emancipation struggle they were exercising it in a new and concerted way. Charges of clerical intimidation in elections, though not entirely without foundation, missed the mark in trying to explain this influence. It rested, in general, on the unique position of leadership which the priest held in the community — often a curious amalgam of spiritual leader, legal adviser and political organiser. The nature of the struggle ensured the participation of the priests in electoral politics in the 1820s and theirs was to remain a crucial influence for almost 50 years afterwards.

O'Connell used the aftermath of the 1826 election to add to the strength of his New Catholic Association; a fighting fund was set up to give legal aid to freeholders victimised for their insubordination in the elections. The outlook in Parliament was not without promise. There had been little anti-Catholic feeling shown during the general election in Britain and the Commons was fairly evenly divided on the issue. When Canning took over from Liverpool as Prime Minister in early 1827 Catholic hopes rose and even after Canning's sudden death it was hoped that the favourably disposed Goderich would grant emancipation. However, all these hopes vanished in early 1828 when the Wellington-Peel Ministry took over, pledged to oppose emancipation. After a temporary lull in activity the wheels of agitation began to move again. When Goulburn's Act expired at the end of 1827 the Catholic Association resumed full action on the old model. The opening weeks of 1828 saw great meetings held throughout the country. A new scheme was devised for revitalising the Catholic rent. By mid-1828 the Association was beginning to invade the jurisdiction of the Government itself. Lawyers were dispatched from Dublin to give legal aid to victims of 'Orange tyranny', and a variety of arbitration boards were set up. A confrontation situation had been reached between the Association and the Government. The Clare election of July 1828 provided the flashpoint.

The Catholic Association had already decided to oppose at an election any candidate who supported the Wellington regime. In June 1828 William Vesey-Fitzgerald, one of the MPs for Clare, was appointed to a cabinet post and had to seek re-election. Though Vesey-Fitzgerald was in fact sympathetic to the Catholic cause the Association decided to stand by their pledge and to oppose him. They had difficulty in finding a candidate, the Clare gentry being virtually unanimous in favour of Fitzgerald. Eventually O'Connell himself agreed to stand. Despite his initial reluctance he soon warmed to the task and the Clare election campaign of 1828 remains one of the most colourful elections in modern Irish history. The 40/– voters were well drilled, and in an extraordinary display of self-discipline there was an almost total abstinence from drink for three full days — a phenomenon which left the eyes of commentators wide with amazement. Still, O'Connell in full flow against Wellington and Peel was good value, and amid scenes of unparalleled excitement he easily beat Fitzgerald. Scenes of jubilation were widespread and the Government became terrified at the pitch which popular excitement had reached. The likelihood of violence between Catholics and 'Brunswickers' (in response to the Catholic agitation the Protestants in many places had formed themselves into Brunswick Clubs to resist emancipation) was very great. The Clare example might be repeated and the problem for the Government was to decide whether they could afford, even with a garrison close on 35,000 men, to defy such an expression of popular will, thereby risking a possible rebellion. These fears of violence were confirmed by the priests and by the leading agitators who spoke of the increasing danger of the movement going out of control. This calculated brinkmanship was decisive. Wellington and Peel were not prepared to risk provoking rebellion and so they decided to bow to what many observers had for a long time seen to be the inevitable. They advised the King to grant Catholic emancipation.

A last ditch stand by the die-hard anti-emancipationists, and a blocking campaign by a King outraged at so gross an apostacy, were unavailing, and by April 1829 the Act had received the King's signature. The desire of the Ministry to forestall the rise of any popular anti-Catholic campaign in Britain was a major factor in securing so swift a passage for the Act. Their anxiety may have been unnecessary. Popular politics in Britain had by the late 1820s different preoccupations, and even the more prudent Irish Protestants had by this stage decided against further resistance. If the democratic demon were to be fought, they had best pick more favourable grounds on which to fight him. Thus in 1829 the King and the Ministry, backed by a minority die-hard element and faced with a largely in-different public at home and an entire mass movement on the brink of rebellion in Ireland, decided to bow to the inevitable. Fear and political expediency had won the day.

THE SIGNIFICANCE OF THE VICTORY

Any analysis of the significance of the passing of Catholic emancipation must proceed from an understanding of what exactly the Act conceded. The old oaths of allegiance and abjuration were abandoned and were replaced by an oath of allegiance to the Crown and the Protestant succession. Catholics were now eligible to hold all offices of State, with the exception of that of Regent, Lord Chancellor of Ireland or England, or Lord Lieutenant of Ireland. They were still forbidden to hold religious celebrations outside their houses or churches; their bishops could not assume titles of sees already held in title by the Established Church; and all members of religious orders who should in future enter the country were liable to banishment. From the outset most of these restrictive clauses were ignored. To accompany the Emancipation Act the Catholic Association dissolved itself, and an Act was immediately passed disfranchising the 40/– freeholders by raising the franchise qualification to £10 freehold (an action which reduced the Irish electorate from over 100,000 to around 16,000). O'Connell and his followers, having made the necessary protesting noises at these clauses, welcomed the Act. The way was now clear for Catholics to enter Parliament.

Some of the more direct consequences of emancipation are obvious. The ambitious Catholic middle-class and gentry could now aspire to all but the highest positions in the land. This is not to say that there was any immediate Catholic invasion of office, high or low. The complex mesh of privileges and procedures through which members of the Protestant establishment had fortified their positions could not be easily penetrated, and it wasn't until the mid-1830s that Catholic participation in central and local appointments became significant. Nor did the dissolution of the Association signify an end to mass agitation, as the 'Repeal' agitation was soon to show.

As for the disfranchisement of the 40/– freeholders, its immediate effect was to cut the electorate to about a sixth of its former size. Many subsequent nationalists and historians argued that this Act resulted in the widespread consolidation of holdings, with consequent eviction and misery, as the landlords decided against the further existence of a now politically useless tenantry. More recent research has modified this picture considerably. It is true that the ruling classes had decided that a turbulent voting lobby who had defied their landlords could no longer be trusted and would have to be disfranchised. Moreover, the English radicals were not alone in regretting this raising of the franchise qualifications. Some of the Catholic leaders, though not O'Connell himself, were beset with feelings of guilt and dissatisfaction. But this is a long way from asserting that the 40/– freeholders were thrown to the wolves when their political usefulness was over. The loss of the vote may have been the final factor behind a sentence of eviction for a certain minority. But in the struggle between landlords, seeking to consolidate holdings, and the tenantry, fighting (often literally) to hold on to the subdivided lots, the dictates of economic interest and the deterring force of secret societies were more important to the outcome than the possession or loss of a 40/– franchise. Indeed in the new electoral situation which the agitation had created, with the traditional landlord dominance now challenged by the priests and the agitators, it is arguable that the loss of his vote may have been a blessing of sorts to the insecure tenant, caught as he was between these two stools of influence and intimidation.

The wider implications of emancipation have provoked a variety of interpretations, though on some aspects there is general agreement. The impact of emancipation on the British Constitution was considerable. The theoretical framework of the Protestant Constitution — i.e. the concept of the Established Church as the conscience of the State — had already undergone many modifications, as legislative safeguards were provided for the rights of Dissenters. But the rights of Catholics constituted a more thorny problem, since the demands of the Church of Rome seemed to be intrinsically irreconcilable with the very essence of the Constitution. Accordingly the concession to Catholics in 1829 of the right to participate fully in the legislative process may be seen as a major event in the erosion of the Erastian base to the British Constitution. On a more practical level, the *modus operandi* of the Catholic agitation served as a model for many subsequent pressure groups in British politics, most notably, the Birmingham Reform Union and, later on, the Anti-Corn Law League.

The emancipation struggle was no less an event in the context of contemporary Europe, representing as it did proof positive that Catholicism and reactionary conservatism were not necessarily synonymous, and that liberalism and the advance of popular rights need not mean godlessness and anti-clericalism. For this the Catholic liberals of Europe, such as Montalembert and Lacordaire, gave full credit to O'Connell.

Apart from its constitutional implications, the main impact of emancipation on Anglo-Irish relations centred on the manner of its achievement. The Government had yielded through fear what it had refused to the force of rational argument or basic justice. The lesson was obvious — Britain would not concede anything to Ireland except under the threat of revolution. The policy of brinkmanship received the seal of success.

The consequences of the emancipation struggle for the domestic history of Ireland are more problematic. The mobilisation of the peasantry into a coherent political force was a major stroke in political tactics. But the use made of this new force poses some questions. The fact that the first mass movement in Irish politics was for a Catholic grievance, and that its leaders at grass-roots level were often priests, went a long way towards consolidating the growing sectarian hostility between Catholics and Protestants which had been part of the eighteenth-century legacy. The abortive attempts of Lawless to rally support for emancipation in Ulster, where the concentration of Protestants was heaviest, showed clearly how deep were the sectarian divisions. The struggle for emancipation did not, of course, create sectarian divisions in Irish life *de novo*, but by its very nature it accelerated polarisation in political life on a sectarian basis. The violent language used by both sides left lasting scars. O'Connell's own professions of religious tolerance were perfectly genuine, but for his excited audiences his tirades against the 'insolent Orange faction' left the more abiding impression. O'Connell made a national movement out of what was, at base, a sectional grievance. By so doing, he institutionalised that association of Irish nationalism with Catholicism which was to severely handicap not only his own Repeal movement, but also the attempts of later generations of nationalist ideologists seeking to formulate a doctrine of Irish nationalism acceptable to all elements of Irish society.

But how avoidable was any, or all, of this? What other options were there? Certainly, given his background and temperament, one can hardly be surprised at O'Connell's desire to win full Catholic emancipation. Not only that, but given the fact that effective leadership was crucial for any successful mobilisation of the Irish peasantry, it is highly doubtful if any other issue could have called forth the same corps of effective leaders in the early nineteenth century. It hardly seems fair to blame O'Connell for the numerical and regional imbalance between the different denominations in Ireland, or, indeed, for the violence of the opposition which his movement encountered. No other cause had parliamentary prospects quite as bright as emancipation at that time. On no other issue could a union of the classes be effected. The most vital issue in pre-famine Ireland may well have been the crisis through which peasant society was passing, but in the debate on this crisis there were as many remedies as there were evils. A mass agitation cannot prosper on divided counsels and competing wares.

Finally, it is often suggested that the agitation for emancipation had a lasting influence on Irish popular attitudes to politics. Certainly O'Connell's style of leadership was highly personal. The sense of what he represented, the political pose which he struck; these, and not the ideological content or consistency of his politics, were what mattered to his followers. These, and his proven ability to succeed. It is not by accident that the name by which O'Connell was most widely known among the peasantry was 'the Counsellor'. They trusted him because he was indeed a Daniel who could enter the lion's den of the enemy's Courts and emerge triumphant; because he was, in Seán Ó Faoláin's apt phrase, 'a hero-personification of themselves'. O'Connell, by flattery, cajolery and incessant preaching of the need for self-respect, succeeded not only in making the peasantry aware of their rights, but also in convincing them of their ability to succeed in claiming those rights. Only Luther King in our own day attempted or achieved as much.

Emancipation has been described as a 'token of national rehabilitation'. A token it certainly was. The politically-ambitious Catholic middle-class were the only ones to reap a tangible harvest from the great struggle. The masses of the peasantry were made aware of their power, but their condition remained unchanged. Emancipation may indeed have been but a symbolic victory for the mass of the people, yet pride and self-respect were germane to its achievement. And, most important of all, it *was a victory*, with profound repercussions on the collective psychology of a people long used to defeat. In the making of Yeats's 'indomitable Irishry' the marshalling of the forces of the 'hereditary bondsmen' in the agitation of the 1820s should not be slighted. To regret that this new energy was not harnessed in a bid to save rural society from collapse is understandable. But it is, perhaps, to wish for the stars.

03 | THE STATE AND THE PEOPLE

The Act of Union was responsible for far-reaching changes in the way in which Ireland was governed. The abolition of the Irish Parliament was the most important of these. Yet the constitutional yoking together of two very differently constituted societies presented problems of government and administration which called, in many instances, for solutions involving a new interpretation of the responsibilities of the State towards the people. In the following pages we will locate, and discuss briefly, some of the main areas of contact between the State, as governing agent, and the people. In this way some general statements can be made about the involvement of the State in the lives of the people in pre-famine Ireland.

CENTRAL AND LOCAL GOVERNMENT

After the Union all major decisions on Irish legislation were taken by the Government in London. However, geographical factors and an indecision at the time of its inception about what exact mode of administration would best serve the purposes of the Union, both combined to produce an Irish administrative machine which had a distinctive style and sphere of action. The nerve-centre of this machine was Dublin Castle, the window through which the Home Secretary and the cabinet viewed the Irish landscape.

As royal representative, the Lord Lieutenant was the titular head of the Irish Administration. For the greater part of the year he lived in the Vice-Regal Lodge in the Phoenix Park, and his presence was expected at all State ceremonies in the Castle. To the Chief Secretary fell the lot of defending in the Commons the Irish policy of the Government of the day. The relationship between these two offices, in terms of political power, varied throughout the nineteenth century, as the exigencies of party and the force of personality might dictate. A seat in the cabinet was a reliable index of primacy of influence. Not surprisingly, friction occurred at intervals, though not as often as might be expected from an arrangement with such inherent tensions. The Lord Lieutenant was usually a nobleman who had already attained distinction in politics or diplomacy; the kind of man who by birth and service could represent the Sovereign with dignity and satisfy the social cravings of the Irish gentry. The Chief Secretary tended to be a young politician with ambitions to satisfy and a reputation to make. The demands of the Irish office made it essential for its occupant to be a man of enormous stamina and not a little patience; and if the Irish Secretaryship proved to be a baptism of fire for many future Prime Ministers (such as Lord Melbourne, Sir Robert Peel and Arthur Balfour), it also proved to be the rock on which the reputation and the health of many incumbents foundered. Holding the brief for the Government's Irish policy in the House of Commons, he needed to be well informed on all aspects of this policy. Consequently, during his visits to Dublin, usually when Parliament was not in session, the Chief Secretary was generally occupied in assembling information for answering queries and in drafting legislation with the Lord Lieutenant and with the permanent officials at the Castle.

The permanent officials centred around the Under-Secretary, whose business it was not only to act as liaison with the Chief Secretary in London, but also to keep the Lord Lieutenant fully informed and to oversee the routine correspondence between the Castle and its vast army of correspondents throughout the countryside. Again, the measure of influence which the Under-Secretary enjoyed varied throughout the period, depending on the willingness, or otherwise, of the Lord Lieutenant and the Chief Secretary to surrender the initiative to him. But at all times his influence in the routine business of the Castle (appointments, decisions on magistrates, etc.) was quite important, due no doubt to his unrivalled familiarity with situations as they developed on the ground.

The Irish law officers were often consulted on policy and as the maintenance of law and order occupied so much of the attention of the Administration throughout this period, their contribution to the policy debate at Castle level was considerable. Additionally, a litany of people of various degrees of influence offered their advice to the Castle on details of policy and administration. These advisors included the Lord Chancellor and members of the judiciary, the Irish landlord interest, bishops and ministers of the Established Church and Provosts of Trinity College. During the later 1830s, with the Whigs in power and a popular Administration installed at the Castle, the O'Connellites had for a short time some influence there, and the views of the Catholic hierarchy were canvassed more frequently as the period progressed. These shifts in influence were reflected in official appointments.

The network of patronage controlled by the Castle was quite significant. Although in the more important appointments the wider political considerations involved London's sanction, the Castle nevertheless had an effective control on appointments to the Bench, the bishoprics, certain grades in the army, certain offices on the corporations, and a large number of sinecure offices and clerkships. The top-heavy edifice of jobbery which the Irish civil service represented came under close scrutiny soon after the passing of the Act of Union, as the drive for efficiency in the machinery of government, which had emerged in late eighteenth-century England, was applied to the Irish Administration. The consolidation of various agencies — e.g. the two Exchequers in 1816 — gave opportunities for substantial pruning, and improved control of expenditure by the Treasury further reduced the incidence of institutionalised peculation.

For the first thirty years after the Union this entire complex of officialdom was recruited almost exclusively from the Protestant community, and most frequently from that section of it most unpopular with the mass of the people. The law itself, up to 1829, specifically excluded Catholics from some of these offices, and in any case the claims of the Protestants to preferment rested on their unswerving loyalty to the constitutional arrangement which begot the Castle system. Had an attempt been made early to offer a measure of Catholic participation in the workings of the Castle, the system might have had some chance of popular acceptance. This, however, did not happen, and the Castle came to epitomise for the people all the injustices of which they were becoming daily more conscious. As an instrument for gaining popular confidence in the Union, the Castle was killed at birth by its own friends.

In county government the administrative authority was the Grand Jury. The civil powers of this body chiefly involved providing for the construction of roads and public works in the county. The system was unsatisfactory in many ways. In the first place the Grand Jury was a non-elective body, selected by the Sheriff. Prior to 1816, appointment to this latter office was virtually in the gift of the local MP supporting the Government, and even after the adoption of the English method of selecting Sheriffs from lists supplied by the Assize judges, political considerations still counted for much. The Grand Juries would sanction certain schemes of public works, have a surveyor estimate the costs, then at the subsequent Assizes make presentments for the sums involved, which the presiding judge would duly ratify. When the works were completed the expenses were liable to be levied, as county cess, on all occupiers of land in the various baronies of the county. The main objection to this system was that the actual payers of county cess were not consulted when the money for these schemes was being voted. However, the practice, no less than the principle, of the system was open to serious objection. The Grand Juries were notoriously careless in making presentments, the works were often indifferently carried out, and the Jurors frequently manipulated the system to their own advantage.

All these abuses came under close scrutiny in the early nineteenth century; a succession of Government-appointed committees made their enquiries and found the system in many instances unjust and at all points inefficient. The difficulty lay in finding acceptable remedies. An Act of 1817 provided for specially qualified County Surveyors and laid down new procedures for the examination of presentments. This went some way towards eliminating the grosser forms of corruption, or at least towards ensuring some efficiency in the actual construction of the works. Eventually an Act of 1836 gave cess-payers some control, by decreeing that they be represented at the Special Presentment Sessions to be held in each barony to discuss proposals for public works before their submission to the Grand Juries. This was a significant improvement. Nevertheless the representation remained inadequate, the procedures proved cumbersome, and the cess continued to fall exclusively on the occupiers of the land. After 1839 elective Boards of Guardians were responsible for the administration of the new Poor Law, and their responsibilities increased during the famine crisis. Yet the 1836 Grand Jury Act remained at the base of county government in Ireland until the end of the century, part of a system aptly described as 'government by confusion'.

The local government in the towns was, if anything, worse than the system operating in the counties. The vast number of closed corporations, created in earlier days for political purposes, had dwindled to about 60 in the immediate post-Union period. The corporations were compact, generally non-elective and almost exclusively Protestant bodies. There were no uniform rights of admission. Freemen were often admitted only by the special favour of existing members. The rights of freemen included possession of the borough franchise, although after the 1832 Reform Act had conferred the franchise on the £10 householders the votes of freemen were only of significant proportions in a minority of towns (including, however, Dublin). The judicial functions of the corporations — with their corporate magistrates, sheriffs and juries — had all the defects which one might expect of self-elective, politically-inspired, sectarian bodies. The corporations controlled a considerable amount of patronage and, in some cases, of property. Not, indeed, that they were very wealthy; the reverse was more often the case. Poor management of corporate funds was quite common, and flagrant misappropriation was not unknown.

The poverty and incompetence of these bodies meant that they were unable to provide many of the services which one might nowadays expect of corporations. This was realised only too well by contemporaries and in 1828 an Act had been passed permitting the inhabitants of any town with houses of £5 valuation or over to elect a board of commissioners who could levy rates for such municipal purposes as cleansing, lighting and watching. This Act was widely adopted. However, the Whigs during their reform activity of the 1830s completed a reform of corporations throughout Britain. The Irish corporations could not escape. In 1835 a Government Commission, having listed the abuses which the corporations were found to contain, concluded that they were:

> in many instances of no service to the community;
> in others injurious; in all, insufficient and inadequate . . .

A complete reform was recommended. The Government had already, in 1835, reformed the Scottish and English boroughs. To refuse to deal with Irish municipal reform in as liberal spirit would be to give political ammunition to the Repealers. Accordingly late in 1835 the Government proposed a Bill, which, though it safeguarded the rights of existing freemen, and laid down substantial property qualifications, effectively suggested making elective bodies of the corporations and giving them a vital role in the government of the towns. The Bill encountered strong opposition and was dropped. The vested interests rallied their forces, the Tories determined that the corporations should not become the centres of popular agitation (as O'Connell had indiscreetly forecast), and for the next five years the question became enmeshed in the party warfare which plagued the Irish policy of the Melbourne ministry. Eventually in the Corporations Act of 1840 Dublin, Belfast, Cork, Limerick, Derry, Waterford, Clonmel, Sligo, Kilkenny and Drogheda were given elective town councils. Elsewhere the existing corporations were abolished and their property and duties vested in boards of commissioners elected under the 1828 Act (where such boards existed). In towns with less than £100 property annually, local government was handed over to the Poor Law Guardians. For the liberals the Act was a disappointment. Even in the towns incorporated, the powers were restricted and the high elective franchise qualification of £10 was considerably less liberal than that adopted in the English reform. The Act was an improvement, yet by the mid-century Irish municipal government was still in need of reform.

LAW AND ORDER

The principal responsibility which the Government discharged was the maintenance of law and order in the country. This involved a wide range of activities. All officers of the law were appointed by the Government; from the judges in the higher courts in Dublin, down to magistrates who presided at the Courts of Petty Sessions. It was chiefly at these lower levels that the ordinary man came into contact with the system and he could not have been favourably impressed with either its efficiency or its justice. The problem was that the mass of people simply had no trust in a system from which all members of their own creed were excluded. Those who presided at the Courts were Protestants, often Orangemen; the Sheriff was a Protestant and the juries which he was responsible for selecting were very likely to reflect his political bias. In these circumstances it is hardly surprising that the Catholic peasant was so reluctant to trust the law. Its functionaries differed from him not only in creed but also in class, and the hostility with which a Catholic peasant encountered the law administered by the Protestant landlord or his agent was a too familiar feature of the Courts in Ireland.

Before 1829 Catholics were, of course, excluded from the higher offices in the judiciary. However attempts to reform the system had been made long before this. The lists of magistrates were revised in 1822 and Peel's tenure of the Chief Secretaryship saw important improvements made in the methods for selecting Sheriffs. Not only the personnel but also the regulations of the lower Courts came in for attention. In 1823 the Government began to insist on the magistrates acting in concert rather than individually at Petty Sessions. More significantly, an Act of 1814 empowered the Lord Lieutenant to appoint a special stipendiary magistrate in particularly disturbed areas. In 1822 this was extended to include any area where local magistrates requested a stipendiary magistrate. This new departure was significant. The stipendiary magistrate was a paid man, an employee of the Government who could be expected to be reasonably free of those prejudices which prevailed among local magistrates; in short, a professional among amateurs. In the later 1830s the use of stipendiary magistrates became more widespread; in many instances they were used more as a substitute for than as a complement to the local unpaid magistrates. This increasing use of stipendiary magistrates indicates not so much a new awareness of the inadequacy of the existing system (this was realised by all post-Union Administrations), as an increased disposition on the Government's part to try to remedy the situation.

During Peel's tenure of the Chief Secretaryship, reforms were undertaken in many areas of administration. But the main reforms of the judicial system in pre-famine Ireland took place during the period 1835–40, when the famous Thomas Drummond was Under-Secretary at Dublin Castle. During these years there were few corners of the Irish Administration which did not feel the winds of change. Certainly the spirit of reform was evident in the changes in the legal apparatus of the State. Liberal lawyers were appointed to vacant judgeships, and Catholic liberals like Sir Michael O'Loghlen and David Pigot became law advisors to the Government, before going on to fill the chief positions on the Bench. Nor was it only the highest levels of the law that felt the effects of the new policy. The proceedings at Petty Sessions, Quarter Sessions and Assizes were brought under increased Government surveillance; the compilation of jury lists and the protection of witnesses were all subject to new regulations. Through increased use of the stipendiary magistrates and the sessional Crown solicitors, the Administration showed its determination that the law be enforced efficiently and impartially. It was assumed that once the law was seen to function without favour the peasantry would soon begin to place their trust in it, and it was hoped that the appointment of Catholics to positions in the legal system would give evidence that the law was for the protection of all.

The industry of the Administration during the Drummond era did indeed make some impression on the popular imagination; O'Connell's speeches gave full credit to the regime for its efforts during these years. However, the interval of reform was short, the number of appointments limited, and the counter-action of vested interests powerful. Deeply-rooted fears are not easily dispelled, and although by the early 1840s the implementation of the law had been purged of many of its earlier abuses, it still lacked the trust of the mass of the people. One important consequence of this was the special relationship between the people and the secret societies. These societies, often enforcing their rules on land-occupation by violent methods, did have some kind of moral sanction for their actions among the more desperate peasantry. In fact this adherence of a section of the people to a code of conduct based on terrorist methods of enforcement indicates forcibly the distrust of the law so widespread among the Irish peasantry. Even in the 1820s when the Catholic agitation produced a corps of Catholic lawyers ready to advise the people on their legal rights, the confidence that was reposed in these lawyers, such as O'Connell and Sheil, often owed more to admiration for their forensic skill than to any new belief in the intrinsic justice of the system.

The Drummond era was a brief glimpse of what might have been, had an effort been made over an extended period to enforce the law impartially but effectively. Yet it is open to doubt whether even this would have been enough. Many of the tensions in Irish society, and above all the land problems, owed their origins to causes more fundamental than could be remedied by simply overhauling, however thoroughly, the operations of the criminal law. So long as these tensions remained, the maintenance of public order in Ireland would owe more to the constraining influences of the military and the police than to the effective functioning of the Courts as a moral force in Irish society.

Like the incidence of special coercive legislation, the changing strength of the military presence was a reliable index of the peaks and slumps of popular agitation throughout the nineteenth century. During the French wars there were at one time over 30,000 regular troops stationed in Ireland, and even with the return of peace, the number rarely fell below 20,000. In 1828 the total force of the garrison in Ireland was almost 35,000. This total garrison force included not only the regular troops, but also the police, militia, waterguards and revenue police. In addition, there was the Irish yeomanry, a body of volunteers who might be called upon to act in an emergency. Raised and officered by the local gentry, the strength of the yeomanry corps at the start of the 1830s was about 36,000. The yeomanry were badly disciplined and the method of recruitment gave them something of the character of a private army of the gentry. Their involvement in the bloodshed of 1798 had left a bitter memory and throughout the early nineteenth century they remained an unpopular force. Eventually they were disbanded by the Whig Government in 1834. The militia had already been disbanded at the end of the war, although a number of officers were retained in the county towns.

The army played an important role in Irish life. It offered a livelihood to many who might otherwise have joined the throngs of the unemployed in pre-famine Ireland. Apart from a sprinkling of officers, some quite distinguished, thousands of Irishmen were to be counted among the rank and file. From the 1830s the recruitment in Ireland accounted for one-third of the yearly intake of the British army. No doubt restlessness or boredom sent many an adventurous youth into uniform, but the low pay, harsh discipline, and poor accommodation made it more likely that the struggle for survival was the main stimulus to enlistment.

However, the role of the army in Irish life was not confined to offering the chance of employment. In fact its activities in Ireland extended far beyond what might be expected of an army in peacetime. Apart from the routine duties of drilling and marching, the military were heavily committed to acting in aid of the civil power. This was a subject of much controversy throughout the nineteenth century, above all during the anti-tithe agitation of the early 1830s. Indeed throughout this period the threat of public disorder, arising from any one of a host of causes, brought the army into almost continuous operation. Aiding the civil power might involve (in Dr McDowell's words): 'Supplying detachments to escort prisoners, to protect sub-sheriffs executing judgments against defaulting tenants and tithe-payers, to guard wrecks, to keep the peace at fairs and race meetings, to stop Orange processions and take down Orange arches, and to search the country for arms.'

As some of these activities had unmistakable political connotations, the use of the military in such actions depended to a considerable degree on the discretion of the Administration. After clashes between troops and peasants during the early 1830s, the Administration showed some reluctance in committing the soldiers to aiding the serving of processes for tithe arrears. Yet, all in all, the use of the military in the preservation of the peace had a beneficial effect. The arrival on the scene of a force of troops in disciplined formation often dispersed excited crowds, thereby preventing what might otherwise have erupted into violent clashes.

The first half of the nineteenth century saw a major reform of the police forces in Ireland. At the close of the eighteenth century the police force in rural areas was confined to baronial constables under the effective control of the Grand Juries. They did not give satisfaction and it soon became clear that a more effective force was needed to cope with the frequent outbreaks of agrarian disorder. In 1814, Peel took steps to improve the system. By an Act of that year the Lord Lieutenant was empowered to appoint a chief police magistrate, with a specially appointed force under his command, to function in specified areas proclaimed to be disturbed. Though this force — the Peace Preservation Force — only applied to disturbed districts, its creation signified the tendency of central government to assume powers and responsibilities which had hitherto been left to local interests. A further reform followed in the Constabulary Act of 1822, by which the Lord Lieutenant was empowered to appoint a chief constable for each barony and to call on the local magistrates to provide a certain number of constables for each district. In the event of the magistrates not complying with the request, the Lord Lieutenant himself could appoint these constables. This was a significant advance, yet certain obvious faults still remained. The Peace Preservation Force still remained and the two forces were often in disagreement on questions of jurisdiction. The existence of four provincial heads was unsatisfactory, making it difficult to obtain uniform standards of discipline or modes of action. By the early 1830s the constabulary numbered nearly 7,700 officers and men, while the detachments of the Peace Preservation Force stationed in ten counties amounted to about 600. The need for a tidying up operation was obvious and it was equally obvious that this would have to be done by the central government. Already in 1829 Peel had given as his opinion that:

> *The best plan will be to take the nominations of all offices, high and low, in the police force into the hands of the Lord Lieutenant.*

It was left to Drummond to complete this process of centralisation. By an Act of 1836 the entire force was placed under the command of a single Inspector-General, stationed at the Castle. An improved system of recruitment was adopted. Recruits were required to take an oath disclaiming association with any secret organisation, and cases of misconduct were severely punished. The force was recruited on a non-sectarian basis. The bulk of the officer corps came initially from the army and this, together with the initiation of a compulsory training-period for recruits, made for high standards of discipline from the outset. The Castle was to be kept informed on the state of the country through regular reports from the police in all districts.

This comprehensive reconstruction of the rural police owed

much to the unceasing industry of Thomas Drummond. It was not without its birth pains. Problems of authority between the Lord Lieutenant and the Inspector General were a cause of early friction; and certain adjustments had to be made to improve the prospects for promotion within the force. However, the new force was undoubtedly a major contribution to the preservation of public order in Ireland. By 1841 it had a total force of over 8,600, distributed throughout the country in those compact barracks which were gradually becoming familiar features of the landscape of rural Ireland.

Finally the 1830s saw the reform of the two other police forces in Ireland, namely the revenue and the metropolitan police. In 1836 the former were transformed from an irregular band of armed guards into a disciplined force which soon numbered 1,000. At the same time a major police reform drawing on the example of London at last provided Dublin with an efficient police force.

HEALTH

In this brief discussion of local government and the maintenance of public order in pre-famine Ireland, there is one aspect which forces itself repeatedly upon our attention, namely, the increasing tendency of the central government to assume control over functions which in contemporary England were left to the initiative of the local gentry. The main reason for this development was simply that the Irish gentry had neither the will nor the way to carry the same administrative burden as their English counterparts. Insufficient in number, inadequate in resources of wealth and intelligence, this class had little hope of powering an efficient system of local government. This presented the Government with a problem. The supporters of the Union, at the time of its inception, had forecast that its effects on Ireland would be in every way beneficial. Yet it soon became apparent to all intelligent observers that the social problems of Ireland, chiefly poverty, ignorance and violence, were becoming, if anything, more acute as time went on. For those whose task it was to govern Ireland in the decades after the Union, the only alternative to an absolute reliance on repression was for the Government to take the initiative in areas of social administration which in contemporary England were left to the voluntary efforts of local interests. These areas of State involvement included health, public works, education and providing for the poor.

The extent of the State's involvement varied in different areas. In the case of hospitals, the contribution of central government was originally in the form of a grant to supplement private endowments or funds raised locally through the Grand Juries. However, with a rapidly expanding population, requirements in medical services became ever pressing. The ability of the local contributions to meet the cost of this expanding demand fell increasingly into arrears, so that the Government was obliged not only to continue but to increase its contribution. During the early years of the nineteenth century, state-aided public dispensaries rapidly dotted the countryside (there were over 600 in existence on the eve of the famine), and a striking expansion was also evident in the provision of fever hospitals. In providing for the mentally ill the State's role was even more important. In 1817 a committee of inquiry found that provision for lunatics throughout Ireland was primitive and inhuman. Legislation followed through which special asylums were established in ten centres. By 1835 this building programme had been completed; uniformity of standards was ensured through the appointment of an inspectorate. Thus, by the middle of the century, Ireland, unlike her near neighbour, had a reasonably comprehensive and highly-centralised system of health services.

PUBLIC WORKS

The inadequacies of local initiative and the resulting demands on central government are well illustrated by the system for constructing public works. The economic orthodoxies of the classical school sanctioned a limited degree of State expenditure on the provision of those elements in the economic infrastructure which were deemed indispensable to the spontaneous growth of economic activity. Services, such as bridges, roads and harbours, which private enterprise would be unable or unwilling to undertake, certainly came within the pale of what enlightened opinion considered healthy State intervention. The intention, however, was simply to provide the minimum necessary to induce capitalist economic development. These principles could not be rigorously applied in an Irish context, where economic expansion was insufficient to absorb the ever-increasing surplus labour force. It was suggested (though most orthodox economists rejected the idea) that public works should be used as a device to create jobs, so that by putting money into circulation the rural economy would be reactivated. More important than this doctrinal speculation was the problem created by the frequent distress caused by partial potato failures. These partial famines, which left many of the subsistence tenants and labourers virtually destitute, forced the Government to make substantial grants to public works with the object of putting some purchasing power back into this depressed class. The scope of these operations was extensive, yet at all times they were confined to such works as would not demonstrably interfere with the market options for investment. When suggested schemes seemed likely to encroach on the domain of private enterprise — as in the case of land reclamation or the construction of railways — the vested interests in parliament and the political economists combined in a firm rejection.

Yet despite these inhibitions, public works on an ambitious scale were undertaken in pre-famine Ireland. The prime responsibility for such works lay with the Grand Juries. However, many schemes were so big as to be outside the competence or jurisdiction of any one Grand Jury. Since the eighteenth century, grants from public funds had been made in such cases. In 1800 a Board of Directors of Inland Navigation was given a grant of £500,000 to devote primarily to the laying out of lines for canals. This board gradually took control of the Royal Canal Company, the Shannon navigation, and the Newry and Tyrone canals. From 1819 the Board was charged with the responsibility for encouraging Irish fisheries, to which was added, after 1825, the control of various western roads built as public works in the aftermath of the partial famine of 1821–2.

It was during such periods of acute distress that the frontiers of State involvement were pushed forward to new limits. In the aftermath of the 1817 potato failure £250,000 was made available from the consolidated fund, to be administered by special commissioners. Some £30,000 of this was spent in the construction of public works. During the financial crisis of 1820 the remainder was put at the disposal of yet another special board for the support of commercial distress. This latter case illustrates in a striking way the accommodation of official thinking and economic orthodoxies to the exigencies of Irish economic difficulties. The potato failure of 1821–2 is yet a further example of this tendency, when £50,000 was voted for schemes of road-building. Funds were also made available (on the security of county rates) to local committees set up to relieve distress. Within a matter of months they disposed of £65,000.

All these boards represent a considerable State interest, but it was a rather untidy interest, and by the end of the 1820s plans were being made for bringing some kind of order into the system. Accordingly in 1831, a new Board of Works, consisting of three special commissioners, was constituted, taking over the functions of all existing boards. Some £500,000 was put at their disposal to be used as loans to Grand Juries or private individuals, and an additional fund of £50,000 was provided for use in the form of grants toward the construction costs of roads and bridges in areas too poor to enable local Grand Juries to undertake such projects. From the outset, the Board earned praise for efficiency and imagination; high standards were ensured through employing professional engineers. By 1845 the loan fund had reached £980,000 and an additional £125,000 had been laid aside for grants. This represents a substantial investment and when the role of these schemes as a determinant of wage-rates in the rural countryside is taken into account, the full impact of public works on the Irish economy begins to emerge. The famine crisis was to present new problems to the Irish Board of public works, but already, in the previous twenty-five years, the construction of public works had become a significant element in the Irish economy.

EDUCATION

Perhaps the most striking example of the growing collectivist role of the State in Irish social life is presented by the growth of a state-sponsored system of elementary education. It was a widely-held belief that one of the main factors which made for the social distress of the Irish masses was their lack of education; ignorance acted not only as an impediment to practical schemes for the improvement of their condition but also prevented their developing habits of industry and systematic thinking, the lack of which left them an easy prey to the rhetoric of agitators. It was assumed that a properly conducted system of elementary education could only lead to an increasing awareness of the benefits of the Constitution. Acceptance of the desirability of the goal led to increasing State subsidisation of endowed agencies; as the resources of these agencies became increasingly inadequate the State began to play the dominant role. The shift in the balance of influence was a gradual one.

By the early nineteenth century there were many agencies engaged in providing elementary education in Ireland. The Tudor parochial schools had only begun to function with any show of regularity in the early nineteenth century, and, as Established Church foundations, they found it impossible to overcome the suspicions of Catholics. The trustees were not always attentive to their obligations (funds were often mismanaged). By 1823 the total number at these schools was estimated at 36,498 (21,195 Protestants, 15,303 Catholics). The educational role of the Established Church was more favourably advertised in the schools of the Erasmus Smith Foundation, 150 of which were operating with a quiet efficiency by the close of the eighteenth century. Apart from these endowed foundations a certain group of schools were from 1733 onwards in receipt of grants from the State. These were the Charter schools — run by the Incorporated Society in Dublin for Promoting English Protestant Schools in Ireland — whose missionary role was on behalf of the Protestant faith and the English tongue. Between 1745 and 1832, these charter schools received a total of over £1 million in State grants. Yet a further Protestant missionary organisation — the Society for the Discountenancing of Vice — began operating schools in the early years of the nineteenth century and it too received Government aid.

Since these schools were considered by the majority of Catholics as proselytising agents, it is not surprising that their combined efforts catered for only a fraction of the children of school-going age. The great majority of children, at the close of the eighteenth century, were receiving their experience of education in the hedge-schools. These schools owed their name to the habit of holding classes in the open air during the fine weather of the summer. During winter a landlord or farmer might provide a barn in which the schoolmaster could teach his classes. The curriculum of the hedge-school was based, for the most part, on the three r's. There was a clear occupation-orientated bias in much of the curriculum. Apart from giving potential seminarians a good grounding, the system seemed designed to fit pupils for jobs as clerks, store-keepers or similar occupations.

In many schools smatterings of Latin and Greek, and history and geography, found their way into the curriculum. Increasingly English, the language of commerce and of social mobility, became the language of the hedge-school, though elements of the native *béaloideas* seem to have been encouraged by some schoolmasters. Obviously in such a system as this the conditions, the curriculum, and the standards attained all varied considerably. Though the hedge-school system had probably passed its hey-day at the time of the Union, it nevertheless survived long into the nineteenth century. By the mid-1820s it was estimated that close on a half-million children, of whom four-fifths were Catholics, were being taught in the hedge-schools.

Finally, the dismantling of the penal laws and the growing assurance of the Catholic establishment in the late eighteenth century manifested itself in the growth of an exclusively Catholic system of education. The first priority was the training of priests and by the turn of the century seminaries had opened at Carlow, Kilkenny, Killarney and, of course, Maynooth. However, at an elementary level there was also considerable activity; a number of teaching orders set out to provide the poor with a Catholic education. Nano Nagle's Presentation nuns (1793) and Edmund Rice's Christian Brothers (1802) soon began to expand their operations. By the end of the first quarter of the nineteenth century the Presentation, Poor Clare, Ursuline and Carmelite nuns were providing education for upwards of 6,000 girls and there was a similar growth in the number of Catholic schools for boys.

The Catholic expansion owed not a little of its urgency to the need to counter the proselytising activities of the endowed and State-aided schools. In fact the role of the State in this educational activity was debated at some length throughout the first quarter of the century, and there was a consensus of opinion favourable to the State's assuming a dominant role in extending a nation-wide system of elementary education. This seemed the most satisfactory course to follow. The subsidisation of missionary schools was causing much ill-will, and it was unacceptable that the State should endow an exclusively Catholic system. Consistency seemed to demand either full control or complete disengagement, and the former seemed the more preferable course. A State-run system of elementary education, by reaching the minds of the native peasantry at a formative stage, might, in time, effect a cessation of disaffection.

In 1812 a committee of enquiry had recommended the establishment of a State-controlled, centralised, system of elementary education. The Government of the day was not prepared to go quite so far and contented itself instead with providing a subsidy for a Society which had begun operations in 1811. This was the Kildare Place Society, which had been founded to provide a system of undenominational elementary education. Although under Protestant control, it initially enjoyed the support of the Duke of Leinster, Lord Cloncurry and even O'Connell. By confining religious instruction to simple Bible readings, without comment, it was hoped that controversy on sectarian lines would be avoided. In 1815 the State awarded a subsidy of £7,000 to the Society and this grant was increased annually until it reached some £30,000 in 1831, by which date 137,639 pupils were being instructed in the Society's 1,621 schools.

Within a decade of its foundation, however, allegations were made that members of the Society were involved in proselytising activity and that the schools were being used for similar purposes. The initial benediction of the Catholic leaders turned to loud condemnation and Catholics were advised to avoid all contact with the Society's schools. In the mid-1820s, further Government committees of inquiry found that the allegations for proselytising were well-founded, and recommended yet again that the State should sponsor a national system of elementary education. As the Wellington-Peel Ministry entered its closing days, the plans were already prepared for a phasing-out of the grants to the Kildare Place Society but, as with public works, the major overhauling of the system had to await the advent to office of the Whigs. In 1831 Chief Secretary Stanley announced the Government's decision to establish a National Board of Education to administer a centralised system of undenominational elementary education.

The main denominations in the country were represented on the Board and schools in receipt of subsidies from the Board were to be run by mixed local committees. The curriculum was to be secular in content, though provision was made for separate religious instruction at special stated times. The Board gave assistance to local committees in building schools; published texts; and made the major contribution towards teachers' salaries. In time, a paid inspectorate was set up to ensure uniformity of standards. A teacher-training school was established in Dublin and within a decade, over five hundred teachers had been trained under the Board's aegis. Model schools were set up gradually throughout the country and an important extension of the Board's activities resulted in the establishment of a model farm at Glasnevin. Soon some of the model schools were giving some attention to agricultural instruction, though efforts in this area were never in any sense adequate to meet the needs of pre-famine Irish society.

The Board's income was in the form of a grant voted annually in Parliament. In 1831 the grant was £30,000; two years later it had fallen to £25,000 only to rise to £50,000 in 1837, and eventually to reach £100,000 in 1847. The annual vote of these funds provided the Board's critics with an opportunity to attack its operations on a wide front. The main area of criticism centred, predictably, on the place of religious education within the system. In the Established Church, the favourable attitude of Archbishop Whately of Dublin (from the outset one of the most influential members of the Board), was not widely shared. In 1832 seventeen bishops joined in condemning the scheme, whose episcopal supporters, including Whately, only numbered five. Opinion among ministers and laity, and especially among the evangelical wing, was also weighted heavily against the new departure. The action of the State was seen as a dereliction of duty, as a result of which the initiative in education was to be surrendered to the agents of Rome. In such a climate of opinion it is hardly surprising that a section of the Established Church resolved to have no dealings with the Board. In 1839 the Church Education Society was established. Its declared object was to maintain an independent system of schools conducted on the principles and under the auspices of the Established Church. By 1850 it had 1,800 schools (educating over 100,000 pupils) affiliated to it. A minority (through inclination or financial necessity) continued to work under the National Board, but it was clear by the mid-century that the Established Church intended to maintain its own system of elementary education.

The Presbyterian attitudes to the new education scheme were more complex. Lacking the resources of the Established Church, it was clearly in their interest to seek a formula which would enable them to participate with an easy conscience in the workings of the new system. Such a formula was not easily come by, particularly as the Presbyterian body itself was at this time experiencing much internal agitation. Since the close of the eighteenth century Irish Presbyterianism, like Protestantism in general, had seen a great increase in the influence of the evangelical interest. By 1830 the orthodox Presbyterian evangelicals, led by the fiery demagogue Henry Cooke, had gained the initiative within the Synod of Ulster and within five years they had succeeded in driving from the Synod the old-style liberal Presbyterians of the Henry Montgomery stamp. Thus it was a combative, Cooke-controlled Synod of Ulster which considered what attitude should be adopted by the Presbyterian body towards the new education scheme.

The scheme offered obvious benefits, but there were regulations concerning religious instruction with which the Presbyterians could not agree. The Board's object was to provide combined literary and separate religious education, but the manner of achieving this objective presented many problems. There was dissatisfaction about restrictions on the use of the Bible in the schools, on the visiting rights of ministers of denominations different from that of the majority of the pupils and, above all, about the manner in which parental demands concerning the withdrawal of their children at the special times allotted for religious teaching could best be met. At first the Board was reluctant to concede much to Presbyterian demands and for a short time in the 1830s the Synod of Ulster recommended that its members have nothing further to do with the Board. But, gradually, through shrewd negotiation, the Synod forced the Board to compromise on the points at issue. By the mid-century, the Presbyterians were receiving State aid for what was, *de facto*, virtually a self-contained system of denominational schools.

The Catholic response to the new system in the decade was one of initial, though by no means unanimous, support, which gradually gave way before an increasing volume of criticism. The system at first enjoyed the support of the majority of the bishops, including Crolly of Armagh, Murray of Dublin and Doyle of Kildare and Leighlin (known as JKL). They judged that the scheme gave Catholics a good opportunity to acquire a subsidised elementary education and were hopeful that the regulations of the Board would provide sufficient guarantee against any attempt at proselytising. On the other hand a sizeable minority, among whom Dr McHale (from 1834 archbishop of Tuam) soon emerged as the most vocal, had grave misgivings about the new departure.

By 1838 these misgivings had turned to open hostility. McHale believed that the scheme was anti-Catholic and anti-national. In principle opposed to a nondenominational system of education, he asserted that the experience of education for Irish Catholics should be characteristically Irish and exclusively Catholic, and he pointed out, correctly, that the actions of the Presbyterians showed that they too were aiming at providing an exclusively Presbyterian education for their own children.

From the late 1830s the noises of discontent within the Catholic body became increasingly loud. In contrast to the Presbyterians the Catholics had not succeeded in gaining many concessions from the Board. The hierarchy's dissatisfaction covered many aspects of the scheme — the hiring and firing of teachers; the selection of texts; and the trusteeship of school property. The internal divisions among the bishops, particularly between McHale and Murray, spilled into the public press and the matter was referred to Rome; however, Rome's non-committal reply contented itself with giving each bishop the right to decide for his own diocese, and requested that the bishops avoid public controversy on the matter. Nevertheless, attitudes were hardening. The monastic schools, which had from the outset made no more than a token participation in the scheme, severed all connection with the Board. The accession to the Papacy of Pius ix in 1846 and the appointment of Paul Cullen as Archbishop of Armagh three years later, heralded the beginning of a new phase in Church-State relations in Ireland, but already on the eve of the famine, the demands of the Catholic bishops on elementary education were becoming increasingly uncompromising.

Yet, though tossed about in the storm of religious controversy, the record of the Board's activity is by no means unimpressive. The number of schools under its control in 1833 was 789, catering for 107,042 children; by 1849 this total had jumped to 4,321 schools with close on a half-million pupils. Much of this increase represents the absorption into the system of many existing schools. There were also regional variations in the Board's activity. McHale's hostility meant that in Tuam, and in several other areas in the west, the provision of primary education continued for some time to furnish a theatre of war for the rival activities of Catholic teaching orders and Protestant missionary societies. While the Board may have lacked little in administrative rigour, and while religious controversy could hardly have been avoided in any educational policy proposed at this time, it is rather more difficult to judge the quality of the education which it provided. Here McHale's claim that the system was anti-national is undeniable; no Irish history, language or literature was taught; as far as the texts of the Board were concerned, Ireland was merely a geographical expression. The smatterings of the classics which many of the old schools had encouraged found no place in the new curriculum. The texts were uncontroversial and inexpensive, but dull and unimaginative. Large chunks of platitudes on polite behaviour (modesty; deference to one's betters) represented a turgid amalgam of social ethics and political docility. In this way it was hoped to inculcate a loyalty to the State and to the *status quo*.

Yet the system undoubtedly made major inroads into the high percentage of illiteracy, which in 1841 stood at seventy-two per cent; and during the second half of the nineteenth century the increase in literacy in Ireland, when related to *per capita* income, compared favourably with European levels. More directly, perhaps, for many of those thousands of Irishmen forced to emigrate to America or Australia or to Britain, a basic literacy in the English language was not the least of the meagre assets which they took with them into the brave new world.

Finally a few words about the State's role in post-primary education in pre-famine Ireland. At the secondary level the story is a brief one. True, the long-established endowed foundations were gradually subjected to more rigorous inspection by a professional inspectorate. But apart from this, the Government was content to leave secondary education to the efforts of voluntary societies. In the first quarter of the nineteenth century diocesan colleges began to operate at Wexford (St. Peter's), Waterford (St. John's) and Tuam (St. Jarlath's), and the network was gradually extended. The older endowed agencies of the Established Church were soon joined by Catholic teaching orders like the Jesuits, Christian Brothers and Sisters of Mercy, in the field of intermediate education. Likewise, the Presbyterians showed considerable enterprise, as evidenced in the opening of the Belfast Academical Institution in 1814. This was a two-tier institution with a primary section and a collegiate department, which latter, it was hoped, would eventually gain university status. The radical proclivities of some of its teachers caused the Institution to lose its State grant in 1816; yet it continued to flourish on the voluntary contributions of Presbyterians.

At the beginning of the nineteenth century, university education in Ireland was confined to Trinity College, Dublin. Since 1793 Catholics were entitled to take degrees at Trinity, though still excluded from holding fellowships. In the wake of emancipation efforts were made to abolish these restrictions. More important was the development in the 1830s of a demand for university education in the provinces. The ubiquitous Thomas Wyse pressed for the establishment of provincial academies and local interests in Cork, and to a lesser extent Limerick, claimed attention in the provision of higher education. Then in 1845 Peel proposed the establishment of the Queen's colleges; three colleges were to be established at Belfast, Cork and Galway; all appointments were to lie with the Crown and the colleges were to be strictly non-denominational. The Catholic bishops met to consider the scheme and this time Crolly and Murray found themselves in a minority in their willingness to 'co-operate'. The majority backed McHale in demanding sweeping changes, including a fixed quota of Catholic professors, changes in the appointments procedures, and dual professorships (Catholic and Protestant) in such disciplines as history, philosophy and anatomy. When the Government refused to meet these demands the hierarchy, backed by Rome, pronounced against the colleges, and this decision was confirmed in unequivocal terms at the Synod of Thurles, held in 1850 after Cullen's return from Rome. An impasse had been reached. Thus, at university as at primary level, the mid-century heralded the beginnings of a new phase in the crucial debate on the legitimate roles of the Church and State in Irish education.

THE PROBLEM OF POVERTY

Before concluding this discussion of collectivist experiments let us examine the efforts of the State to deal with what was, in size and significance, the greatest social problem of pre-famine Ireland — the problem of poverty. Certainly on this topic legislators could hardly complain of a lack of information. Descriptions of hordes of Irish poor swarming around coaches are standard in the travel-books of most foreign visitors from the close of the eighteenth century; more systematically quantified evidence was at hand in a succession of official enquiries throughout the opening decades of the nineteenth. The Report of 1836, estimated that the number of labourers who were unemployed for thirty weeks of the year was not less than 585,000, whose dependants would number at least 1,800,000. The question was, what, if anything, ought the State do about this? The sick and the lunatic poor benefited from improvements in the provision of infirmaries, asylums, dispensaries and fever hospitals in the decades before the famine. The problem of the able-bodied poor was more difficult.

It is impossible to grasp the complexity of the problem without briefly mentioning the assumptions about the economy and society which underpinned the debate on Irish poverty among the governing classes. The most widely accepted analysis, though there were important exceptions, proposed that the twin roots of the problem lay in excess of population and scarcity of capital. Population pressure, at once a cause and an effect of excessive subdivision, was an impediment to improved agricultural cultivation. The objective, it was argued, should be to consolidate holdings into viable economic units, a process which demanded that the smaller uneconomic farmers be made to release their hold on the land and to join the labour force. Rent inflation, the product of unnatural competition among subsistence farmers, would be halted, with resulting benefit to the stability of society and of the land market. Curtailment of subdivision would act as a brake on improvident marriages, and hence on population increase. Improved cultivation of economic land holdings would induce capital formation and this, as well as foreign capital, would find profitable outlets for investment in the new stable society. Thus, in time, a satisfactory equilibrium would be reached in the distribution of labour to economic resources.

Yet it still left the Government of the day with the more immediate problem of coping with the massive ranks of the poor already in need of help. Nor was it denied that the transition of the Irish land economy from uneconomic subsistence holdings to a consolidated capitalist-farming system would bring with it many problems, as many thousands of dispossessed cottiers would be thrown on to the already overstocked labour market. Many suggestions were made about the best way of dealing with these casualties of displacement. State-aided emigration schemes, massive public works projects, land reclamation; all found advocates among the ranks of the political economists. There was also an influential body of opinion which held that the problem of Irish poverty called out for the enactment of a Poor Law for Ireland. Ireland, unlike England, had never at any stage had a Poor Law; one consequence of this was that any discussion of the pros and cons of such a provision for Ireland was conducted with the English law as the reference model. Prior to 1834, this meant a system of outdoor relief, based on the parochial unit. The advocates of an Irish Poor Law argued on the assumption that the poor had a moral claim on the support of society as a whole. They themselves produced a variety of 'solutions'; there was general agreement, however, on the desirability of a Poor Law. A system of outdoor relief (by giving wages for work done) would enable the labourers to reach at least subsistence level; this, it was hoped, would break the spiral of despair, so that the prospects of improvement would lead to a more prudent marriage pattern. This view was most forcibly argued by Bishop Doyle. For him, as for George Poulett Scrope and other advocates of an Irish Poor Law, what was involved in poor relief was essentially a programme of public works which would, in Dr MacIntyre's words, 'increase the country's prosperity, lessen insecurity and stimulate investment'.

Those who opposed the introduction of a Poor Law into Ireland, including O'Connell, argued that it would further demoralise the poor and rupture old ties of charity. Above all, however, it was held that a Poor Law would merely aggravate further the problem of Irish poverty by placing an impossible burden on the rates, thereby devouring the rental of the country. The Irish land economy stood in need of a transfusion of capital, a Poor Law seemed more like a deadly haemorrhage. Predictably this view found plenty of support among Irish landlords. As late as 1830 a Select Committee recommended against a Poor Law, suggesting instead a combination of public works, emigration and county government reform. However, within a few years the context of the debate was to be changed significantly, following a major reform of the English Poor Law, carried out by the Whigs in 1834.

Since Tudor times the English poor found support in a system of outdoor relief work financed from parish rates. However, during the late eighteenth and early nineteenth century the system came under severe pressure. Population increase and the impact of the early stages of the industrial revolution caused serious dislocation in the work-cycle of many labourers. Complaints were heard of the rising cost of the relief system and it was claimed that its methods were demoralising the rural labourers. In 1832, a Royal Commission was appointed to investigate the question, and two years later Parliament, acting on the Commission's main recommendations, enacted the Poor Law Amendment Act. This Act showed unmistakably the influence of its efficiency-conscious Benthamite architects. The parochial outdoor relief was replaced by a centralised (though with important concessions to local agencies) system based on the workhouse. These workhouses were to be administered by special Boards of Guardians elected by the ratepayers of a certified union of parishes. From the outset the new institutions were unpopular and, particularly in the North of England, provoked violent resistance. This was not surprising. The workhouse system was planned on what became known as the 'less eligibility' principle; that is, in order to ensure that only the really destitute would seek refuge within its doors the workhouse conditions were designed so as to be less comfortable than the conditions enjoyed by any worker supporting himself in the labour market. The deepest resentment centred on the rules requiring the separation of families — wives from husbands, parents from children.

Meanwhile yet another Commission was appointed in 1833 to investigate and make recommendations on the condition of the Irish poor. The Commission was a representative one and it conducted its investigation with great thoroughness. Its report rejected the workhouse system as a model for Irish poor relief; with close on two and a half million people in distress for over half of every year the cost of the workhouse system would be ruinous. For the same reason it rejected a system of outdoor relief. Instead the report recommended a series of measures which amounted to a programme for reactivating the depressed sector of the Irish economy; a state-subsidised system of organised emigration; land drainage and reclamation and a comprehensive system of agricultural education, all to be administered by special Boards of Improvement; a programme of public works; and institutionalised relief for the disabled poor. These proposals constituted the outlines of an ambitious economic plan; but this was not what the Government required. The proposals were controversial and the only consequence which could be forecast with certainty was that they would stir up a veritable hornet's nest of vested interests. Accordingly, Lord John Russell (Home Secretary) set aside the report, and sent George Nicholls, an English Poor Law Commissioner, to Ireland to see if the workhouse system could be established there. Within a matter of weeks he reported that it could. Predictably the members of the Commission of enquiry were outraged that the fruits of exhaustive enquiries should be set aside in favour of Nicholls's hastily prepared report. But the Government's mind was made up — the workhouse system was to be transplanted to Ireland. In this view the ministers had the support of the great body of public opinion in Britain. No doubt part of the British concern for the Irish poor derived from humanitarian impulses. But economic self-interest also loomed large. There was increasing alarm at all levels of British society at the ever-increasing flood of Irish paupers who crowded into the ghettoes of the new industrial towns. As Thomas Carlyle warned,

> *There abides he (i.e. the Irishman), in his squalor and unreason, in his falsity and drunken violence, as the readymade nucleus of degradation and disorder.*

British opinion not only favoured the establishment of a Poor Law in Ireland, it also believed that the Irish landlords should meet the costs. As to the form of poor relief, the Nicholls scheme had many advantages; it was straightforward and a model for its implementation already existed in England. Opposition to the Nicholls scheme was not over-impressive. The Irish landlords were divided on the issue, but a majority were hostile; however, any alternative scheme yet suggested seemed equally likely to involve a raid on their pockets. O'Connell, after several uncomfortable bouts of indecision, eventually swallowed his basic convictions and supported the Bill; his followers were divided on the matter. The Churches were unhappy at the institutionalised form (i.e. the workhouses) of the proposed poor relief, but neither they nor any other of the scheme's critics exerted themselves sufficiently to prevent its adoption.

Accordingly, in 1838, a Poor Law was conferred on Ireland. A Central Board was established in Dublin to administer the system (subject to the control of the English Board of Poor Law Commissioners); the country was divided into unions, each of which was to have an elected Board of Guardians. These Boards were charged with erecting the workhouse, administering it, and raising the levy (half from the owners and half from the occupiers of land) to meet the costs. The commissioners were empowered to employ a number of assistant commissioners to help in setting up the system. Unlike the English experience, there was little initial opposition in Ireland to the construction of the workhouses. The total lack of any previous system of poor relief in Ireland may explain to some extent this contrast. The Irish operation also gave the Central Board greater control than in

England, and Nicholls was certainly not deficient in administrative capacity. Absence of violent resistance should not imply popular acceptance for the workhouses; on the contrary, the evidence suggests that they were viewed by the mass of the people as more detestable than the jail.

Certainly the application of the less eligibility principle to Irish conditions, i.e. devising a workhouse system less attractive than the lot of the Irish labourer on the eve of the famine, was a policy requiring the greatest administrative ingenuity. Nevertheless the workhouses were built, and dire necessity ensured that they were not left vacant. In 1841 there were thirty-seven workhouses in operation and during that year over 30,000 people sought relief within their doors. By 1846 all 130 unions were operating and on the closing day of that year there were 94,437 people lodged in the workhouses. By this time, however, the entire system was in the grip of a larger crisis. The administrators of the Irish Poor Law had made it clear that the system was designed to meet the normal demands of Irish poverty, but was not equipped to deal with any major catastrophe. Yet, within a very few years of the scheme's inception just such a catastrophe struck rural Ireland.

CONCLUSIONS

These, then, were the main efforts made by the State to exercise a beneficial influence on the condition of Ireland in the half-century before the famine. We may notice the absence of activity in areas for which there was no shortage of suggestions. For example, despite a persistent lobby of support, a major scheme for state-aided emigration was not attempted. A very modest experiment in 1823–5 (about 2,000 were sent to Canada at a cost to the Government of over £20 a head) caused misgivings about the prohibitive costs of such schemes, and in any case the increasing flow of voluntary emigration suggested that State intervention was not needed in this area. More significant, however, was the State's unwillingness to tamper in any way with that which most vitally affected the condition of the people — the land system. This is only to be expected. The inviolability of private property rights was one of the cardinal principles of the age, and while a landlord was expected to know instinctively his social obligations, how he disposed of his property ought in no way to be interfered with. In vain might Sherman Crawford, William Blacker and other reformers propose their schemes of tenant-right and small holdings. They were swimming against a relentless tide.

The extent of State activity may, when measured by present-day standards or even by the enormity of the problems of pre-famine Ireland, seem totally inadequate. Yet by the standards of the time it was quite extensive; more than was being attempted in most of Western Europe and, in some respects, spectacularly more than was being undertaken in England itself. For example, England had to wait until 1870 for even the beginnings of a national system of education. This State intervention in Ireland was not the systematic implementation of any pet theory on the functions of Government, rather was it a response to the problems needing most urgent attention. Nevertheless the limits of intervention, highlighted by the 'untouchability' of land, do indicate that certain basic assumptions underlay much of this activity. The premise most widely shared was that if English conditions could be established in Ireland, if law and order could be made to prevail there, and if a capitalist form of agriculture could be encouraged, then the resulting social stability would provide the necessary inducement for the investment of capital and the growth of the economy. Yet, however defensible these assumptions were in theory, the sorry mesh of socio-religious and political tensions in which the performance of the Irish economy was embedded could not be resolved simply by applying to Irish social problems palliatives designed to meet the needs of a different society. Paradoxically, the attempt to create 'English' conditions in Ireland involved in most instances (Poor Law is a notable exception) the adoption by the State of roles significantly different from those which it fulfilled in England.

Speculation on how a native Parliament might have dealt with the problems of pre-famine Ireland is no task of the historian. What can be said is that the response of Government to Irish problems in these decades was conditioned by the notions of

property and policy which prevailed at the seat of power —
Westminster. On the other hand, these very notions were
themselves modified, often significantly, as a result of the
problems encountered in dealing with Ireland. The explicit
questioning of the normalcy of English conditions lay yet in the
future, but already experiments of State intervention in pre-
famine Ireland provided ample grounds for a revaluation.

04 | THE ECONOMY AND THE CONDITION OF THE PEOPLE

THE INDUSTRIAL SECTOR

At the beginning of the nineteenth century, the prospects for the Irish economy seemed by no means discouraging. There was a sustained increase in agricultural output, for which the increasing population in Britain seemed to guarantee an expanding export market. The farmers were getting good prices for their produce. Profits and savings seemed likely to provide a sufficiency of investment capital. A growing domestic population promised at once a home consumer market and an adequate labour supply. The industrial base did not seem in any imminent danger. Industries like brewing and glass had already shown their capacity to adapt to new forms of production and organisation. In the north-east the skills and resources which caused the linen industry to flourish in that area throughout the eighteenth century were now being applied to the new lord of the textiles — cotton. In 1811 it was estimated that in the Belfast district some 50,000 people were employed in cotton manufacture. Elsewhere in the country, the textile industry was still heavily based on local markets and small-scale production. Spinning had scarcely begun to move from the home. Weaving was still confined to the handloom, although the semi-independent weaver (working on a fixed quantity of spun yarn supplied by the dealer) was by this time becoming as common as the old-style independent weaver (whose home and family constituted a self contained unit of production). Many small-scale farmers lived through combining part-time domestic textile work with their farm labour, though full-time weaving was the norm in many areas. Yet, some disturbing trends were already in evidence. Chief of these was the growing imbalance in the structure of the agricultural community. Population increase was largely among the labouring and cottier classes; and as their relative size within the agricultural community increased there was a corresponding decline in their condition. A disproportionately large number were living at subsistence level on a potato diet. Yet the full significance of this trend was not realised in 1800, and at the time of the Union there was a widely shared confidence that the Irish economy could look forward to continued expansion. This confidence proved, in large measure, to be misplaced. Why was this so?

Until quite recently, it was widely held that the retardation of the Irish economy in the first half of the nineteenth century was a consequence of the abolition of protective tariffs in the decades after the Union. Let us see what grounds there were for this belief. By the terms of the Union, Ireland and Britain were to be henceforth a single free trade area. However, it was conceded that certain Irish industries would need time to adjust to the new arrangements. Accordingly it was agreed that an *ad valorem* duty of ten per cent be retained by some eighteen articles until 1821. These articles included leather, glass and furniture. Woollen and cotton goods were allowed even more favourable terms of adjustment. In 1820 these duties were reviewed and the Government first suggested that the ten per cent duties should remain until 1825, then be phased out prior to final abolition in 1840. However, the Huskissonite free traders in the Government secured the total abolition of the duties in 1824. Irish industry now faced English competition unprotected.

The decades before the famine were, in fact, to witness, with certain significant exceptions, the gradual decay of wide areas of

Irish industry. From the 1820s on there was widespread distress and unemployment throughout much of the country as industries based on small-scale handcraft gradually gave way before cheaper mass-produced articles. The silk industry was an early casualty. Continuous contraction soon saw the woollen industry virtually confined to Dublin and, to a much lesser extent, to county Cork and the Suir valley. Distress was widespread. In Bandon the number of weavers fell from about 2,000 to a mere 150 in the years between 1815 and 1840. In Drogheda in 1840 some 1,900 linen-weavers were on part-time employment at 4/– a week, and many of them would not have survived were it not for their potato patches on the outskirts of town.

No doubt the apparent coincidence between the onset of this long cycle of industrial decline and the dismantling of the tariffs prompted the belief in a causal relationship between the two. Such an explanation, however, fails to take note of Ireland's 'economic situation' in the age of the industrial revolution. For Ireland's economic problems in these decades were, in many respects, similar to those being encountered in certain areas within Britain and throughout much of Western Europe as the industrial revolution traced its pattern of economic growth. Regions hitherto prosperous began to decay and new centres of industry, wealth and population arose with staggering rapidity. This dramatic change in the balance of regional economic activity owed its origin to the supply and use of the natural resources of industrial expansion; it was a function of the location of the sources of industrial power and energy. Individual inventiveness, the supply of capital and labour, foreign markets, and entrepreneurial capacity, changed spinning and, a generation later, weaving from domestic to factory industries. But crucial to the acceleration of output and the reduction of unit costs was the change from water to steam power, a change already under way before the end of the eighteenth century. Easy access to supplies of coal and iron was now a major determinant of industrial expansion. Watt's steam engine helped to improve pumping in the mines, and the increased output of vital fuel supplies, together with the development of the new puddling and rolling processes in the iron industry, powered Britain's expansion in the heavy industries. As the improvements in mining and mechanisation gathered momentum, industry began to be localised near the main sources of coal and iron. This was to be the pattern of industrial development throughout much of western Europe. Old centres of industry, which had relied on water-power and local markets, decayed, and new industrial towns grew up close to the mines. In Britain itself, this development is illustrated in the decline of the west and much of the south, and the rise of the great industrial towns of the north and midlands.

Viewed within this context, the fate of Irish industry in the early nineteenth century becomes more intelligible. The resources of coal and iron in Ireland were very poor, and consequently in the steam age Irish industry was faced from the outset with certain handicaps in any competition with her near neighbour. Raw materials could, of course, be imported, and they were. But this added to costs and, within the Irish economy, placed those ports facing Britain in a relatively favoured position. English factory production, particularly in textiles, became increasingly mechanised and with the combination of increased output and a reduction of unit costs, English manufacturers were able to meet and beat any other manufacturers sharing the same market. Could an Irish Parliament have devised a tariff scheme which would have ensured that Irish manufacturers did not have to meet the competition of cheaper British goods on the home market? Could a 'common-market' situation have been avoided? Recent research tends to offer a negative reply to these questions. Ireland's proximity to Britain, then the first industrial nation in the world, was a crucial factor in her economic problems. The selling-price of mass-produced British goods was so much cheaper than the corresponding Irish products that it is likely that they would eventually have succeeded in jumping even the most prohibitive of tariff walls.

British industry's invasion of the Irish market also owed much to the growth of quicker and cheaper transport facilities. From the 1820s, the installation of a packet-steamer service between the two countries heralded a major reduction in transport time and costs. However, the most important stage in the penetration of the Irish market had to await the coming of the railway. Before the advent of the railway, internal transport in the Irish economy was by road and internal waterways. Already at the end of the eighteenth century, the principal internal markets of the country were well serviced by an impressive road network. Further improvements followed in the pre-famine decades. Yet, impressive though it was, this road network had, in economic terms, certain shortcomings. The surface of the roads was suitable for light traffic, but not for the carriage of heavy loads. The roads facilitated the proliferation of commercial travellers and contributed to the growth of tourism, but for heavy goods, in the pre-railway age, water-carriage was the mode of transport.

There had been considerable canal-building in the late eighteenth century. By 1817 Dublin was linked with the Shannon by both the Royal and the Grand Canals. In time many additional lines were linked to the main arteries. In the north-east, a network of canals was constructed linking Belfast, Newry, and Lough Neagh with their hinterland. The main freight cargo on the southern canals was of agricultural produce — corn, flour and provisions — going to Dublin for export, and of manufactured goods coming down the country from Dublin. This traffic stimulated economic activity in market towns like Tullamore, and the countryside which surrounded them. Passenger traffic encouraged the building of hotels on the routes; warehouses and flourmills were in evidence at many stopping-stations. Yet, for all that, the Irish system of inland waterways never realised the regenerative economic role which its advocates expected of it. This was partly due to inefficiency in the construction and operation of the system. The Grand Canal cost £2,000,000 to construct, £12,000 for each of its 160 miles. Freight rates were discouragingly high. Accordingly, Ireland in 1830 had only 600 miles of navigable inland waterways, compared with England's 4,000 miles.

The railway was as yet in its infancy in Ireland at the time of the famine. The first Irish railway, the six mile suburban line between Dublin and Kingstown, was opened in 1834, and eight years later Belfast was linked with Lisburn and Portadown. In the interval, a royal commission had recommended the construction of an elaborate network of railways in Ireland. Its recommendations were ignored, partly because they were in many respects impractical, but chiefly because the State was unwilling to trespass on the domain of free enterprise. The result was a marked sluggishness in the development of Irish railways in the eighteen-thirties and early 'forties. During the famine crisis the Government found it inadvisable to rely entirely on private enterprise for railway investment, and in 1847 a Railway Act was passed which enabled the Government to lend over £600,000 to railway companies. The next six years were boom years in railway construction, as Dublin was connected with Cork, Galway and Belfast. The following table gives some idea of the change of pace:

Year end 30 June	Miles open on 1 Jan. each year	Passengers Number	Passengers Amount in £	Freight cargo in £	Total receipts in £
1836	6	1,237,800	35,316	105	35,421
1840	13.5	1,358,761	36,176	414	36,590
1842	13.5	2,046,901	54,219	2,520	56,739
1844	31	2,588,096	62,608	8,886	71,494
1845	65	3,481,707	104,712	14,636	119,398
1846	65	3,610,506	105,469	18,274	123,743
1847	120	3,866,294	149,581	35,000	184,581
1848	209	4,374,749	211,593	60,215	271,808
1849	361	4,963,856	283,481	121,694	405,175
1850	475	5,181,794	315,341	159,963	475,304

The railway, opening up the interior of the country, and drawing remote areas into the mass market, was to have a profound impact on Irish life in the latter half of the nineteenth century.

From the foregoing remarks on transport facilities a clearer light is cast on the time-scale of Irish industrial decline. The expansion of transport services and reduction of costs was a gradual process, and accordingly, so also was the penetration of the Irish market by the cheaper English factory goods. Difficulty of access gave some industries temporary insulation in their local markets, and it was the advent of the railway which finally made Britain and Ireland a single integrated market economy. As late as 1841, over 700,000 gave their occupation as textile workers. However, in order to compete with cheaper imports, these workers were having to sell their products at a lower price, or to work for a lower wage. There can be no doubt that their living standards declined appreciably in the 1820s and 1830s. Many full-time weavers became unemployed; those who had combined part-time weaving with small farming were driven to a total reliance on the land. For those who could not find work or a potato patch there was only the emigrant ship as an escape.

The localisation of industry was also apparent within Ireland itself. Dublin, the origin of all the major transport networks, supplied evidence that the larger unit of production, selling at lower prices, could eliminate or absorb its smaller competitors. In brewing, the house of Guinness, with expanding output for export as well as home consumption, gradually eliminated its rivals, first in the Dublin region and in time throughout much of the country. In the Cork region, Beamish and Crawford became the dominant brewing concern. Dublin was also the centre of the distilling industry, though towns like Cork, Limerick, Dundalk and Tullamore had also major distilleries. Many other Dublin industries survived because the railways provided them with a national market, encouraging them to expand and become more competitive. This process usually meant the extinction of smaller units in rural towns. However, the most important example of the localisation of industry in nineteenth-century Ireland is not Dublin, but rather Belfast and the north-east.

During the eighteenth century Ulster, with Belfast as its regional capital, had become the main centre for the production of linen in Ireland. Apart from its natural resources — a good harbour, fast-flowing streams, a plentiful supply of flax — the region had in addition a supply of able entrepreneurs and a distinctive rural economy in which agricultural cultivation was attuned to the work habits of the domestic linen workers. In the 1770s cotton manufacture was introduced into Ireland and it centred in the north-east, where many of the techniques already acquired in the production and sale of linen could now be applied to the new material. Capital was forthcoming and cotton mills were sprouting throughout the Belfast region before the end of the century. By 1810 there were over 20,000 employed in cotton spinning alone, and large numbers also found employment as weavers, mechanics and textile printers. Belfast rapidly increased its imports of coal and the boom stimulated activity in engine construction, iron production and other ancillary industries. The town was spoken of as the Irish Manchester. However, the cotton era in the north-east was short-lived. Protected by tariffs and based almost entirely on the home market, the industry faced a succession of crises in the early 1820s from which it never recovered. The agricultural price slump after Waterloo led to a severe contraction of the consumer demand for cotton manufactures on the home market. Then in the early 1820s the abolition of protective tariffs left the industry open to the cold winds of Lancashire competition. It failed to meet the challenge largely because, in Dr Goldstrom's words,

> ... the industry had been producing inferior goods, inefficiently, at high cost.

Unable to gain new markets, it soon lost its own.

Luckily for the economy of the region, the collapse of the cotton industry coincided with the recovery of the veteran staple of the area — linen. During the years of the cotton boom, the linen industry had declined in relative importance. In the Belfast area workers, attracted by higher wages, transferred to the cotton mills. Moreover, Irish linens were from the 1790s facing sharper competition from English and Scottish rivals, who increasingly adopted the new machines for spinning coarse yarn. The abundant supply of cheap labour seriously retarded the mechanisation of the Irish linen industry. However, the growing popularity of cheap cotton was causing linen manufacturers to fear for their future and when the development of the wet-spinning process in the 1820s made it possible for fine linen yarn to be spun by machine the manufacturers of the north-east resolved to act. They invested heavily in the new machines, installed them (in some instances in recently deserted cotton factories) and set about expanding their export markets. With plenty of capital, a skilled labour force and a plentiful supply of flax, the industry rallied, so that by 1841 Belfast and its neighbourhood had nineteen factories for spinning yarn.

The changed organisation of the industry had important social as well as economic consequences. For one thing, the industry soon became confined to Belfast and its surrounding area. As late as 1817 as much as a fifth of the total value of Irish linen production came from outside Ulster; Louth, Longford and Meath, Sligo, Mayo and even parts of Munster were involved in the industry. By the mid-century these pockets of linen production had all but disappeared. Within Ulster itself, the localisation of the industry in the Belfast region was equally marked. In 1821 the value of goods sold at the brown linen markets in various counties was as follows:

Monaghan	£142,952
Derry	£231,219
Antrim	£345,504
Down	£214,199
Armagh	£570,348

Yet by 1850 Antrim had thirty-six factories for spinning and Down eleven, as against Armagh's four and Derry and Monaghan's two each. The factory system, though cotton had already trained a generation to its disciplines, was not popular with the spinning operatives. Hand-spinning, however, could not compete with the factory and accordingly many spinners abandoned the rural cottage for the shelter of the belching chimney. In weaving also there were important, if less spectacular, organisational changes. Power-looms did not appear in Ulster until after the famine; yet although the handloom was still in control, the old independent farmer-weaver was rapidly displaced by the employee-weaver who worked on materials provided by the manufacturer. In due course, this branch of the industry also became mechanised and Belfast soon developed a network of industries to service its backbone. The 1850s were to see the beginnings of the city's famous ship-building industry, but already by the mid-century Belfast, with its mills, factories and expanding population, was clearly Ireland's only recognisable Victorian industrial city.

THE AGRICULTURAL SECTOR

From this account of the impact of the industrial revolution both on the relative compatibility of Irish and British industry in a common market and on the pattern of internal industrial growth, it is apparent that, for Ireland, the key to economic progress lay in concentrating on those areas of economic activity in which she possessed certain basic advantages. These advantages might, as, for example, in the case of linen, brewing and distilling, involve special skills, good management and prompt adaptability to new processes of production and organisation. In these cases the industries expanded, captured valuable export markets, and prospered. However, few of the manufacturing industries were of this sort. In these circumstances, the state of the Irish economy hinged on the profitable use of those resources with which nature had endowed the country — the resources of the land. Agriculture was the corner-stone of the Irish economy.

To those who tend to imagine the famine as the final collapse of an agricultural economy which had long been chronically ill it often comes as a surprise to learn that the output in volume in Irish agricultural produce increased almost consistently in the half-century before the famine. This seeming contradiction can be explained as the product of several closely interrelated factors, of which the most important are prices, population, the system of land tenure, and changes in the structure of agricultural output.

The fifty years or so before Waterloo were, excepting set-backs in the 1770s, a period of rising prices for Irish agricultural produce. A continuously expanding demand in the British market and the attractions of high prices, particularly in the boom war years, encouraged Irish farmers to increase their output. Not only the volume, but also the structure of Irish agricultural output changed significantly. From the 1770s, there was a marked increase in tillage and the volume of corn exports showed continuous increase during the Napoleonic wars. The increased tillage was accompanied by rising exports of pigs and pigmeat. In the five years ending in March 1793, the annual average export in pigs (live and dead) amounted to 232,265; whereas by the five-year period ending in January 1813, it had risen to 520,138. Changes were also evident in the output from pasturage. The continued expansion of dairying was reflected in increasing exports of butter and calf-skins. Exports of beef did not share the expansion boom, despite increased British demands. To some extent this was due to the loss of much of the colonial market (in the West Indies) in the face of American competition. From the early nineteenth century there was also a sharp rise in the export of live sheep.

This general increase in output at a time of rising prices undoubtedly meant increased prosperity for somebody; the question is, for whom? The landlords certainly benefited. There was a significant increase in rents between 1760 and 1815. One estimate puts the increase as high as fourfold in places, but the average was probably lower than this. Not all the profits, however, could be creamed off by the landlord. In some instances he was prevented from raising the rent by the existence of a lease; consequently from 1760 onwards, as prices rose, it became less profitable for the landlord to give long leases. Nevertheless, even with substantial rent increases and more frequent demands for lump-sum fines on the renewal of leases, the tenant-farmer was still able to share in the profits. He did this through profitable sub-letting, or through reducing labour costs to a minimum, both of which devices were made possible by the demographic situation obtaining in the country.

The eighteenth-century population growth in Ireland continued right up to the famine. From 4,753,000 in 1791 it rose to 6,802,000 in 1821 and by 1841 had topped the eight million mark. In 1841 about two-thirds of this huge population depended on the land for a living. Obviously this led to a high population density in rural Ireland. The census of 1841 estimated that the average density per square mile of arable land (excluding towns) was about 335 people, though there were marked regional variations. The provincial breakdown was:

Ulster	406 per arable square mile
Connaught	386 per arable square mile
Munster	332 per arable square mile
Leinster	247 per arable square mile

The combination of small-farming with spinning and weaving for the linen markets explains Ulster's high density. In the rest of the country, the pattern was an increase in density as one travelled from East to West.

This massive population increase was both a condition and a consequence of the expansion of agricultural output in the half-century before Waterloo. The expansion of tillage acreage required a high labour density; increased yields in cereals were best achieved in Ireland through healthy crop rotation, and this in fact meant extended cultivation of a good root-crop — potatoes. Both these requirements were met by population growth. However, the rate of acceleration of this growth was so great that intense competition for land led to inflated rents and to a rapid reduction in the rewards for labour. This explains why the profits of higher output at a time of rising prices did not reach the labourer, the cottier, or many of the smaller farmers. As Dr Crotty puts it:

Provided people were prepared to live largely on a potato diet, the provision of land for potato growing assured farmers of very cheap labour. Alternatively, provided under-tenants were willing to subsist to a large extent on potatoes, it paid landlords or their agents to accept or even to encourage the fragmentation of holdings.

Population pressure, with its resulting hunger for land, ensured that people *were* prepared to live largely on a potato diet. Moreover, the high nutritional content of such a diet, and the acre-economising nature of the potato crop, ensured that not only could the high labour density survive on a potato diet, but that it could do so without appreciably eating into the acreage of the profitable cereal crop. These factors combined to maximise the returns to the rent-receiver and to reduce to an absolute minimum the rewards for labour.

The increase in population, then, was chiefly among the small-farmer, cottier, and labouring classes, and this affected the rural class-structure and the pattern and size of holdings. Here again there were regional variations. In Ulster, small farms predominated; and the fact that farm income was to a considerable extent supplementary to income from spinning and weaving meant that, in general, Ulster tenant-farmers enjoyed a comfortable standard of living in the decades before Waterloo. Moreover, better landlord-tenant relations secured the general recognition throughout the province of the right of a tenant to compensation for improvements made by him to his holding. This gave the farmer some measure of security and contributed to social stability in the province. In much of Leinster, particularly in Wicklow and Wexford, there was a high quota of small but solvent tenant-farmers. Rents did not absorb the entire profit margin; subdivision was not excessive and the incidence of rural poverty was relatively low. The midlands, east Munster and parts of east Connaught contained wider differences in economic and social conditions within the rural community. There was a high incidence of large holdings, commercially farmed, and a high density of cottiers and landless labourers. In the counties of the Atlantic seaboard, subdivision was general, the land generally poor, and dire poverty widespread.

This bald statement conceals wide varieties of social relationships and institutional structures within the agricultural community. First in importance in this community was the landlord, the owner of the land and the receiver of the rents. In pre-famine Ireland about a third of these landlords were

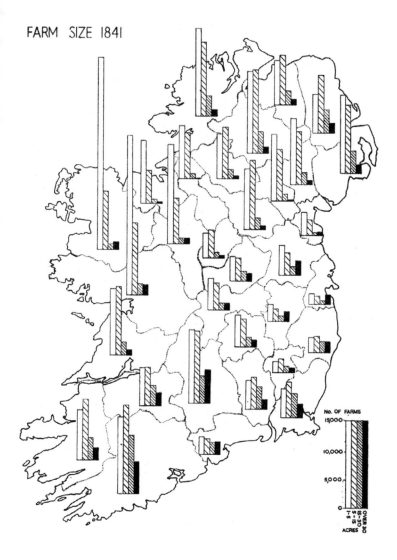

The proportion of farms of each size is shown for each county. Map from
T. W. Freeman, Pre-Famine Ireland, *Manchester University Press.*

absentees, who left the management of their property in the hands of an estate agent. Interpretation of their economic and social role varied considerably among resident landlords (and, indeed, among the agents of absentees). Some of them showed a paternalistic concern for their tenantry, often contributing to improved housing and methods of cultivation. These were the minority, however, and for too many, interest in their property extended no further than the extraction from it of maximum rents. Unlike their English counterparts, most Irish landlords were not responsible for capital investments in such areas as farm-buildings, fencing and drainage. In fact improvements undertaken by the farmer to enhance the value of his land very often triggered off demands for increased rent. Farmers who possessed leases obviously stood to benefit in a period of rising prices. For many farmers, renewal of a lease might mean a considerably higher rent demand, and very often the payment of a hefty 'renewal' fine.

Despite rent increases and tenurial disadvantages, the tenant farmer of modest means was not the chief victim of economic exposure in the decades before Waterloo. This distinction rested, in descending order, with the occupiers of minutely subdivided lots, the cottiers and the labourers. Subdivision enabled the poor tenant to provide his large family with the means of subsistence; for the land-hungry peasant willing to subsist on potatoes it seemed at least an insurance against starvation. Some landlords were prepared to tolerate widespread subdivision (they were often unable to curtail it); it may have meant harder work for the agent but so long as it didn't interfere with the rent it was permissible. Many of the shrewder landlords, however, saw the dangers of excessive subdivision — particularly the risk of damage to the land. Yet such was the passion for a foothold on the land, that efforts to curtail subdivision were to a considerable extent unavailing. Subdivision was most prevalent in the areas of highest population density and poorest land. Its most extreme version was to be found in Mayo and Donegal in the rundale system — whereby a number of families farmed holdings in partnership.

The labour demands of some small-farmers were met by the members of their own families. The bulk of the labour force, however, were cottiers and landless labourers. The cottier usually paid the rent of his tiny plot partly in labour, partly by the sale or surrender of his slight crop. In good times his surplus might allow him to keep a pig, fed from the potato patch which also provided his own food supply. The pig was a saver against hard times, when a poor crop or a rent increase might mean the cottier's having to sell his pig in order to pay his rent and thus retain possession of his patch, his means of subsistence. The landless labourers, the rural proletariat of the pre-famine economy, were in every respect its most unfortunate victims. Yet even within this depressed class there were varieties of experience. A small minority were still housed and fed by their farmer-employer, while yet another group gave their labour in return for access to a potato plot. The most insecure class, however, were the labourers who rented plots for a cash rent and hence were obliged to find adequate wage-paid employment if they were to survive. All of these labourers were in a perilous economic situation in pre-famine Ireland, where the labour market was greatly over-supplied. Some sought wage-paid work through seasonal migration; from the poorer West the *spailpín* hopefully set out, spade in hand, for the rich farm lands of Leinster and east Munster in the busy spring and summer months. Yet this market also had often a labour surplus, and an increasing number sought seasonal employment in England and Scotland. Schemes of public works also provided a limited amount of much-coveted employment. Finding wage-paid employment was not the only source of anxiety for the landless labourer, he also had to pay an exceptionally high rent for his food-supplying plot. This was due to having to rent these plots under the conacre system which, in Dr Black's description,

> *amounted to a letting for a single crop, the land being generally measured and prepared for seed by the lessor, and the lessee paying a money rent for it.*

Competition and the lessor's outlay in preparing the land both contributed to raising the rents on conacre land above the average, and a labourer leasing potato ground in conacre was in a very vulnerable position indeed.

This institutional structure was not, of course, frozen in a state of equilibrium. Population increase and the casualties of competition continuously augmented the ranks of the lower classes, and the frontiers between the poorest sub-tenant, the cottier and the labourer were constantly shifting. A bad harvest or a high rent increase might drive a one-time poor tenant onto the open labour market. Likewise, the social tensions of the economic system could not always be contained and the governing code of regulation was often a violent one. The evicting landlord, the tithe proctor, or the bailiff — all these forces may have enjoyed the backing of the law of the land, but in the violent methods of the secret societies the land-hungry peasantry had a remedy that was more summary and often no less effective. This runaway society with all its contrasts of affluence and squalor, poverty and plenty, depended for its continued existence on two key factors: (1) the continued high price-level of tillage crops, and (2) the continued health of the potato crop. After 1815 the first of these conditions was no longer satisfied, and the fulfilment of the second became a source of rising anxiety.

The slump in agricultural prices after Waterloo seriously altered the prospects for Irish agriculture. The slump was general, but prices dropped more for tillage than for grassland products. And this despite the efforts of the Government (through the enactment of the Corn Laws) to ensure a minimum price for Irish and British corn producers, by protecting them against foreign competition. On the Dublin market the annual average price per cwt of wheat in the period 1812–15 was 17/6, by 1816–20 it had fallen to 15/11 and for 1821–5 it was down to 11/6. Moreover, though grain prices were somewhat erratic over the next twenty years, returns from livestock farming showed a long-term improvement relative to tillage returns. These price-changes had profound effects on the Irish farming community. Most immediately, it became extremely difficult for many farmers to keep up payments of high rents. A minority of landlords made some downward adjustments to meet the new situation. But this was not the general practice and, as rents pressed hard, some farmers found themselves falling heavily into arrears. Leases were renewed with difficulty and tenancy-at-will became increasingly widespread. The more prosperous farmers had the capacity to meet the new circumstances, albeit with a tightening of the belt; but for many small farmers there was really no further economy that they could make, and accordingly they either fell heavily into debt or else lost their hold on the land. The cottier and labourer encountered a growing reluctance on the part of farmers and landlords to permit subsistence plots to encroach on profitable land.

The farmer's attitude reflected his response to the post-war market situation, where grassland farming was more profitable than tillage. Ireland's maritime climate made her soil particularly suitable for grazing, and, when the long price-rise for tillage produce finally ended, Irish farmers responded by endeavouring to increase their pasture. The most striking evidence of this new response was the expansion in livestock exports from the 1820s; the annual average number of live cattle exports for the five-year period 1821–5 was 46,714; in 1835 the figure was 98,150, and in the period 1846–48 the average had jumped to 190,828. This expansion in livestock was also evident in the rising export figures for live sheep. The shift to livestock was accompanied by a marked drop in the provision trade, particularly in beef. The change was facilitated by the introduction of steam shipping between Ireland and Britain and by the extension of the railways throughout Britain. Livestock were now a more convenient export than provisions (which required processing) and the improved transport facilities enabled live cattle to be transported long distances without appreciable deterioration in condition. Moreover, the eighteen-twenties and thirties saw the final capture by the Americans of the old colonial markets for beef. Butter exports remained high and the gross output from dairying suggests that cow numbers also increased in these decades. By the mid-century total output from Irish grassland was high and still rising.

At first sight it might seem from these figures that landlords did, in fact, succeed in satisfying what the post-war prices and markets clearly indicated as their self-interest, namely, transferring from tillage to pasture through consolidating holdings and setting them down to grass. This, however, would be a false reading of what actually happened. True, there was some consolidation of holdings, and both the Ejectment Act of 1816 and the Subletting Act of 1826 testify to the landlords' desire to hasten consolidation. Yet tillage continued to expand in output and acreage from Waterloo to the famine. The reason for this was simply that the population continued to expand; the land had more people to support, more mouths to feed. From 6,802,000 in 1821 the population rose to 7,767,000 in 1831 and by 1841 it had reached 8,175,000. This population increase was accompanied by a continuous expansion of tillage and the rising output of cereals and potatoes and other roots lasted right up to the famine. Part of this tillage increase was achieved through reclaiming land hitherto uncultivated. Plots were extended onto the sides of mountains, and to this day the vestiges of pre-famine cultivation can be recognised in those fading lines which mark many an Irish hillside like old surgical scars. Increased potato cultivation reflects not only expansion of acreage but also increase in yields, as cultivation of the inferior quality 'lumper' potato became more widespread. This simultaneous increase in output in both tillage and pasture may have been partly caused by increased density of stocking on grazing land. Whatever the cause, the fact of increased production in tillage and pasture is beyond doubt. By the early 1840s the total cultivated acreage, at an estimate, was about 14.5 million acres, of which some 8 million acres were in grassland, about 3.75 million in cereals, a further 2.5 million under potatoes and the remainder in other roots.

Increased production did not, as we have already noticed, mean a widening of the base of those sharing in its profits. In fact throughout the eighteen-twenties and thirties there was a marked increase in economic hardship and social disorder. Ejectments became more common, as did the incidence of forceful distraining of goods in lieu of arrears. Landlords were anxious to clear their estates of insolvent tenants and to re-let lots by auction to the highest bidders, recognising no occupancy rights whatever. Rents for subsistence plots were determined by desperate land hunger rather than by the productivity of the soil; and access to conacre land became more difficult and more expensive. Even more serious was the fact that the continued health of the potato crop could not be relied upon. In 1817 there was a serious potato crop failure and distress and hunger were severe. Again in 1821 there was widespread failure of the crop west of a line from Derry to Cork, with distress particularly acute along the Atlantic coast. On both occasions, private charity was augmented by State grants (in the form of public works schemes) in efforts to alleviate the misery. Throughout the thirties there was scarcely a year when partial failure of the crop was not reported from some area in the West. These signs were portentous.

The increase in the incidence and intensity of economic hardship had as its concomitant a serious escalation in rural disorder. Agrarian secret societies, like the Rockites, Whitefeet and Terryalts, were active over wide areas of the countryside. Land hunger and the struggle to survive were the forces which drove the cottiers and labourers into the secret societies. Threatening notices, maiming cattle, burning hay, ploughing up grassland and personal assault and battery — these were some of the ways in which cottiers, labourers and subsistence tenants attempted to prevent eviction, to discourage tenants from occupying holdings from which others had been evicted, to keep down rents, to discourage the tithe proctor, and above all to ensure that landlords and farmers did not convert conacre tillage lots into grass for bullocks. Though few areas were entirely free of outrage, the secret societies were strongest in such places as Tipperary, Laois, Kilkenny, Cork and Limerick, where good land made farmers reluctant to yield any of it in plots to cottiers or labourers. George Cornwall Lewis described the societies as 'a vast trades union for the protection of the Irish peasantry', and the penalties for breaking union rules were felt by landlord and farmer alike.

Rural disorder did not go unchecked and the Government passed a succession of insurrection and Whiteboy acts to deal with the situation. The military and the police were brought into play with increasing frequency. Clashes were frequent and members of secret societies who were brought to trial and convicted often faced, like the famous Connerys of the Déise, the convict hulk and a long trip 'thar na fairrigí go dtí na New South Wales'. These agrarian disorders were symptomatic of the serious difficulties which racked the agricultural economy in the decades before the famine. Production continued to increase, but so also did the extent of poverty. The contradiction rested on the distribution of shares in the rewards of increased output. To resolve the dilemma meant either a fundamental redistribution of resources, or a massive reduction in the non-productive, dependent sector of the population. To carry through the former would, in the circumstances, have required a revolution; in the event, a deadly famine achieved the latter.

COMPLICATIONS AND CURES

In this discussion of the pre-famine economy we have, for convenience, discussed the industrial and agricultural sectors separately. In reality, of course, both sectors were interdependent. The most obvious illustration of this was the domestic unit where family income depended on the combined returns from small farming and domestic textile work. In more general terms, a bad crop or low prices meant a reduction in demand for manufactured goods; the collapse of an industry meant a further rise in the tide of unemployment in both town and country. Of major importance was the ebb and flow in the supply and demand of capital from one sector to the other. Yet, even when examined separately, both industry and agriculture illustrate certain common features of the pre-famine economy. One immediately thinks of the regional variations — variations in the size of holdings and in the structure of agricultural production on the one hand, and on the other, the localisation of industry in favoured locations and its eclipse in other places. The north-east reflects both these tendencies in marked form — a distinctive system of land tenure and a gradual localisation of industry in the Belfast area — but there were also significant variations throughout the rest of the country.

The role which the supply of money played in the post-war economic recession is more difficult to assess. During the French wars, a serious inflationary situation developed in Britain and Ireland. In 1797 the Bank of England suspended payment in gold and the Bank of Ireland immediately followed suit. The rate of inflation was higher in Ireland than in Britain and the exchange rate of the Irish pound depreciated considerably (in 1803 it stood at a discount of twenty per cent to the English pound). With the return of peace the Government elected to abide by a 'sound money' policy, and a period of severe deflation followed, during which the Irish pound was gradually revalued. The Bank of Ireland kept a tight rein on note-issue, and a shortage of credit contributed to the collapse of several banks and industries. Gold payments were resumed in 1821 and the exchange rate remained steady until the assimilation of the Irish and English currencies in 1826. Speculation on what might have happened had an alternative monetary policy been pursued may be interesting, but can lead to no firm conclusions. What can be safely stated is that the post-war deflationary policy contributed its share to the economic difficulties of the pre-famine decades.

The cumulative effect of many factors — minor potato failures bringing famine, fever and death in their train; chronic unemployment in town and country due to surplus labour and industrial decline — began to register in the eighteen-thirties. There was a drop in the *rate* of population growth. The total still rose, but the rate of increase had dropped. Alongside this drop in the growth rate, the Irish population in the eighteen-thirties lost an increasing number through emigration. It is estimated that about 1.1 million Irishmen emigrated to the United States and Canada between 1780 and 1845, about 400,000 of whom went during the decade 1831–41. Emigration to Britain was also increasing. In 1841 there were about 420,000 *Irish-born* in Britain, some 100,000 of whom had arrived during the preceding decade. Few of them brought any skills with them, except, perhaps, in the doomed craft of handloom weaving. The vast majority formed the lowest level of the British labour force, doing the heaviest manual labour available. In London, Manchester, Liverpool, Glasgow and many other towns, the Irish ghetto became a permanent feature of the Victorian industrial landscape. Frederick Engels gave this description of the 'little Ireland' ghetto in Manchester in 1844:

> *The cottages are old, dirty and of the smallest sort, the streets uneven, fallen into ruts and in part without drains or pavement; masses of refuse, offal and sickening filth lie among standing pools in all directions; the atmosphere is poisoned by the effluvia from these, and laden and darkened by the smoke of a dozen tall factory chimneys. A horde of ragged women and children swarm about here, as filthy as the swine that thrive upon the garbage heaps and in the puddles. In short, the whole rookery furnishes such a hateful and repulsive spectacle as can hardly be equalled . . .*

Yet for all its squalor, the English urban ghetto at least offered the Irish peasant the prospect of employment, which the mud cabin in the cutaway at home did not. Accordingly, he emigrated.

The performance of the pre-famine economy, as we have described it, emerges as having been conditioned by a number of key determinants — population pressure, the availability of natural resources, the social structure, and the transformation of the market through price movements and through the revolutionary changes in the means of production and distribution of consumer goods. The interaction of these factors was at all times complex, and ultimate consequences were seldom predictable. At the same time State intervention remained a permanent possibility, and it was in such interventionist terms that many contemporaries sought to provide a prescriptive critique of Irish economic problems. Currency and customs policy are obvious examples; for many Repealers tariffs and bounties seemed the best way of reviving ailing Irish industries, and currency reformers were never scarce. A more challenging analysis argued that the social system itself, or certain aspects of it, was the crucial impediment to Irish economic health. There were many voices in this choir and they were seldom in harmony, but the core of the argument can be stated as follows: that the economy suffered from a shortage of capital, due to *(a)* the outflow of absentee rents, and *(b)* the reluctance of investors to sink capital in an unstable society whose faulty land system led to frequent disorder. O'Connell led the loud cry for a tax on absentee rents, and W. Connor, W. Blacker, W. S. Crawford and F. Lalor are but the most important of a multitude of land reformers. What substance was there in their case?

In the first place, it is not true that there was an absolute shortage of capital in pre-famine Ireland. The extent of Irish investment in Government stock, joint-stock banks and, later on, in the railways, may be taken as proof of this. True, much of this capital consisted of relatively modest amounts widely dispersed. But it did exist; the question is, how was it used? The answer, in a phrase, is: with extreme caution. Unwilling, for the most part, to put their money at risk, Irish investors acted with an eye on security and status. For example, it was not until after English capital had borne the early risk, and returns had begun to look enticing, that native capital flowed into Irish railways and banks. Land, of course, was the epitome of both security and status; accordingly, there was a tendency for many successful merchants and manufacturers to pull their profits out of business in order to buy their way into landed society (the alacrity with which encumbered estates were snapped up in 1849 is a good illustration of this). For the devout Catholic capitalist investment in the Church must have seemed like the ultimate gilt-edged security, and, indeed, the evidence suggests that investment in the heavy post-1830 church-building programme, absorbed a not inconsiderable amount of Catholic capital. Land, the Church, and the professions — these were the havens of security which drew off a considerable part of the capital from Irish industry.

Rents, of course, represented a major drain on native capital. In this respect it is doubtful if there was really any difference, in economic terms, between absentee and ordinary rents. The former, it is true, were a total loss to investment in Ireland. But many resident landlords were having to devote an ever-increasing share of their rental to servicing the debt on mortgages held on their land. Much of their expenditure was on imported luxury goods. In general they did little to generate investment in Ireland. Nevertheless, rent wastage notwithstanding, there was a supply of capital in the pre-famine economy.

Furthermore, credit facilities underwent dramatic improvement from the eighteen-twenties. The Bank of Ireland's monopoly of commercial banking was broken in 1821 by an Act permitting the operation of joint-stock banks outside a radius of fifty miles from Dublin (this latter restriction was removed in 1845). Within a short time commercial banks, like the familiar National, Provincial, and Ulster Banks, were sprouting throughout the countryside. The economic role of these banks was essentially a passive one; that is, they did not seek out investment opportunities, they waited for the customers to come to them. True, interest rates tended to favour the man of substance — the large farmer or merchant — but ultimately the verdict must be that lack of credit is no more convincing than lack of capital as a satisfactory explanation of the low investment level in the pre-famine economy. Indeed, there is probably no single-cause explanation for this phenomenon. There seems, nonetheless, good reason for concluding that lack of confidence and of enterprise did much to inhibit investment in Ireland.

Failure to exploit such obvious sources as fishing, or the ancillary products of agriculture (e.g. leather, cheese, etc.) indicates a clear lack of enterprise. This leaves us with the problem of explaining why such a lack of confidence should have existed; why investors were so unwilling to invest in Ireland. Divining the origins of confidence in capitalist investment is, at the best of times, a hazardous pastime. It is no less so in the context under discussion. Doubtless, many were tempted by the prospect of greater security and higher profits to seek investment outlets in Britain. But it seems likely also that the internal tensions of Irish society did act as a deterrent to investment. Certainly this view was widely held at the time. It is open to question, however, what measure of success would have attended the application of many of the remedies suggested. The case for the economic feasibility (no less than the social desirability) of small holdings was forcibly argued by both Blacker and Crawford, and the merits of their suggestions seemed well advertised not only in Belgium and Prussia but in their native north-east Ulster. Crawford's tenant-right proposals would, if adopted, undoubtedly have given some increase of security to the tenant-farmer. An even greater measure of security might have followed the adoption of William Connor's proposals for fixity of tenure tied to the payment of fixed rents. Yet the subsequent inclusion of these measures in the land legislation of the late nineteenth century should not lead us to assume that they would have provided the key to the pre-famine rural crisis. It may not be unreasonable to assume that, in time, these measures, if adopted, would have lent stability to the social context of rural life. But it is difficult to see how exactly they would have benefited the cottiers or the labourers — the class whose struggle for survival lay at the very root of rural disorder. There is little reason to suppose that security for the tenant-farmer would have conferred any immediate benefit on the cottier or labourer. On the contrary, it is arguable that after 1815 the improvements which security would have encouraged the shrewd tenant-farmer to undertake would most likely have taken the form of increased investment in cattle, and not in grain. There was little security or comfort here for the subsistence tillage man. In short, the problems of chronic poverty, economic imbalance, and social disorder in the pre-famine decades are unlikely to have been solved simply by piecemeal tenurial reform favourable to the tenant-farmer. To have any hopes of success, an attack on these problems would have involved a fundamental redistribution of resources — a gigantic piece of social and economic engineering. Even in the age of Keynes and Mao its chances of success could not be guaranteed. In the early nineteenth century they were nil.

LIFE IN THE COUNTRYSIDE AND IN THE TOWNS
Let us conclude this chapter with a more intimate picture of the condition and life-style of the human element in this economy.

Of course, this process must be selective; but this need not deter us from undertaking some discussion, however defective, of the experience of living in pre-famine Ireland.

As four-fifths of the population in 1841 were rural-dwellers, it seems sensible to begin with a discussion of rural society. The resident landlord, living in the Big House and frequently owning the adjoining village, was the king-pin of this society. Apart from his role as landowner he was very often the main source of employment in the area; the Big House itself employed servants and estate workers, its needs gave work to the local artisans (blacksmith, stonemason etc.), and it was not unusual for the landlord to own the local grain-mill. Obviously enormous power rested with such men. And in the post-Union decades, it would not be difficult to compile an impressive list of landlords who showed a commendable involvement in the welfare of their tenantry. The Edgeworth estate was perhaps the best example of this attitude at work.

Visitors to Mitchelstown were likewise impressed by the neatness of the cottages and by the general signs of comfort, all of which owed much to the paternalism of Lord Kingston. The ladies of the Big House often busied themselves on local committees, promoting education, inculcating thrift and, with increasing frequency, distributing charity to the poor.

Yet to suggest that these instances of enlightenment represented the norm would be a gross distortion. The prototypal landlord of propaganda — bleeding his tenants of rent while recognising no responsibility to them — too often corresponded to the reality. This state of affairs owed as much to indifference as to malice. As numbers rose and prices fell, problems multiplied, and many landlords closed their eyes and ears and asked no more of agent or head-tenant than that the rents be paid in full and on time. Drummond's famous reminder to the gentry of Tipperary — that property had its duties as well as its rights — might have been heeded by many more of their class throughout the country.

Yet even the best-disposed gentry encountered difficulties in attempting to gain the confidence of the peasantry. Quite apart from consciousness of a conflict of economic self-interest, the peasantry and most of the gentry were separated by strong social and religious barriers. Most landlords were Protestants; the minister dined with them regularly, they worshipped in his church on Sundays. Their country houses were the fixed points around which revolved a social whirl of parties, hunting, shooting and fishing; picnics for the ladies, as they gossiped of family and fashion, while the men played at croquet and talked of honour and horses. In general the career-routes of the young gentlemen were predictable — school in England, then Trinity, Oxford or Cambridge, or a commission in the army; an estate and politics; the Church and the Bench. This somewhat rarified cultural syndrome was, of course, expensive, and in the post-war decades many landlords found it increasingly difficult to stand the pace. Some could not and had to mortgage their estates.

The contrast between the life-style of the world of the Big House and that of the mass of labouring peasants was enormous. Indeed so enormous and stark was it that some observers, like de Beaumont, tended to make of this main theme the whole story. This was an over-simplification. The distinctions between tenant-farmers and labourers, and among the various strata of tenant-farmer, were no less real for being more subtle. The substantial farmer enjoyed a comfortable standard of living. His house was well built and well furnished. A spacious farm-yard, well-kept outhouses, and a hunter among his horses might all be taken as reliable indexes of prosperity. He kept a good table. Carleton's employer Pierce Murphy had a hog-yard 'upon a tremendous scale' and

> . . . no day ever passed, so long as I was there, that we had not a goose, turkey, pair of ducks, or a couple of fat fowl for dinner.

He could afford twelve guineas a year for private tuition for his children. This illustration, it must be added, comes from prosperous Leinster; Ulster's small-farm economy boasted few of this sort, and in the counties along the west coast, Pierce Murphy would indeed have been a *rara avis*. The sons of comfortable farmers might aspire to careers in the Church, the legal or the medical profession; the daughters were provided with a good wardrobe and a genteel education, and were expected not to marry beneath their station.

This picture, of course, represents only the highest level of tenant-farmer; there were many grades beneath this. Those whose means were more modest and less secure lived accordingly. They had fewer comforts of diet or dress, and their children's job opportunities were more limited. For the son of the thrifty Catholic small-farmer, entrance to the seminary was probably the ceiling of his ambitions, though pensionable clerkships and, later on, posts as national teachers, were also coveted. However, the lowest level of small-farmer was scarcely distinguishable from the cottier and labourer. The depth of poverty among this latter class is indisputable. Housing conditions give us some idea of the situation: in 1841 some forty per cent of the houses in Ireland were one-room mud cabins, while a further thirty-seven per cent had between two and four rooms. Again the regional variations showed that housing standards declined from east to west. The one-roomed mud-cabin had usually the natural earth as a floor; the smallest of them were about twelve feet wide and from twelve to twenty feet long. The roof consisted of sods of earth laid on wooden rafters and covered with a thatch of straw. Many had neither window nor chimney, so that the smoke from the fire escaped through the open door. Furniture in these mud-cabins was spartan — a súgán chair; a bed of straw, sometimes in a scooped-out hollow on the floor; occasionally a crude table and stool. At this low level cooking utensils were few — a potato pot, a can for carrying water from the well, and plates and mugs made of delph or wood.

Labourer and cottier shared a potato diet, with buttermilk as a luxury in good times. Only at Christmas was there a chance of their tasting meat. The poorer small-farmer's diet was less restricted and, in addition to potatoes, it might include milk, oatmeal and wheaten bread. Dress was a further index of the relative prosperity of the various elements of peasant society. The comfortable farmer had well-cut knee britches, waistcoat, shirt and cravat, tailcoat, warm stockings and sturdy boots, while his wife's ample cloak covered a dainty bodice, 'midi'-skirt and shift. The lower grades had generally the same cut of clothes, but they had to last longer and were consequently more ragged and patched. Few of the labourers had overcoats and their womenfolk and children generally went barefoot. Among the very poorest, clothing was little better than rags. Furthermore, as the home-made woollen and frieze garments gradually gave way to the cheaper and more stylishly-cut (but less warm) cotton, the cast-offs for the poor tended to become more and more threadbare. The main luxuries of the peasantry were tobacco and drink. Consumption of the latter was of gigantic proportions in pre-famine Ireland; on every special occasion (or on none!) there was sure to be heavy drinking. Beer and labelled whisky were both cheap, but in the early nineteenth century the illicitly distilled *poitín* enjoyed wide popularity. However, in the late thirties and forties the increased efficiency of the excise men and the impact of Fr Mathew's temperance crusade both combined to effect a reduction in the consumption of *poitín*.

Pre-famine peasant society, for all its poverty, had plenty of sport and gaiety about it. Music and song were woven into the very fabric of society and the fiddler and uillean-piper were kept busy at weddings and wakes, fairs and markets. There was no shortage of dancing; hurling was widely popular, as were other tests of strength and skill, such as weight-lifting and bowls. Fairs, pattern days and regattas provided numerous *foci* for social activity and merriment. The excitement of the fair lay as much in its fringe activities — jugglers, entertainers, music, dancing and drink — as in the actual business of buying and selling cattle and horses. A feature of many fairs in the early decades of the century was the faction-fight, in which groups of men would club each other with cudgels, sometimes to settle a feud between families or villages, but more often simply as a sort of bravado exhibition of strength. During the late 1830s a concerted effort was made by Drummond to curb all such disorderly conduct, as a result of which there was a sharp decline in faction-fighting. Pattern days (special feast-days of the patron saint of an area) were more local and more numerous than fairs, and, together with the regattas, they added gaiety and life to rural society.

The economic relationships between the various strata of rural society were based on two fundamentals — rents and labour. Conflict of economic interest was scarcely avoidable, though the well-managed estate of a responsible landlord might blunt its edge. But of no less significance than these economic tensions were the social and political cleavages which widened with increasing bitterness throughout rural society in the decades before the famine. The Protestant gentry reacted strongly against O'Connellite popular politics. They saw such politics as vulgar, convulsive and corrupt; the mendacity of O'Connell, the despotism of the priests and the insolence of the *parvenu* Catholic merchants were combining to dupe an innocent, if feckless, peasantry and to subvert the old ties of loyalty and deference which, in their view, were the very essence of rural politics. The growl of the democratic monster was becoming louder every day, conjuring up the spectre of '98, or worse. Maria Edgeworth put it succinctly:

> *The French Revolution gave us enough of the majority of the people.*

The bulk of the gentry agreed, and, under the banners of *Property* and *Law* and *Order*, moved steadily to the right.

Of course they exaggerated the danger, and those who saw O'Connellism as the prelude to a general assault on property institutions seriously misinterpreted it. O'Connell's agitation simply aimed at changing the personnel for whose benefit these institutions operated. It was a power-struggle about displacement and not about destruction. The impact of this struggle on rural community relations was profoundly disruptive, and in the decades before the famine it contributed more than its quota of strife to the community relations of rural Ireland.

If wide contrasts were a marked feature of living conditions in the countryside, this was no less true of conditions in the towns. One obvious contrast was that of size. The census of 1841 counted

Population of Towns 1841

Map based on T. W. Freeman, Pre-Famine Ireland, *Manchester University Press.*

one-fifth of the population as town-dwellers; but as this category included any settlement exceeding twenty houses, the figure is somewhat misleading. In fact only five centres had more than 20,000 people, thirteen had between 10,000 and 20,000, and a further thirty-two had between 5,000 and 10,000 (see map). Over 700 of the towns included in the census had less than 500 people. The maritime ports were the largest centres of population and of economic activity. Dublin, the capital, with its 232,726, was easily the biggest port, while Belfast (75,308 and still expanding) already dominated the north-east. Cork (80,720) was the main port for agricultural Munster, but Limerick (48,391) and Waterford (23,216) were also considerable trading ports. In the West, towns (like everything else but poverty) were scarce, and Galway (17,275) and Sligo (12,272) shared the bulk of Connaught's maritime trade.

In all but one of the maritime ports, food exports formed the backbone of overseas trade, though all of them engaged, with varying degrees of success, in various kinds of manufacturing industry. Belfast alone placed its main reliance on the export of manufactured goods. The inland towns were chiefly market centres, situated at a road junction or on a canal. Trading was their mainstay, but many of them had some kind of workshop, industry, mill or distillery. In 1841 the town of Trim, for example, had a weekly market, five fairs annually, a small flour mill, a brewery and a tannery. Many of the towns were administrative centres; a good example was Ennis, the county town of Clare, whose public buildings in 1841 included a jail, barracks, courthouse, police station, workhouse and several hospitals. From the 1830s onwards an increasing number of county towns could boast of a joint-stock bank amongst its public buildings. There were wide variations in the prosperity of different towns; the collapse of an industry meant severe distress.

Virtually every town had a high quota of unemployed labour, due not only to the failure of local industries or to the natural rate of increase within the towns, but also to the massive influx of unemployed labourers from the countryside. This was often the cause of much bitterness, as labourers from the countryside were usually prepared to work for lower wages than their town cousins, a situation of which employers were not slow to take advantage. In Dublin (where the trades unions were particularly powerful) the surplus of labour led to particularly unpleasant industrial relations. Mr James Fagan, a timber-merchant, told a parliamentary enquiry into trade combinations in 1838 that the wages for unskilled labourers in Dublin was about 8/– or 9/– a week, whereas agricultural labourers in the rural hinterland could at best look forward to only eight or ten pence per day. Accordingly combinations of journeymen were locked in battle with the employers to prevent the introduction of cheap labour into the skilled trades. Equally important for the unions was the strict control of the number of apprentices in each trade. These regulations led to frequent clashes with the employers. However, some of the unions, like their English and Scottish counterparts, were very much in the nature of benefit societies for their members. The Dublin printers' union in 1838 had 260 members, with 180 boys apprenticed; the committee met every Saturday night in a pub, and the union had a fund from which contributions were made towards unemployment or sickness benefits and towards the funeral expenses of deceased members. The printers were fairly typical of the official combinations, which, whatever their militancy, generally sought to settle their differences with the employers through negotiation. On the other hand the *modus operandi* of certain other unofficial groups relied much more heavily on violence. The Billy Welters in Dublin were particularly notorious, while in Belfast (as throughout much of industrial Britain) the early machinery plants in the textile industry came in for some unwelcome attention from the workmen. In town as well as countryside, the struggle for survival in a changing market was a hard one, and violence was never very far below the surface of community life.

Housing conditions in the main towns reflected differences in prosperity between the various classes. There were few towns which did not have a 'decayed' sector, where poor housing and squalid living standards reflected congestion and high unemployment. In Limerick the old 'island' showed all the signs of decay — houses in disrepair, appalling sanitary conditions and chronic congestion — while across the bridge the elegant terraces of Newtown Pery, well-cleansed, paved and lit, testified to the prosperity of the merchant and professional classes. In Belfast the manufacturers were just beginning to move house to the outskirts of the expanding town, while the maze of narrow low-cabined streets that housed the operatives, was gradually spreading out like a giant stain from the shadows of the factories. Moreover, religious antagonisms were imported with rural labour, and separate settlements of Catholic and Protestant proletarians faced each other suspiciously across the great sectarian divide.

But the greatest contrasts were in the metropolis itself. Dublin in 1841 was bounded north and south by the two great canals. At the core of the old city the narrow streets of the 'Liberties' were in a state of advanced decay, overcrowded and unhealthy, their jobless inhabitants in abject poverty. In sharp contrast, as one moved eastwards from the Castle, were the wide roads and elegant squares of Georgian Dublin. Engels described the contrast:

> *The city, too, possesses great attractions, and its aristocratic districts are better and more tastefully laid out than those of any other British city. By way of compensation, however, the poorer districts of Dublin are among the most hideous and repulsive to be seen in the world.*

The slum cancer was already spreading in the pre-famine period; the north-west area was quite dilapidated. Meanwhile the march of the staid well-kept terraces towards the canal ring continued unabated, while just a little further out cosy pockets of respectability, like Rathmines and Ranelagh, beckoned invitingly. Population density was already an acute problem in the slums and the situation was not getting any better.

Yet this does not mean that there wasn't considerable building activity during these years. In fact if one were to seek a paradigm for some of the main themes in Irish history in the pre-famine decades, the nature and pattern of building developments in Dublin would prove quite useful. The building of stately residences did not come to an abrupt end in 1800. Mountjoy Square was not completed until 1818, Fitzwilliam Square in 1825. Yet, for all that, the aristocratic era was in its twilight, and in the succeeding decades, as the upper middle classes came to dominate the life of the capital, the new buildings began to reflect their preoccupations. The G.P.O., the King's Inns, and the College of Surgeons — clerks, lawyers, and medical men — are landmarks of the changing ethos. The expansion of the Catholic establishment was reflected in a spate of church-building, of which the pro-Cathedral and St Andrew's in Westland Row are good examples. And while all these monuments were a-building, the city's poverty problem became progressively more acute. These contrasts were to emerge starkly in the latter half of the century. But already by the late 1840s the lines of future development were unmistakable.

TRAVEL

Those who wished to see and perhaps write about Ireland benefited from improved travel facilities in the pre-famine decades. Since pre-Union days the mail coaches provided a passenger service between the large towns. Fares were expensive, however, and the labourer who had a long distance to cover did so on Shank's mare. The early passenger service on the canals was likewise slow and relatively expensive. Under the stimulus of competition, the companies introduced faster 'fly-boats' and on the eve of the famine, upwards of 100,000 passengers were using the canals annually. The competition which prompted these improvements came chiefly from Bianconi's stage-coach service. Charles Bianconi was an Italian immigrant who had travelled Ireland in the early nineteenth century selling prints. His experiences convinced him of the need for a cheap and speedy passenger coach service. Beginning operations in 1815 with a coach service between Clonmel and Cahir, Bianconi was soon carrying the mails between towns on secondary and tertiary routes not served by the main post office coaches. Within twenty-five years his network of coach services covered most of Munster, south Leinster and Connaught. The service was cheap, fast and efficient; fares were as little as 1.5d. a mile; average speeds of around eight miles an hour were reached. Bianconi's service reached its peak in the mid-forties, when upwards of 3,500 miles were covered daily by over 100 of his cars. The service was gradually eclipsed in the fifties and sixties, when the railway network began to spread across the country. Bianconi himself was quick to size up the new situation; he bought railway shares and redeployed his coaches so as to provide supplementary services to the main railway lines. Such commercial acumen was, unfortunately, not widely shared in the Ireland of his day.

LANGUAGE

Finally, let us turn our attention to changes which were taking place throughout the period in the most immediate of all forms of communication — the language of the people. In 1800 Irish was the language of about half of the population and on the eve of the famine some four million Irishmen spoke it. Yet by 1851 less than a quarter of the population spoke the language and only five per cent were monolingual Irish-speakers. This drastic reduction was but the start of a long cycle of decline during which the Irish language retreated towards the Atlantic seaboard, while here and there (in counties Waterford, Cork, Louth and Meath, for instance) inland pockets fought a long rearguard action.

The motives behind this language-change were quite straight-forward. English was the language of the law, of commerce, and of politics. Increasingly, after the foundation of Maynooth, and as the Catholic revival gathered momentum in the early nineteenth century, it became the language of the pulpit. English was essential to upward social mobility, Irish was a mark of poverty. Already by the turn of the century, the Catholic gentry and middle classes had made the change. The peasantry soon got the message; to get on in the world they would have to speak English. English was also a major asset to the intending emigrant. Responding to these pressures, parents connived with hedge-schoolmasters in forcing children to abandon Irish for English, and after 1830 the national schools system accelerated this process. Despite the long-term factors making for the change to English, the *absolute* number of Irish-speakers continued to rise up to 1845, due to population increase. They were heavily concentrated, in class and regional terms, among the poorest sections of Irish society, and when the famine came they were decimated. Famine mortality was highest among the cottier and labourer classes, the main custodians of the Irish language. In the diaspora that followed, the emigrant-ship bound for Boston or Liverpool usually had a heavy quota of Irish-speakers aboard. By 1851 the percentage of Irish-speakers in the country had dropped to 25 per cent, and it was to continue to fall.

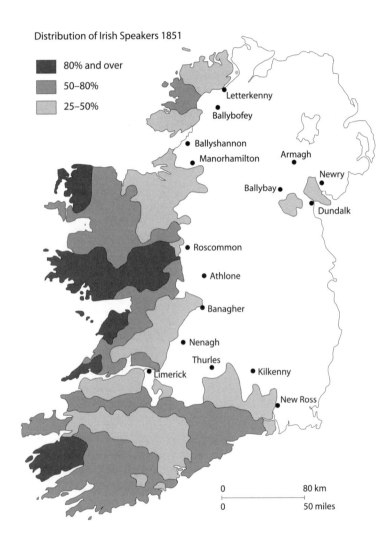

Distribution of Irish Speakers 1851

- 80% and over
- 50–80%
- 25–50%

Letterkenny

Ballybofey

Ballyshannon

Manorhamilton

Armagh

Newry

Ballybay

Dundalk

Roscommon

Athlone

Banagher

Nenagh

Thurles

Limerick

Kilkenny

New Ross

0   80 km

0   50 miles

Based on A View of the Irish Language *edited by Brian O Cuiv.*

05 | REFORM AND REPEAL, POLITICS 1830–48

REPEAL — THE FIRST PHASE

At the conclusion of the emancipation struggle O'Connell was unquestionably the greatest single political force in Ireland. He was to retain this position, despite occasional slumps in popularity, for the best part of two decades. To enable him to become a full-time politician O'Connell gave up his practice at the Bar, a step involving considerable financial sacrifice. To compensate for this loss of earnings a scheme was devised by which a special collection (called the 'O'Connell Tribute') was to be made every autumn to defray his heavy political expenses. This collection, which varied in amount depending on popular enthusiasm for whatever 'cause' O'Connell happened to have in hand at any given time, was collected annually from 1830 to 1947, and in its best years it topped £16,000.

This unrivalled position of influence was one which O'Connell determined to turn to good account. Emancipation was, in effect, to be but the first step — a necessary preliminary — in his plans for effecting sweeping political changes in Ireland. In late 1829 he revealed that what he wanted was that the Government should 'give the Emancipation Act its natural effect'. This meant admitting to positions of power those ambitious Catholics hitherto excluded from them. His wishes in this regard, however, were ignored, and in the early days of 1830 O'Connell founded his Society for the Repeal of the Union. Since this issue was to dominate, to a degree, Irish political life during the next decade and a half, it seems appropriate at this point to discuss briefly what O'Connell meant, and did not mean, when he spoke about 'Repealing the Union'.

There were three main sources to O'Connell's Repeal fervour; the conviction of a constitutional lawyer, the faith of a political radical, and the instinctive response of an Irish Catholic. As a constitutional lawyer O'Connell's case for Repeal was the Grattanite anti-Union case restated, i.e. an assertion of the historic identity of the Irish Parliament, and a denial of the competence of the Parliament of 1800 to vote itself out of existence. This was perhaps the aspect of the Repeal demand which over the years O'Connell argued with the greatest force and coherence. Here his legal erudition and considerable powers of advocacy were employed to best effect.

As a radical O'Connell believed that good government meant representative government. His support for such demands as the ballot, household suffrage, and shorter Parliaments, all derived from this basic faith. The more immediate the link of representation the more healthy, in O'Connell's view, would be the general state of the body politic. He was a firm supporter of self-government for the more advanced colonies. Ireland's claims, in view of her history, her distinctive needs, and her geographical unity, seemed to him unanswerable.

O'Connell's political radicalism was reinforced in the Irish context by his being a Catholic, a member of a majority as yet enjoying no more than token participation, at any level, in the administration of the country. In an Irish legislature, elected on the popular franchise envisaged by O'Connell, the 'Catholic viewpoint' would be assured of a more than adequate representation. This did not imply a leaning on O'Connell's part towards exclusive sectarian politics; simply the logical expectations of the consequences of political democracy in the existing denominational structure.

So much for the sources of O'Connell's Repeal convictions. Let us now turn to the actual *content* of the Repeal demand. A letter written in early 1833 provides a useful general guide to O'Connell's concept of the term; he writes: . . . 'I would not join in any violation of the Law. My plan is to restore the Irish Parliament with the full assent of Protestants and Presbyterians as well as Catholics. I desire no social revolution, no social change. . . . In short, salutary restoration without revolution, an Irish Parliament, British connection, one King, two legislatures.' This extract gives us a general view of the extent, and the limitations, of O'Connell's concept of Repeal. It was certainly not separatist in intent. O'Connell's regard for the merits of the British constitution was quite genuine, as was his deeply personal loyalty to the monarchy. Similarly, O'Connell's emphatic repudiation of any suggestion of social change was also the product of deep-rooted conviction. After all, O'Connell was a landlord, as unrelenting in his defence of private property rights as in his condemnation of agrarian secret societies; an exponent of utilitarian and *laissez faire* views, a vigorous opponent of trade unions and factory laws. There can be no doubting these bona fide credentials of social conservatism. Some slight changes, of course, would be inevitable; but these would be changes (e.g. church reform and absentee tax) which a considerable section of radical and moderate liberal opinion in Britain might be expected to favour. No major structural change was contemplated. In social terms O'Connellite Repeal meant, in essence, the old system under new and better management.

Yet, for all O'Connell's social conservatism, no sizeable group in British politics gave any thought of support for Repeal, or contemplated treating it other than as a revolutionary movement. Why was this so? Obviously there were those ascendancy extremists who simply refused to believe anything O'Connell said. More rationally, to those whose interests, both family and class, were bound up with the maintenance of the political status quo in Ireland the idea of 'a change of management' was anathema. Most interesting of all, perhaps, was the anti-Repeal attitude of those radicals and moderate liberals who, while acknowledging the need for reforms, refused to accept that a national legislature was a prerequisite of better government in Ireland. This latter view was, in a sense, simply a manifestation of colonial paternalism. But the liberal-unionist position had also more solid and defensible foundations.

A Parliament in Dublin could have serious constitutional and strategic consequences. It would mean a new constitutional arrangement between Ireland and Britain; and many agreed with Peel that, for all O'Connell's protests to the contrary, it would be the thin edge of the separatist wedge. A Parliament in College Green, however limited its powers, would be a separate (possibly a rival) focus of loyalty and authority for Irishmen. There would inevitably be disputes between the two Parliaments. Indeed, in the event of Britain being at war with a foreign power, it was not inconceivable that an Irish Parliament would seek its own advantage in the situation, even to the extent of befriending Britain's enemy. This was a strategic danger which Westminster could not permit to exist. Even in the economic sphere there could be no effective guarantee, for all O'Connell's *laissez faire* rumblings, that an Irish Parliament under strong pressure at home would not be driven to protectionism and bounties in an attempt to achieve the industrial regeneration which the people had been told would follow in the wake of Repeal. In addition to these disagreeable possibilities, there was the certainty that under a reformed franchise the electorate for this suggested Irish Parliament would have a majority of Catholics. In view of the involvement of priests in the emancipation episode, this was a prospect which even liberals who held no special brief for the maintenance of the Protestant ascendancy found profoundly disturbing.

Some of these misgivings were more justified than others, but they all derived from a common source — mistrust — which the conduct of the Repeal agitation in Ireland did much to strengthen. Presented in Westminster as an agent of economic and moral revitalisation, a generous act of justice which would replace an empty paper Union by a genuine 'union of hearts' between the two peoples, Repeal seemed to assume a different identity when advocated from an Irish platform. Here popular enthusiasm was tapped by recalling old memories, evoking pride of race, and by generally creating a millenarian mood through presenting Repeal as a panacea for all the country's ills. It is true that the difference was often more a question of tone than of content, but this difference of tone was marked enough to confirm the suspicions and mistrust of British politicians.

The result of all these factors was that when O'Connell canvassed support for Repeal in British political circles he ran up against a blank wall of hostility. Unlike emancipation, all groups in Parliament (excepting, of course, O'Connell's Irish supporters) were united in their opposition to Repeal, and, as the events of 1843 were to show, were prepared to call on all their resources to ensure its defeat. In this sense the Repeal movement as conducted by O'Connell (i.e. as a constitutional agitation aimed at securing a parliamentary victory) was doomed to failure from the very outset. There was simply no chance of a majority at Westminster agreeing to the establishment of a Parliament in College Green.

No such fatalism, however, clouded the enthusiasm with which O'Connell in 1830 embarked on the first phase of his Repeal campaign. It was to be a fitting encore to the emancipation struggle, with the same formula for victory. This attitude seriously underestimated the depth of anti-Repeal feeling at Westminster. It was equally over-sanguine about the prospects of launching the campaign on the home front. In the first place most of the liberal Irish Protestants who had accepted emancipation as a timely concession of 'civil rights' drew the line at any attempt to tamper with the Union. And, of course, there were the Presbyterians of the north who, as we have seen, had become the staunchest defenders of the Union soon after its inception. O'Connell's efforts to woo these groups from their anti-Repeal position met with little success. Finally, even among the Catholic middle classes, whose leadership had been crucial to the success of the emancipation struggle, there were many who were in no hurry to plunge headlong into the Repeal campaign. They had fought for full civil rights and their immediate objective now was to see their newly-won political status translated into practical terms — preferment, government appointments and contracts. They also believed that their energies would be better spent in pressing for reforms in such areas as local government, tithes, and law enforcement, where the need for reform was urgent and the prospect of early success encouraging. This attitude was shared by most of the Catholic bishops. O'Connell had the sympathy of most of the lower clergy, but frequent episcopal exhortations to the priests not to become involved in the politics of Repeal were an acute embarrassment to him.

Underlying the preference of all these groups for immediate reforms was the conviction that the seriously disturbed condition of the country demanded a reduction, not a rise, in the political temperature. For, during the early eighteen-thirties a situation close to anarchy existed over wide areas of rural Ireland. The crime-list for 1832 (over 9,000) showed 242 murders, over 300 attempted murders, and 568 cases of arson. This latest episode in the long chronicle of Irish rural disorder coincided with a vigorous campaign against the payment of tithes, which began to sweep almost the entire country during the winter of 1830–1. The anti-tithe campaign enjoyed strong support from the more prosperous and law-abiding elements of the farming community, who relied for success on passive resistance, legal ingenuity, and parliamentary redress. For all that, efforts to defeat the campaign frequently led to violent clashes involving police, proctors, process-servers, soldiers, and the peasantry. Of greater consequence, however, in terms of the threat to law and order, was the fact that among the more desperate peasantry opposition to tithes was but part of a general disposition to subvert the entire oppressive social system. From parts of the country, particularly the west, there were reports of peasants demanding rent-reductions, or, in extreme cases, total abolition of all rents, rates and taxes. Not surprisingly, desperate men often used desperate methods. Bitterly realising that the Emancipation Act, from which they had expected much, had in fact left their condition totally unaltered, many peasants turned again to the familiar agents of 'instant remedy' — the secret societies. Accordingly, Whitefeet in south Leinster, Terryalts in Clare and Limerick,

Ribbonmen elsewhere — all these bands renewed their activities with assaults on persons, property, and livestock. Clearly, those who feared that the country was on the verge of revolution had ample grounds for their fears.

Under these turbulent conditions it was inevitable that the question of law and order would become a central issue in the political debate on Ireland. The Government's position was clear — order had to be restored. A wave of revolution was sweeping all Europe west of Russia, rocking the fragile world bequeathed by the settlement of Vienna. The 'July revolution' of 1830 toppled the Bourbons in France and established a moderate liberal government; Belgium won independence from Holland and set up a similar liberal regime; a revolt of the Poles was suppressed by the Russians; it required Austrian intervention to put down revolts in parts of Germany and Italy; while Switzerland and the Iberian peninsula were racked by civil strife. In Britain the frightened Whig Government decided to head off trouble by pushing through a cautious measure of parliamentary reform. In doing so they encountered strong die-hard opposition, especially in the House of Lords. More seriously, in the popular clamour for reform there were many radical voices whose demands were considerably in advance of Whig intentions, and this, allied to popular discontent arising from widespread social distress, presented the Whigs with a potentially explosive situation. Clearly, one development which they could not tolerate was the risk of a major upheaval in Ireland. Accordingly, between 1830 and 1832 the law and its agents were stretched to the limits in a drive to keep Ireland under control. A battery of existing criminal laws were resorted to; the military and police were used in the implementation of the civil law. Above all, a concerted effort was made to crush the Repeal movement, considered by the Government as the most threatening agent of revolution. A succession of variously titled Repeal societies (O'Connell showed considerable skill in reconstituting his Repeal organisation under different names) were proclaimed the moment their organisational structure began to show any signs of permanence. Prosecutions were undertaken by the Government against newspapers advocating Repeal. In early 1831 O'Connell himself was arrested and a long litany of charges (later dropped) brought against him. The Government obviously meant business.

Yet the Irish policy of the Government during 1830–2 did not consist solely of a tough line on law and order; there were carrots as well as kicks. A scheme of State-sponsored elementary education was started; the Board of Works was overhauled; an attempt was made in 1832 to solve the tithe question; and Ireland was included in the plans for parliamentary reform. The Government's hands were not entirely free in dealing with O'Connell himself. In the reform struggle in Parliament the moral support of O'Connell was invaluable, and the numerical support of his followers indispensable to the Ministry's survival. Tentative overtures were made to tempt him with office, and, though abortive, they indicate that at least some members of the Government realised that their task in Parliament no less than in Ireland would be easier with O'Connell in the role of friend rather than foe. In addition the Government, anxious to retain O'Connellite support in Parliament, decided in May 1831 to avail of legal loopholes and allow the charges pending against O'Connell to lapse.

That O'Connell was prepared to give parliamentary support to the Whigs at this time may seem surprising, until it is realised how difficult and complex was his tactical position during 1830–2. On the home front he was as anxious as the Government about social disorder, as vehement as the bishops in condemning secret societies. But he was equally determined that neither he nor his legitimate political agitation would be put down by ministerial edict. Having raised the Repeal standard he kept it flying, but he was shrewd enough to broaden the base of his support by agitating, either under the Repeal umbrella or independently, for a wide range of reforms which moderate liberals, radicals and Repealers sought in common, and by the wholesale denunciation of all government appointments. On the parliamentary front however his options were very restricted indeed. He could, and did, denounce the Whig policy for being oppressive and unjust, and for failing to attack the sources of disorder. He could also rail against Government appointments. But at least the Whigs were committed to parliamentary reform, and O'Connell, from principle and from the expectation of political advantage, felt that this entitled them to his continued support in Parliament. After all, parliamentary reform was to include Ireland, and O'Connell originally expected the Irish bill to be a sweeping measure, lowering the franchise, increasing the representation, transforming the borough constituencies and strengthening his influence on the counties. He may also have hoped that a reformed Parliament might prove more sympathetic to the demand for Repeal. All these expectations were soon disappointed.

The Irish reform bill proved a timid measure. Only five extra seats were conceded (one each to Belfast, Limerick, Waterford, Galway, and Trinity College); there was no disenfranchisement; high franchise qualifications ensured that there would be no major transfer of electoral power in the constituencies. Bitterly disappointed, O'Connell redoubled his efforts to make Repeal the key issue in the general election of 1832. It is a measure of his genius for mobilising popular discontent that, despite all the difficulties, he returned to Westminster at the head of thirty-nine MPS pledged to support Repeal. However, the 'reformed Parliament' soon showed that it had even less sympathy with Repeal than its unreformed predecessor. Alarmed by the soaring crime figures of 1832, and despairing of the adequacy of existing laws to effect an improvement, Parliament in early 1833 passed one of the toughest Coercion Acts of the entire century. The Lord Lieutenant was empowered to proclaim districts where no meetings of any sort could be held; even meetings to petition Parliament could be banned unless the Lord Lieutenant had been given ten days notice and granted his permission; he was also empowered to suspend *habeas corpus*. These powers were initially to remain operative for one year. In vain O'Connell inveighed against the 'Algerine Act'. The need for some extraordinary powers to crush crime had already been acknowledged by many Irish bishops, English radicals, Irish liberal and even Repeal members, and the promise that substantial reforms would follow enabled them to stomach, however reluctantly, the coercion dose of 1833. It was otherwise with O'Connell. His own fears of social revolution had prompted him to call for military reinforcements. But he realised that the clauses of the Coercion Act relating to public meetings would effectively paralyse his political movement in Ireland. This was precisely what the Government intended and expected. And so it transpired.

The Coercion Act, even allowing that there were other contributory factors, had a considerable effect in reducing the incidence of rural disorder. It also put the shackles, temporarily, on the kind of popular politics which O'Connell practised in Ireland. Finally, the total futility of raising the Repeal question in Parliament (which O'Connell had long realised) was confirmed in April 1834 when, reluctantly yielding to the pressure of some of his supporters, he eventually raised the question at Westminster. His motion merely asked for a House Committee to enquire into the effects of the Union. The motion was defeated by 523 votes to 38. The verdict could hardly have been more final. To O'Connell the lesson was quite clear. On the home and parliamentary fronts Repeal was, temporarily at least, a dead issue. It was time to concentrate his energies exclusively on extracting the maximum reforms possible under existing constitutional arrangements. And already in 1833 forces were stirring which gave him hope that his efforts in this direction would not be wasted.

REFORM

The hostility between O'Connell and the Grey Ministry reflected conflicts of personality as well as policy. During 1833 there were changes in both areas. In March of that year Edward Stanley retired from the Irish Secretaryship; six months later the Marquess of Anglesey departed from the Viceregal Lodge. Both had spent their taxing terms of office virtually at war with O'Connell. Anglesey was the more unfortunate; as a champion of emancipation he had enjoyed a certain popularity in Ireland, but when he strongly opposed Repeal he was abused, quite unreasonably, by the O'Connellites. Within the Government, what little influence he possessed was exerted in advocating sweeping measures of Irish reform; but his temperament was not suited to the prevailing turbulence in Ireland; under pressure he too often lost his composure, and by the date of his departure the O'Connellites regarded him with a certain superior contempt. Stanley, however, was in a different category. Ice-cool in crisis, brilliantly incisive in debate, the staunchest defender of Church interests, the most unyielding believer in strong coercion, Stanley seemed totally impervious to Irish criticism. Indeed, like Arthur Balfour and the Home Rulers later in the century, he seemed almost to relish the vilification heaped upon him by the Repealers. Between O'Connell and Stanley there existed a profound mutual loathing.

Clearly the departure of Anglesey and Stanley from the Irish scene constituted in itself the removal of a major obstacle to some form of conciliatory dialogue between O'Connell and the Ministry. Relations between the new Chief Secretary and O'Connell were cordial from the very outset. There were also indications that the eruption of long-standing disagreements within the cabinet might soon bring changes in the Government's Irish policy. Cabinet tensions were largely the product of personal rivalries working on basic conflicts of outlook as to what a 'reforming Government' ought properly to be doing now that the Reform Act was on the statute book. Opinions were particularly divided as to what ought to be done about Ireland and what attitude the Government ought to adopt towards O'Connell. And it was appropriate, if not inevitable, that it was the reform of the Irish Church that brought the first serious threat of disruption to the Grey ministry.

The need for reform in the Established Church in Ireland had long been the cry of reformers both sides of the Irish Sea. With four archbishops, eighteen bishops, 2,000 clergymen, and a gross annual income of nearly £1 million, it seemed both over-staffed and over-endowed for an establishment ministering to the needs of less than a seventh (800,000) of the population. Within the Church itself there were many irregularities. Pluralism and sinecurism were not uncommon; there were clergy stationed in parishes where congregations could be counted on one hand; and there was a huge disparity between the almost princely incomes of some of the bishops and the pittances paid to many curates. It is true that for most Catholics and Dissenters total disestablishment and disendowment was the ultimate goal. But even among defenders of the State Church, including Peel, there was an admission that something would have to be done to correct abuses.

In 1833 something was done. The Irish Church Temporalities Act suppressed ten bishoprics, abolished Vestry Cess (for which Catholics and Dissenters as well as Anglicans had been liable), and established a Board of Ecclesiastical Commissioners who were empowered to suspend appointments to parishes where no religious service had been held for three years, to divide livings, and to administer a fund comprising the revenues of suppressed bishoprics and the returns from a graduated tax of from five to fifteen per cent on all clerical incomes over £200. The Commissioners were to use this fund to build and maintain churches, and to raise the stipends of the poorer curates. It was, by any standards, a sweeping measure of reform. Paradoxically, however, it was the omission of a key clause from the Act that caused the most immediate political impact. When originally introduced the bill had included a clause which provided for the sale of episcopal lands to sitting tenants, thereby creating a fund from which the bishops would receive the equivalent of their former rents, while any surplus that might remain could be appropriated by Parliament to be used 'for religious and charitable purposes'. It was on this last point, the 'appropriation clause', that controversy arose. It was not the amount but the principle of the appropriation clause that mattered to all concerned. To the O'Connellites, the radicals, and the left-of-centre liberals, the clause conceded the vital principle that the control of Church property and its returns was a matter in which Parliament had the right to intervene. It might easily be the first step on the road to disestablishment. The defenders of the Church were equally alert to this possibility, and demanded the exclusion of the appropriation clause. In 1833 the latter view prevailed; the constant prodding of Stanley in cabinet, and the desire to avoid a confrontation with the heavily pro-Tory House of Lords, combined to persuade the Grey ministry to drop the appropriation clause. The Stanleyite victory, however, was short-lived, for within a year the appropriation principle was again to rear its disruptive head in cabinet. It arose on this occasion in connection with the one major aspect of ecclesiastical revenues which remained a source of communal strife — the payment of tithes.

Opposition to the payment of tithes had been a feature of every outbreak of agrarian disorder from the eighteenth century onwards. This opposition was a compound of religious and economic objections. In terms of conscience, Catholics, Dissenters, Quakers, and other non-Anglicans found it unacceptable that they should have to contribute to the maintenance of a Church of which they were not members, and with whose doctrines they could not agree. These conscientious factors severely aggravated the basic economic objections on which opposition to tithes was chiefly based. Tithe was a tax on the produce of the land; in the case of non-Anglicans a tax for which there was no return whatever. Moreover, prior to 1825 tithes were levied exclusively on tillage land, as pasture had been exempted by an act of 1735. This meant that the burden of tithe fell heavily on the cultivators of small tillage plots, mostly Catholics, while the large graziers, mostly Protestants, enjoyed something like complete immunity. The very methods by which tithes were assessed and collected caused considerable friction: payments might be made in kind, by a fixed annual money payment, or by a payment based on an estimate or 'view' of the value of the growing crop made by the tithe-owner or his proctor. Conditions varied from region to region regarding which crops were liable for tithe, e.g. in some Leinster and Ulster counties potatoes were non-titheable, in Galway the same was true of hay. Against defaulters the tithe-owner had a wide choice of remedy, ranging from the expensive equity bill of the Exchequer Court to summary proceedings before two magistrates for sums below £10, or, most common remedy of all, by distraint, i.e. the seizure and sale of the debtor's goods. Finally, if we add in the considerable venality of tithe-proctors exploiting the many loop-holes in this system it is not difficult to understand why the chorus of protests against the tithe system was such a loud one.

The defenders of the tithe system had two main arguments; firstly, that tithes were a species of private property, with the same inalienable rights as any other form of private property; and secondly, that tithe, though ostensibly an extra tax on an already over-burdened tenant, came ultimately from the pocket of the rent-receiver who took tithe exactments into account when fixing the rent. For the first of these arguments an impressive case could be presented in legal or ecclesiastical law. Moreover, the fact that by the 1830s about one-fifth of the total tithe revenues belonged to lay proprietors indicates that tithes had indeed changed hands as private property. The second argument, however, that tithe was effectively a concealed rent reduction, could hardly be sustained. This may have been true in England, where both parties to a rent agreement had acknowledged bargaining rights. But in Irish conditions, where land occupancy was a matter of survival rather than choice, and where rents were determined not by agreement but by acute land hunger, it was scarcely meaningful to describe tithe as a concealed rent reduction; and those who claimed, probably correctly, that abolition of tithe would lead to further rent increases merely testified to the almost limitless powers of the rent-receiver in the existing market conditions to avail of every opportunity for raising rents.

However, even the defenders of the tithe principle were aware of the need to make changes in the system, if only to remove its most obvious anomalies. Accordingly, in 1823 a tithe Composition Act was passed decreeing that special vestries should negotiate a composition for tithes for the entire parish with the tithe owners. Each side would appoint a commissioner, and these men would fix a sum for the entire parish and for each tithe-payer in it; the exact sum might be reached by simple agreement or alternatively might be based on the average tithe payments or corn prices for the years 1814 to 1821. A further Act of 1824 abolished the exemption of pasture from tithe. These acts brought mixed results. In general, the tithe compositions fixed in this voluntary way were less of a burden to the tithe-payer than the old tithe had been, so that it was not surprising that by 1830 over half of the country's 2,450 parishes had agreed on compositions. But on the debit side must be counted the fact that voting procedures in the vestry sessions were weighted in favour of the large landlord interest, that the reformed system still entailed the collection of small sums of money from a vast number of occupiers, and that the extension of tithe to pasture simply spread the cancer of discontent into the upper levels of the rural hierarchy. The basic objections to tithes remained unaltered.

This was the position when in late 1830 there began in south Leinster an anti-tithe campaign which soon became more widespread and intense than any previous campaign. The propaganda of the emancipation campaign had aroused popular consciousness of 'grievances' in many spheres. Tithe could hardly escape this new critical scrutiny, particularly since many of those who had compounded on the basis of the comparatively high price average of the years 1814–21 were now demanding a revision of their agreements in view of falling prices. The campaign started in the parish of Graiguenamanagh on the Carlow-Kilkenny border. This was by no means a 'depressed' area, but it is possible that its population was particularly sensitive on the tithe question as the local bishop, Dr Doyle (JKL), was perhaps the most influential critic of the system in the whole country. In Graigue the ill-judged attempt by a particularly unpopular Protestant curate to demand tithes from the Catholic priest aroused the indignation of the parishioners. Encouraged by the bishop the priest soon had the entire parish organised in resistance to the payment of tithe. The conditions governing the seizure and sale of goods for distress were such that a well-organised community intent on defying the system was in a very strong position to do so. For example, livestock could only be seized between sunrise and sunset, and could not be touched if under lock and key: thus, a system of signals between neighbours giving warning of the approach of the proctor and his men could frustrate, at least temporarily, the workings of the system. Even in the event of a seizure of goods a conspiracy to boycott or 'fix' the ensuing auction could render it a Pyrrhic victory for the tithe-owner. These devices proved substantially successful in the south-Leinster area, and the resistance campaign soon spread throughout the entire country. By 1833 more than half the tithe arrears of the previous two years were still outstanding. In 1834 only a third of the composition was paid, in the following year less than one-eighth.

The considerable success of the anti-tithe campaign was due to the fact that it enjoyed overwhelming support from all sections of the agricultural community — landlords, comfortable farmers, small farmers, and labourers. Between these groups, however, there were clear differences of objective and method. For the landlords and comfortable farmers the immediate complaint was that existing compositions were too high and ought to be reduced. In pursuit of this goal they were prepared to withhold tithes, to convene and participate in public meetings to petition Parliament, to boycott sales of tithe 'booty', and to encourage townspeople with whom they traded to do likewise. With many of the poorer tenants and labourers, however, the anti-tithe agitation was simply a facet of a more general opposition to the very basis of the social system. The methods of the poorer classes were often direct, desperate, and violent — arson, intimidation and assault. Not for them the well-publicised martyrdom which the seizure of a few cows earned for the prosperous farmer; the cottier's lone cow or pig was his lifeline, and he would fight to keep a grip on it.

For O'Connell and his largely landowning and bourgeois parliamentary group the anti-tithe movement presented both a political opportunity and a problem. Tithe was, perhaps, the only 'social question' on which all sections of the agricultural community, if handled properly, could present a reasonably united front. The minority against whom it was directed (i.e. the tithe-owners) were, for the most part, unpopular and vulnerable. The campaign need not be conducted explicitly as a 'social' agitation, but could be dressed in the safer language of civil and religious liberty. The problem was one of preventing the agitation from developing into a revolt of the have-nots against all rents, rates and the institutions of property; of directing peasant discontent exclusively against tithe. It called for the familiar O'Connell tactics of canalising the frustrations of the wilder men into support for a non-violent political campaign with a strictly limited objective. It was a difficult tactic, especially in view of the continued attraction of the secret societies; it would have been impossible had O'Connell not been able to rely on the constant support of the most commonly accepted leaders of local communities — the Catholic priests.

The Government's first reaction to the anti-tithe campaign was to vindicate the law and protect the tithe-owners. Accordingly, during 1831 soldiers and police were engaged in protecting proctors and process-servers, and in keeping order at tithe seizures and auctions. It was a mistaken policy. The resistance was not defeated. Only a small portion of the tithe was collected 'by force'. The military and police incurred popular hostility for their involvement in maintaining the 'iniquitous impost'. Violent clashes occurred between the police and the peasantry. In mid-summer twelve people were killed when a frightened magistrate ordered the yeomanry to fire on the crowd at a tithe auction at Newtownbarry in Co. Wexford; there were seventeen deaths at a clash in Castlepollard in Co. Westmeath; in December a proctor and a dozen police were killed when ambushed by the peasantry at Carrickshock in Co. Kilkenny. In 1832 the Government adopted new measures in an effort to reach a solution. Firstly, a new tithe Composition Act was passed making composition compulsory (fixed and apploted by a special commissioner), and decreeing that it last at least twenty-one years. The corn prices for the years 1823–30 were to be the basis of calculation, and tenants-at-will and tenants from year to year were to be exempt from paying tithe, this latter provision aimed at eliminating the difficulty involved in levying tithe *directly* on a vast number of subsistence tenants. Finally, a fifteen per cent rebate was offered to any party, from the head landlord downwards, who would undertake the responsibility for paying the composition.

The Act had little immediate impact. To be sure it brought

uniformity to the operation of the system; but the majority still considered the composition to be too high, and the rebate offered was too small to tempt farmers or landlords into paying a composition which they could not be sure of recouping, and which, if they persisted in their resistance, might yet be abolished. So the majority decided to continue the campaign. More unfortunate still, the Government accompanied the Composition Act with a measure making £60,000 available for use in relieving tithe-owners, the money to be recovered by using the police and military to collect the arrears of 1831. The results of this policy were lamentable. The soldiers and police disliked the work, were disliked by the people for doing it, and in any case did it badly. In the course of a year some 43,000 decrees were issued; yet only about £12,000 was recovered, at a cost which doubled that sum. By early 1833 a new initiative was clearly called for. The first priority was how to solve the arrears problem without risking further violence. The Government's solution was to make a million pounds available for advancing to tithe-owners sums in lieu of outstanding arrears (less 25 per cent for the arrears of 1831 and 1832, 15 per cent for 1833). Simultaneously the Government effectively suspended the involvement of its forces in enforcing payment. This was an acknowledgment that the arrears were a dead letter, and it had a calming effect on the situation. But what of the future? After all, there was still widespread refusal to pay composition. Here also 1833 saw the emergence of a consensus in official circles. So long as composition remained identifiable as a distinct tax it was in a vulnerable position. The solution seemed to lie in the conversion of the composition into another, less vulnerable, form, such as a rent-charge. The optimum arrangement, of course, would be for the tithe-payers to buy out the tithe entirely in one money payment, thereby creating a fund which would then be invested to produce the annual revenue needed to pay clerical incomes. By 1834 there was general acceptance in the Commons that this formula — conversion of the composition into a rent-charge, with provision for its ultimate redemption — gave the best basis for a solution. It was also generally accepted that, to make the package acceptable in

Ireland, some degree of commutation would be necessary, though opinions varied as to the right amount. One major bone of contention, however, remained in the way of a settlement, namely, the appropriation issue.

For O'Connell, the radicals, and an influential faction within the cabinet (led by Lord John Russell) a *sine qua non* of any real settlement was an explicit acknowledgement of the right of Parliament to appropriate any surplus that might remain after the payment of fixed clerical incomes. Bested by Stanley in the Church Act crisis of 1833, Russell was determined not to give way on the tithe issue, whatever the cost. In May 1834 he announced in Parliament that he was in favour of appropriation, whereupon Stanley and a number of his followers resigned, much to O'Connell's delight. Nor was this the end of disruption. Chief Secretary Littleton, acting on behalf of the cabinet group who had long favoured a rapprochement with O'Connell, indiscreetly sounded out the Irish leader with a view to finding an acceptable formula for renewing sections of the Coercion Act. These soundings had been taken without Grey's knowledge, and when they were publicly disclosed he resigned. Within the reconstructed ministry, under Lord Melbourne, there was general agreement that to seek an accommodation with O'Connell was both expedient and right, especially in view of Parliament's contemptuous dismissal of his Repeal motion. Initial reservations on both sides soon dissolved; in O'Connell's case by the fact that the surprise dismissal of the ministry in late 1834 made him realise that the bleak immediate alternative to the Whigs was his arch-foe Peel, while Whig losses in the general election of 1835 left them in no position to be choosey in deciding from whom they could accept parliamentary support. So it transpired that in the Spring of 1835 the O'Connellites and the Whigs finally became firm allies. At the pre-session meetings at Lichfield House O'Connell and his followers attended and pledged their full support for the Whigs, who, for their part, committed themselves to providing a tithe settlement with an appropriation clause, as well as a series of Irish reforms in such areas as municipal reform, registration and appointments. There was no written compact;

rather was it a bargain made on the basis of each party's realistic assessment of its immediate political advantage. It was an alliance that was to last for six years, from 1835 to 1841.

The years of the 'Whig alliance' have been described as 'a Saint Martin's summer in the long winter of the Union'. For the first time under the Union the Government of the day enjoyed the full support of the spokesmen of the majority in Ireland; more significantly, perhaps, the Dublin Castle Administration basked in a popularity which it had never enjoyed and was never again to enjoy under the Union. In seeking the basis for O'Connell's unwavering support for the Melbourne ministry we are unlikely to find it in the legislative record of the ministry, especially with regard to Irish measures. In 1838 the tithe question was eventually 'solved' — *without* an appropriation clause. Tithe was converted into a rent-charge amounting to some 75 per cent of the old composition and payable by the head landlord who (deducting a 25 per cent bonus) could then pass on the charge down the line of sub-tenants, with only tenants at will or year to year being exempt. The arrears of 1834–37 were effectively written off. A year later, in 1839, the Irish Poor Law Act was passed; an Act which was repugnant to O'Connell in principle, and which in many crucial details left even the supporters of the principle of an Irish Poor Law extremely unhappy. (In fact it was very much a solution 'imposed' from London.) In 1840, after 5 years of arid debate, a Municipal Corporations Act was passed which not only fell far short of what the ministers had originally intended and O'Connell had expected, but was also far less radical than the corresponding measure of municipal reform passed for England and Scotland some years previously. Finally the electoral system, including the much abused registration, was left untouched by the Melbourne ministry.

The poverty of this legislative record was due mainly to the essential weakness of the ministry in Parliament. In the Lords the ministers were faced by a massive and implacably hostile majority; in the Commons their numerical majority was tiny, particularly after the 1837 elections; they were weak in debating power, while the Opposition was strong in numbers and talent and led by one of the most able statesmen of the century, Sir Robert Peel. Furthermore, the ministers were not popular in the country: radicals were disappointed at the inadequacy of their domestic reform programme, while true-blue Whigs and Conservatives disapproved of their pact with O'Connell. O'Connell was well aware of the ministers' difficulties, and made generous allowance for them. In any case he himself believed that some measure of beneficial legislation, however limited, was better than none. In seeking political objectives he always favoured accepting whatever was immediately obtainable as an 'instalment', and then coming back for more. In the case of the Tithe Act this meant accepting the fact that Appropriation would never pass the Lords, and concentrating on getting the best commutation possible. (The cancellation of arrears, and the diminution of discontent at least among landlords and comfortable farmers as prices picked up after 1835, both facilitated O'Connell's desire to compromise.) The same attitude — that half a loaf was better than nothing — dictated O'Connell's acceptance of the 1840 Municipal Act.

But it would be inaccurate to believe that the Whig-O'Connellite alliance endured because of the latter's gratitude for meagre legislative crumbs or, even less likely, because of his sympathy for the ministerial dilemma, i.e. that they held office but not power. The real cement of the alliance was the liberalisation of the administrative machine in Ireland which was carried out during 1835–40. The process began at Dublin Castle itself where Gregory, a firm supporter of the Protestant ascendancy, was replaced as Under-Secretary by Thomas Drummond. Drummond was a thorough liberal with an inherent sympathy for the underdog; an administrator of prodigious energy he was determined to root out sectarianism from every corner of the Irish administration, and to ensure that the law be enforced strictly but also impartially. In this he had the full support of his superiors, Lord Mulgrave (Lord Lieutenant) and Viscount Morpeth (Chief Secretary), and indeed of the cabinet in London. Accordingly, Catholics and liberal Protestants were appointed to vacancies as they occurred within the judiciary and civil service. A new spirit informed the entire enforcement of law and order. The magistracy list was revised, and those guilty of behaving provocatively were reprimanded or removed entirely from the list. New procedures were adopted for making the operations in all the courts, high and low, more effective and more just. A major reorganisation of the police was undertaken; strict regulations were drawn up and vigorously enforced. Strong measures were adopted for putting down faction fights and secret societies. The Orange Order itself fell a victim to the new broom. In 1836 the disclosure of illegal penetration of the army by the Order gave politicians a shock; a Parliamentary enquiry investigated the matter, but to forestall Government action the Grand Lodge of Ireland dissolved itself, and it was not until 1845 that it openly recommenced activity. In addition, the Administration took every precaution to ensure that the reorganised police and the soldiers would not forfeit the confidence of the majority through excessive involvement in the enforcement of contentious civil procedures (e.g. the Castle frequently refused to commit the law forces in tithe proceedings). In short, the entire style of the Administration was aimed at winning the confidence of the majority of the people.

It is as easy to exaggerate as to belittle the achievements of the Melbourne ministry in Ireland. Government jobs could only be given to the few, and only a minority ever came before the courts; but all were affected by such social legislation as the Poor Law and Tithe Acts. A portion of the Catholic middle classes benefited directly, but, apart from the vicarious thrill of seeing an occasional Orange magistrate humbled, the politics of conciliation brought little change to the lives and worries of the majority of the population. Nevertheless, for a brief interlude an attempt was made to legitimise the regime by gaining for it the active support of the majority of the population. It was a commendable effort, but it was short-lived. In 1840 Drummond died, worn out by his huge exertions in Ireland. A year later the rickety Melbourne ministry finally collapsed. A general election followed, and Peel was returned to power with a comfortable majority. For O'Connell any accommodation with 'Orange Peel' was inconceivable; so he turned once again to Repeal.

REPEAL — THE SECOND PHASE

O'Connell was not exactly unprepared for the fall of the Whigs. Already in 1838 he had founded the Precursor Society, which was to be a prelude to a new Repeal initiative if 'full and prompt justice for Ireland' were not forthcoming soon. In founding this society he was responding to the deep dissatisfaction of a section of his supporters with the inadequacy of Whig legislation, and also to the fact that the cessation of skirmishing between the Government and the 'movement' had caused a considerable falling off in popular interest in O'Connellite politics — a fact reflected in the drastic depletion of the 'Tribute' collection in the late 1830s. But the Precursor Society made little impact, and at the Government's prompting O'Connell dissolved it, maintaining under various titles a skeleton organisation as a forum for airing grievances and for supervising the registration of voters. When at last, in 1840, the days of the ministry seemed numbered, he founded the Loyal National Repeal Association.

The early fortunes of the new Repeal movement were not encouraging. O'Connell's strident 'addresses to the Irish people', warning that the return of Peel would mean a fresh dose of oppression for Ireland unless they stirred themselves for Repeal, seemed to fall on deaf ears. During the years of the Whig alliance many people had lost interest in politics in general, and in O'Connell in particular. In the general election of 1841 the number of pledged Repealers returned slumped to eighteen; O'Connell himself was defeated in Dublin and had to seek refuge in Cork County. It was also true that the appointments 'plums' of the Whig years had made contented liberal unionists of many of those middle-class Catholics whose support had meant so much to O'Connell in the emancipation struggle. Moreover, O'Connell's election as Mayor of Dublin in 1841, though giving him a prestigious platform, not only reduced the time he could devote to agitation but also, because of his conception of the mayoral duties, inhibited his conduct of an essentially partisan campaign. In late 1842, however, the agitation began to gather momentum. That year had seen a bad harvest and there was widespread distress and discontent. The credit for harnessing this discontent in the Repeal interest was largely due to the impact of the propaganda which a group of young recruits to the Repeal ranks began to turn out in the columns of a newspaper called *The Nation*, which commenced publication in October 1842. The three men who launched the paper were Thomas Davis, Charles Gavan Duffy, and John Blake Dillon. Davis, a Protestant, graduate of Trinity College, called to the Irish bar in 1836, was a sensitive and generous man who in his short life (1814–45) held the respect of all who knew him. Duffy was a self-educated northern Catholic who had started his journalistic career in Dublin, then moved to Belfast and returned to Dublin in 1842. Dillon was a Mayo Catholic from a well-off commercial family, who graduated from Trinity in 1840. All three, and many others of similar background who were later to join them in what came to be described as the Young Ireland group, shared certain views on the subject of patriotism, the identity of Ireland, the destiny of the Irish nation, and the duties all Irishmen owed to the nation. The romantic nationalism which they preached reflected many of the ideals shared by young romantic intellectuals in the Europe of their day. They rejected the economic laws of the market-place as the determinants of social relationships. The ideal was that of an organic hierarchical community within the nation-state, with the efforts of each group directed towards the common good of all. The informing spirit in the creation of this idealistic state of harmony was the spirit of nationality. For the Young Irelanders the nation was a spiritual entity in itself. By cultivating the collective consciousness of the people, preaching the essential 'oneness' of the nation, and giving each member of the nation a sense of 'belonging', all activities, whether in trade, commerce or the arts, would assume a new coherence as an expression, indeed a celebration, of the identity of the nation.

The *Nation* writers saw their task as that of creating this national spirit, as being 'the voice of national self-respect'. The paper, in addition to its detailed reporting of Repeal activities, was packed with stories celebrating the heroic past of Ireland; biographies of saints, scholars, and soldiers; all aspects of native culture were encouraged, including exhortations to the people to retain their own language as a badge of nationhood; fragments of the old literature were translated, and new 'patriotic' ballads were published. No man was to be debarred from membership of the Irish nation because of his religion or his pedigree. The tolerance and generosity of Davis are well reflected in his charter for the ideal nation which he strove to make a reality:

> *What matter that at different shrines*
> *   We pray unto one God?*
> *What matter that at different times*
> *   Our fathers won this sod?*
> *In fortune and in name we're bound*
> *   By stronger links than steel;*
> *And neither can be safe nor sound*
> *   But in the other's weal.*

Youth, lofty idealism, earnestness — these were the great resources of the Young Irelanders as they set about 'regenerating the spirit of Ireland'. They thought and spoke in heroic terms. These very qualities, however, were not always as commendable as they may sound. Mixed with youthful idealism was a strong current of political naiveté; lofty earnestness often shaded into self-righteousness; the view from the heroic heights was often a trifle censorious of those on the lower plains of human fallibility. Certainly in terms of political action there was in the Young Ireland attitude of 'high principle' an implicit condemnation of the wheeling and dealing which was a central feature of O'Connell's political style. Here lay the seeds of future discord.

But in late 1842 this lay well in the future. The *Nation* scribes concentrated on spreading the gospel of nationalism, and left the practical politics of Repeal to the experienced campaigner O'Connell. The people responded enthusiastically to the tone and content of the *Nation*; by 1843 its circulation had climbed to a record 10,000, and its readership was estimated as over a quarter of a million. Factors other than the press campaign seemed to augur well for Repeal in early 1843. Many of the bishops followed McHale's lead and expressed support for Repeal; priests throughout the country began to participate fully in the movement. The formal Repeal organisation — broadly similar to the old Catholic Association structure — began to function effectively. A central controlling body in Dublin met weekly and discussed the campaign, grievances, and finance; there were various grades of membership — Volunteers (£10 annual subscription), Members (£1), and Associates (1/–). At local branches throughout the country, supervised by Repeal wardens, collections were taken up weekly, reading-rooms were established in which the nationalist papers and other propaganda were available to members. Moreover, Dublin Corporation, after a three-day debate in which O'Connell excelled, passed a motion in favour of Repeal in February 1843. Press coverage of the debate was so extensive as to make it an event of national interest, and the result had the effect of bringing many moderate liberals from the commercial classes into the Repeal ranks. The subscriptions began to roll in; at the end of May the Repeal rent for one week topped £2,000. Understandably O'Connell was elated; he stayed away from Parliament during most of 1843 devoting all his energies to the campaign in Ireland; others followed his example.

One key tactic in the campaign was the holding of huge meetings at various places, usually of historic significance, throughout the country. During the summer and autumn of 1843 hundreds of thousands attended over forty such meetings in Leinster, Munster, and Connaught. Ulster, for the most part, remained outside O'Connell's 'command'; yet even here some of the advanced liberals were beginning to show some sympathy towards federalist ideas. The monster meetings of 1843 were extraordinary events; crowds often came long distances, they were marshalled by Repeal wardens or by priests; many groups were accompanied by their local Temperance band. The atmosphere was a mixture of fair, football game and evangelical revival. By the autumn of 1843 O'Connell had worked the country into a fever pitch of excitement. At the start of that year he had promised the people that if they exerted themselves they could make 1843 'the Repeal year'. But both they and he misjudged one crucial factor — the response of Peel's Government to the crisis.

During 1841–2 the Government was preoccupied with measures aimed at resolving the general economic and financial crisis which was racking Britain, and had little time for Irish affairs. The Irish Tories, of course, were demanding action against O'Connell, but even if he had wished to do so Peel would have found difficulty in acting immediately. The movement was not breaking the law. As a propagandist movement it was, in essential features, very similar to the Anti-Corn Law League then active in Britain. It would have been dangerous to move against one without touching the other. Still, Peel could not completely ignore the bleatings of his Right wing. In the summer of 1843 a stiff Arms Act for Ireland was passed after two months of bitter debate. In addition the Government began to deprive known Repealers of their commissions as magistrates. In total exasperation at this hardline attitude many moderate liberals went over to the Repeal camp. Perhaps the most important of many such 'converts' was William Smith O'Brien, a distinguished Limerick Protestant landlord MP who had hitherto been very much 'his own man' in Parliament. The summer meetings and the excitement which attended them worried Peel, but he had to be cautious. Nevertheless, O'Connell was living dangerously: in defiance at the dismissal of Repeal magistrates the Association adopted a plan for by-passing the courts and setting up their own arbitration tribunals. Moreover, O'Connell promised to summon a Council of Three Hundred to prepare a Repeal bill. Clearly there was the danger that this would act as the basis of a national assembly. Finally there was the fact that O'Connell's language was becoming increasingly violent; at Mallow in particular he had hinted at a threat of physical force if Repeal were refused. By late 1843 Peel finally decided on his Irish policy — it was to be a crack-down on agitation followed by an extensive programme of reforms. The priorities were important. The show-down came in October 1843. O'Connell had arranged for the biggest meeting of all to be held in Clontarf. On the eve of the 'great day', with crowds already thronging the roads to Clontarf, Peel banned the meeting, and brought in armed troops to prevent its taking place. O'Connell, unwilling to risk bloodshed, called off the meeting. The balloon had burst. A week later he was arrested and charged with conspiracy. In February 1844 a notoriously partisan jury found him guilty: he was given a year's imprisonment and a £2,000 fine. However, in September the Law lords, acknowledging that his trial had been unfair, reversed the decision and freed him.

YOUNG IRELAND AND 1848

The Clontarf show-down marks the effective end of the O'Connell Repeal campaign as a credible political movement, even if many did not realise it at the time. He had repeated the brinkmanship which had won emancipation, only this time he had misjudged the parliamentary situation. He had over-played his hand and his bluff had been called. Realisation that the basic strategy has failed invariably causes disagreements in any political movement. This was particularly true of the Repeal movement. Differences of temperament and opinion which could be contained so long as O'Connell's euphoric generalship seemed likely to carry off the spoils soon forced their way into open controversy when he began to cast about for new options. This did not happen all at once. The Young Irelanders had, after all, agreed with O'Connell's decision on the Clontarf meeting. They were gratified when the high-minded Protestant Smith O'Brien was deputed to preside over the Association while O'Connell was in jail — he was a good advertisement for non-sectarian duty-motivated politics. But with O'Connell's return to active politics after his sojourn in jail the rumblings of disagreement were soon audible. O'Connell's view of the situation was that while Repeal was the best, and would be the ultimate, solution to Ireland's problems, it was simply out of reach at that moment; accordingly efforts ought to be directed towards grabbing whatever benefits seemed within reach. Whether this attitude constituted pragmatism or opportunism was, and is, a matter for debate. At any rate it prompted O'Connell to make overtures in late 1844 to the liberal federalists. They came to nothing; the Young Irelanders strongly protested against any compromising on Repeal, and in any case Sharman Crawford's federalists were as unbending as any Young Irelander and were highly suspicious of dealings with O'Connell. An additional complication was the fact that O'Connell was also engaged in sounding out the Whigs on possible terms of a future alliance, and the Whigs had no time for federalism or any other devolutionary notions.

The Young Irelanders found all this 'bargaining' deplorable. For them Repeal was a great crusade, not negotiable. O'Connell saw things differently. They saw his trucking to the Whigs as sycophantic, he found their inflexibility rather naive; the coarse personal abuse which O'Connell often threw at his opponents seemed to them unworthy of a noble cause, while he found their holier-than-thou attitude somewhat irritating. They disliked the excessive influence of explicitly Catholic views and concerns in the affairs of the Association. They were also concerned at the rather casual attitude of O'Connell towards the Association's funds. Finally, by 1845 O'Connell was 70 years of age; the spell in prison, though every comfort was given to him, had taken its toll of his mental and physical resources. He emerged a tired and testy man. He was forced to absent himself more often from the Association meetings, leaving matters in the hands of his son and political heir John, who had little of his father's skill and between whom and the Young Irelanders there was considerable antipathy.

These deep tensions within the Repeal Association became open disagreements as a result of conflicting reactions to certain Government policies. Peel's policy, as we have said, involved a 'package' of reforms as a follow-up to the smothering of the Repeal agitation. This package included an investigation into the Irish land system, a measure of franchise reform, and a series of measures especially aimed at gaining the confidence of the Catholic middle classes, and particularly of the hierarchy. In late 1843 a special commission was set up under the Earl of Devon to investigate the Irish land system. Its extremely informative Report, presented in 1845, made suggestions for legislation in such areas as land reclamation, public works, grand jury reform, and, most important of all, recommended the recognition in law and the extension throughout the rest of the country of the 'Ulster Custom', that is, the payment to an outgoing tenant of compensation for any permanent improvements made to the holding during his occupancy. The land system, however, was a hornet's nest of political interests, dangerous to him who would disturb it. Accordingly, apart from a timid compensation bill, dropped under pressure from the Lords, Peel's ministry steered clear of the land issue. Franchise reform proved equally unfruitful; a measure introduced in 1844 was dropped under Whig attack. However, Peel did press ahead with his explicitly 'Catholic' measures, with mixed results. In 1844 a Charitable Bequests Act was passed, which set up new machinery for supervising the law on bequests and donations, giving Catholics a greater say in its operation, and generally seeking to safeguard Catholic charities. The Irish hierarchy were divided on the issue. McHale felt that it interfered in the internal affairs of the Church and, in certain particulars, cast aspersions on the integrity of the priests. He opposed it, and so did O'Connell and a section of the priests. But many of the bishops were tolerably satisfied with the Act and it had the general approval of Rome.

1845 brought an even greater concession to the Catholic hierarchy, when an Act was passed raising the grant to Maynooth seminary from £9,000 to £26,000, and decreeing that it be made a permanent grant from the Consolidated Fund. It further provided for more frequent visitation of the College and granted £30,000 for outstanding repairs. The Act outraged Peel's right-wing supporters (as well as many radicals) and almost split the Conservative party. It was warmly received by the Irish bishops. The same could not be said of the final instalment of Peel's Catholic appeasement programme, the Irish University Act of 1845. The Act sought to provide University education acceptable to the Catholic conscience while yet avoiding the endowment of a specifically Catholic denominational University. A sum of £100,000 was voted for the establishment at Galway, Belfast and Cork of three Queen's Colleges, where no religious tests would apply and where chairs in theology would be left to private benefactors. The annual endowment was fixed at £30,000. A minority of the hierarchy held the view that, with additional Catholic safeguards (e.g. control of appointments in certain subjects) the Colleges ought to be given a trial. But most of the bishops backed McHale's outright condemnation of the scheme and his demand for a fully Catholic University.

Within the Repeal Association the Act brought long-smouldering divisions into the open. O'Connell denounced the 'Godless colleges', called for the endowment of chairs of theology and further claimed that Catholic theology should prevail at Cork and Galway, and Presbyterian theology at Belfast. (Protestants were already catered for at Trinity.) The Young Irelanders, particularly Davis, openly opposed this view. They welcomed the Colleges as instruments for bringing Irishmen of all denominations together. The debates in the Association were bitter and left deep scars. The sudden death of Davis in September 1845 brought a temporary break in the acrimony but before long relations between the two groups became even more hostile. The Young Ireland group, it must be stressed, were very much a minority within the Association, though from late 1845 onwards they gained strength from the talents of a number of new recruits. These new men included John Mitchel, the son of a northern Unitarian minister of United Irish sympathies, Thomas Francis Meagher, from a wealthy Waterford commercial family, John Martin, Thomas D'Arcy Magee, Michael Doheny, and Thomas Devin Reilly. They were mainly from comfortable middle-class backgrounds, and Reilly and Martin had had the familiar experience of having their political consciousness sharpened at Trinity College. The crucial source of friction between this group and the majority in the Association was O'Connell's attitude to the Whigs.

By late 1845, when it became apparent that Peel's decision to repeal the Corn Laws would split his party, O'Connell had virtually moved into open support of the Whigs. By the summer of 1846 Peel's party had indeed split. The Whigs kept him in office just long enough to repeal the Corn Laws, and then in June they turned him out in a vote on his Irish Coercion bill. This latter had been introduced in response to the increased disorders caused by the stresses of the famine from late 1845; it was a tough measure with provisions for collective fines on disturbed areas and a possible fifteen years transportation for breaking curfew. Defeating the measure furnished the Whigs and O'Connell with a suitable occasion for combined action. It was effective; and when the Whigs returned to office there were two ex-Repealers among the five Irish MPs given junior ministerial posts. In O'Connellite terms this was a good start to the alliance.

The Young Irelanders bitterly opposed the alliance with the Whigs; they wanted the Irish party to retain full freedom of action. Their continued sniping began to annoy O'Connell once the Whigs actually resumed office, and he determined (with strong prompting from his son John) to force them to submit or withdraw. In a bitter debate in the Association in July 1846 O'Connell demanded an absolute declaration from the meeting that no political objective justified the use of violence; the Young Irelanders, though they had no immediate plans for violence, would not accept this theoretical limitation of the means which the winning of Irish freedom might justify, and so they withdrew from the Association. The O'Connells seemed to have won. The Young Irelanders, little known and with little popular support throughout the country, went into temporary eclipse. The clergy and the majority of the Association remained faithful to O'Connell. 'Old Ireland' seemed to have triumphed.

But this situation was transformed by the total failure of the potato crop in the winter of 1846–7; the Whig alliance became the kiss of death for the O'Connellite forces, and the Young Irelanders were propelled into new directions of action. During 1845–6 famine distress had not been a source of contention between the two groups in the Association. There was general criticism of details of Peel's relief measures, and general agreement on demands for more exchequer funds for relief schemes and public works and for some form of embargo on the export of food. In fact the 'social question' had never been a source of conflict between Young Irelanders and O'Connell up to the end of 1846. Both groups deplored class politics. Both groups hoped that the landlords would see the light and take their rightful place at the head of the national movement. Both sides favoured some form of compensation for improvements and some measure of security for the tenant-farmer. Davis's long-term ideal was peasant-proprietorship, but in achieving these aims the support of the landlords was sought through appeals to their sense of duty. The revival of Irish industries was part of the general national regeneration in which both groups saw the restored Irish Parliament playing a key role. In some respects O'Connell was less cautious than the younger men; unlike them, he supported the repeal of the Corn Laws, and he also advocated a tax on the incomes of absentees. Clearly, at the time of their withdrawal from the Repeal Association, the Young Irelanders could not be considered as an advance guard of social radicalism.

The parsimony of the Whigs in dealing with the famine horrors of 1846–7 totally discredited the Whig-O'Connell alliance. By Christmas 1846 the Government was being criticised by all factions in Ireland. Tentative overtures for a reconciliation with the Young Irelanders came unstuck on personal and policy grounds. In early 1847 the O'Connellites sponsored a meeting of Irish MPS and Peers who resolved on concerted action in the coming session to force the ministry to change its famine policy, but this effort was also short-lived due to conflicts of interest among the participants. The ministers were indifferent to O'Connell's advice. In despair, the broken Irish leader set out on a final pilgrimage to Rome. He died en route on 15 May 1847 at Genoa. The Repeal Association was disintegrating rapidly. True, thirty-nine nominal Repealers were returned at the 1847 general election, but they lacked any coherent policy of action. The hapless John O'Connell struggled to keep life in the old Association, but he had neither funds nor a policy, and communication with the Whigs was rather a dialogue with the deaf. By 1848 the Repeal Association was simply irrelevant in a famine-stricken land.

The famine crisis also brought problems for the Young Irelanders. Land, food, and survival were what mattered to the people. Early 1847 saw the rise of tenant-right societies especially in Ulster where tenants were afraid of any whittling away, by landlord or legislation, of their Ulster Custom. Throughout 1847 evictions caused misery and often provoked violence. In some towns — Dublin, Cork, Limerick and Waterford — politically articulate artisans condemned O'Connell's support for the Whigs and called for condemnation of their famine policy. Yet those who had seceded from O'Connell, and who had formed their own Irish Confederation in early 1847, were confused in their response to the new situation. Smith O'Brien and Duffy had nothing useful to say on the 'social question' — they remained wedded to the 'national revival' gospel which the *Nation* had preached in 1842–3. They feared social disorder, preached class harmony, and had no time for the language of the Chartists in Britain. They wanted the Confederation to concentrate on the national issue. But in early 1847 James Fintan Lalor, the son of a Laois farmer who had been prominent in the anti-tithe campaign, made contact with the Young Irelanders and in a series of letters provided an analysis of the 'condition of Ireland'. Lalor asserted that under existing circumstances an agitation based exclusively on the national issue was doomed to failure; it must also agitate on the land question. Lalor accepted private property rights, but denied that they were absolute. He asserted that 'the entire soil of a country belongs of right to the entire people of that country and is the rightful property not of any one class but of the nation at large'. In Lalor's view the famine crisis had dissolved the existing 'social contract' in Ireland. A new contract was necessary, and the people would confer new and valid titles to land on landlords who recognised their right of occupancy, i.e. to landlords prepared to grant security of tenure to tenants. Such were Lalor's views: they favoured the tenant-farmer, were likely to be opposed by the landlords, and, like virtually all 'solutions' of the land problem, held out little hope in the immediate future for the throngs of landless labourers. Lalor himself became active in setting up militant tenant-right societies in the Tipperary-Kilkenny area.

Lalor's views found little immediate support. Within the

Confederation the majority agreed with O'Brien and Duffy that they were too extreme and would alienate landlord support from the 'national movement'. However, a minority, including Devin Reilly and Doheny, agreed with Lalor. Mitchel had reservations at first, but gradually during 1847, responding to Lalor's preaching and to the harrowing reality of the famine, he moved to the left on the social issue, while also becoming more favourable to the idea of using physical as well as moral force. By late 1847 he was defining tenant-right as a definite property right deriving from mere occupancy (i.e. not depending on improvements), and he was also advocating withholding repayments on loans made by the Government. Duffy and the majority within the Confederation rejected these views, and eventually in early 1848 Mitchel and Reilly broke with the *Nation* and set up the short-lived *United Irishman* as an organ of advanced views. Yet even among those within the Confederation who considered Mitchel's views too extreme (men like Meagher and Doheny) there was considerable unease at the hyper-cautious attitude of Duffy and O'Brien. When the Government, in response to Clarendon's (Lord Lieutenant) demand for increased powers for dealing with rural disorder, passed a strong Crime and Outrage Act at Christmas 1847, there was much resentment when Duffy and the moderates, in an attempt to stand right with frightened property-owners, muffled criticism of the Act in the Confederation.

The division within the Confederation caused by the growing impatience of a left-wing lobby in late 1847 and early 1848 greatly exercised the debating skills of the participants. It also has an interest for historians concerned with the development of Irish nationalist ideology. But it was not an event of overriding importance for the majority of the Irish people in 1848. Though there were Confederate Clubs in most of the large towns, the Confederate leaders themselves had never enjoyed great popularity throughout the countryside, as their dismal showing in the general elections of 1847 had shown. They were blamed by many for having contributed to O'Connell's death, a view not likely to be contradicted by the Catholic clergy who remained strongly O'Connellite. Moreover, the Confederate Clubs in many towns, particularly in Dublin, contained elements whose views were in many respects nearer to Mitchel than to Duffy. All in all, by the spring of 1848 the fortunes of the Confederation were not very promising. A new stimulus was badly needed. In February 1848 the revolution in France provided just such a stimulus.

The initial spectacle of liberals, socialists, republicans, middle classes and lower classes, combining to overthrow Louis Phillipe and establish a popular government raised the spirits of reformers throughout Europe. The continent shook with excitement; between February and May the established order in Paris, Vienna, Berlin and Budapest collapsed. In Ireland Repealers greeted the French revolution rapturously. Meetings were held throughout the country calling for Repeal and sending fraternal greetings to Paris. Mitchel and Meagher now raised the cry for an Irish republic, the first time a republic had been suggested in Repeal circles. Mitchel's paper published articles on military tactics. Even the moderates, while taking care to distinguish their position from Mitchel's extremism, were caught up in the new mood of defiance. Impressed by the discipline and the class-harmony shown in Paris, O'Brien suggested the formation of a National Guard. A temporary harmony, though not a reunion, was restored between O'Connellites and Confederates. Even more remarkably, the Confederates began to embrace the friendship of the hitherto dreaded Chartists. In March joint meetings of Chartists and Confederates were held in the north of England. In the same month a deputation from the Confederation went to Paris. They were cordially received, but Lamartine valued British support for the new regime too highly to place it in jeopardy. On 3 April he gave the delegation a friendly audience, but no encouragement. Despite this, the mood in Dublin remained buoyant; the efforts of Repealers, and the friendly aid promised by Feargus O'Connor on behalf of the Chartists, would force the Government to concede Repeal. In April Duffy issued a manifesto stating that while he hoped that an independent Irish Parliament (with a responsible Irish ministry) under the crown would be established peacefully, he would not, if the Government set its face against this, refuse his support to the establishment of a republic by force. This was escalation with a vengeance. Meanwhile there were reports that some Confederate Clubs were drilling with pikes.

The Government, fearful of the possibility of synchronised action between Repealers and Chartists, decided to move against the Confederate leaders. In March O'Brien, Meagher and Mitchel were charged with sedition. The former two were acquitted, but Mitchel was not so lucky. In April a Treason Felony Act had been passed making transportation the penalty for treason, and it was under this Act that Mitchel was tried in May. After a virtuoso performance of defiance before a hopelessly packed jury he was sentenced to fourteen years transportation, a verdict bitterly condemned not only by Repealers but also by the English Chartists. Duffy, Dillon and Reilly, under a constant stream of advice from Father Kenyon — a Tipperary priest who had been on the extreme wing from the outset — now began to talk of planning an armed insurrection, but spies kept the Government well informed on their movements. Duffy, Meagher, Doheny, and Magee were arrested, but all except Duffy were allowed out on bail. At last, in July 1848, the cabinet finally yielded to Clarendon's persistent demand for the suspension of habeas corpus; in one day, 22 July, Parliament approved the measure. Four days later mere membership of a Confederate Club was declared sufficient for arrest under the habeas corpus statute. In desperation the Confederate leaders who remained at liberty decided on open armed rebellion. It was a hopeless gesture. They had made no real preparations (arms, tactics); they were almost unknown in the countryside; and in any case a famine-torn peasantry had little interest in rebellion. The Confederates, led in a surrealistically chivalrous manner by Smith O'Brien, tried to rouse the people on the Tipperary-Kilkenny border, always a promising area for militant action. But it was useless. At last, in the closing days of July, a brief skirmish with police in a widow's cabbage garden at Ballingarry, brought down the curtain on Smith O'Brien's rebellion. The heroic had turned to burlesque.

The leaders surrendered or were apprehended. They were tried, convicted, and sentenced to transportation. In July 1849 O'Brien,

Meagher, McManus and Pat O'Donoghue set out to join Mitchel in Van Dieman's land. Their departure caused little stir in Ireland. Three years of famine misery had drained the people of any interest in Repeal politics. The 'national issue' was, for the moment, a dead issue. Duffy realised this, and on his release in 1849 turned his attention to the question which was of immediate concern to the people — land tenure. 1849 also saw the appointment of Dr (later Cardinal) Paul Cullen as successor to the deceased Archbishop Crolly of Armagh. In 1850 Cullen presided at a national synod of bishops at Thurles: the 'Godless Colleges' were condemned, and a harder line was adopted on the primary schools question. A new phase in Irish Church–State relations had begun. The politics of the early fifties would be the politics of tenant-right and religion.

However, though in practical terms it had achieved little, the Young Ireland movement left a legacy of ideas which were to have a profound influence on the thoughts and actions of later generations of Irish nationalists. In their different ways Griffith and Pearse were to draw inspiration from Davis — his cultural nationalism, his comprehensive conception of Irish nationality, his emphasis on 'teaching the people', and his incessant preaching of national self-reliance The gospel of Lalor, as expounded by Mitchel, that the 'social question' and the 'national question' were inextricably linked, was later to be taken to heart by Davitt and by Connolly. More immediately, the skirmish of 1848 had given a brief taste of rebellion to a number of young men — including James Stephens, John O'Mahony and Charles Kickham — who were later to play key roles in the Fenian movement. For them 1848 was a humiliating failure. But they survived it, and determined that there would be another day. And there was.

06 | THE FAMINE

THE COURSE AND EXTENT OF THE FAMINE

By the mid-forties the potato was the sole food of about one-third of the Irish people; it was a crucial component in the diet of a considerably larger number. The long-term factors which had created this situation have already been discussed. This alarming dependence on the fate of a single crop was fraught with danger; it left a very large number of people in a frighteningly vulnerable position. Already in the decades since Waterloo a number of partial failures of the potato crop had caused deep distress throughout certain areas of the country; a major failure of the crop would produce a social and economic crisis for Irish society. Between 1845 and 1851 just such a crisis occurred.

In the autumn of 1845 a potato disease, which had already attacked the crop in North America, finally reached Ireland. The south-eastern counties were first affected, and by late autumn the blight had spread to seventeen counties. However, about a sixth of the crop had been dug before the blight struck; the crop yield itself was quite heavy. Accordingly the distress, though acute, was not felt throughout the whole country. Hopes that the blight would not return were cruelly dashed when, after a wet spring and a humid summer, the crop of 1846 was a total failure. In 1847 the blight was less virulent but this brought little improvement; many people, in despair, had neglected to plant seed potatoes; still more, in hunger, had eaten them. The autumn of 1848 brought another failure of the crop, and in this season the situation was aggravated by a very poor grain harvest. In 1849 the blight was less severe, and by 1850, although some counties did suffer a substantial failure, it was clear that the blight was on the wane. By this time, however, the harrowing nightmare of the previous five years had effected some radical changes in the structure of Irish society; and the size, if not the full significance, of some of these changes stood out clearly in the census figures of 1851.

The key change was evident in the population statistics, which showed that between 1841 and 1851 the population of Ireland had fallen by about twenty per cent. In fact during the famine years (1845–51) the population declined by about two and a quarter million. Emigration had accounted for some one and a half million of these. To give a precise figure for deaths during the famine would be impossible; the data in the 1851 census are clearly defective. At the height of the famine the classification system in many institutions had been overwhelmed. More significantly, the deaths of many thousands who expired in cabins or in the fields went unrecorded. All told, it seems that a figure of about 800,000 for famine deaths would not be excessive. The major cause of death was not actual starvation, but such attendant famine diseases as typhus, relapsing fever and dropsy. Moreover, during the first half of 1849 a serious outbreak of cholera (particularly severe in the large towns) added its own grim quota to the death total.

While these figures give some idea of the size of the convulsion which Irish society experienced, they do not distinguish between the different intensities of impact felt by different sections of that society, both in regional and in class terms. Such distinctions are important. In regional terms the famine produced its highest quota of death, suffering and emigration in those counties where dependence on the potato was greatest, sub-division most acute, trade and communications least developed; in short, in the counties of the west and south-west. It is true, of course, that no area of the country escaped entirely the misery of those years — the movement throughout the country of fever-carrying paupers, in search of food or work, ensured this. Conditions differed even within particular counties. But, in general, Sligo, Leitrim, Mayo, Galway, Clare, Limerick, Cork, Kerry and parts of Tipperary, together with Cavan and Laois, were the hardest hit. Counties near the east coast were least affected. Despite high population density, the north-east was not badly hit, due to the better balance in the region's economy. The high mortality in the cities reflected the heavy influx of fever victims from the countryside.

Related to the question of where in geographical terms the famine hit hardest, is the question of where in terms of social groups its effects were felt most severely. Here the evidence is clear. The labourer and cottier classes were the chief victims of the famine, and the small-farmer class scarcely fared much better. Those most heavily dependent on the potato for subsistence, and most vulnerable (through poor housing, bad sanitation, and defective diet) to fever, were those likely to feel the full devastation of the famine. That many of them were also in parts of the country where communications and retail trade facilities were least developed, was a severe handicap to attempts for their relief. Many of the smaller farmers were, of course, farmers in name only, tenants-at-will cultivating minute holdings. Their condition differed but little from that of the cottiers when the blight struck. It was not only the subsistence men, however, who had their numbers reduced during the famine years; there was also a significant thinning in the ranks of small farmers in more comfortable circumstances, cultivators of holdings up to fifteen acres in size. For many of these latter class 1848 was the decisive year. Having survived the ravages of 'black 47' they needed a good harvest in 1848 to restore their faith in the desirability of remaining on the land. When the potato failure in 1848 was accompanied by a poor grain harvest the resolution of many small-farmers to 'hold on' was finally broken, and they set out on the emigrant ship for a 'new start'. Between 1849 and 1852 annual emigration from Ireland never fell below 200,000, and in 1851 it

reached a massive 250,000, of whom small-farmers formed a
sizeable quota. The full significance of the impact of the famine
years on the various strata of Irish rural society emerges clearly
from a table comparing the number (and percentage) of holdings
of various sizes in 1841 with those for the year 1851:

Holdings	1841	Per cent	1851	Per cent
1–5 acres	310,436	44.9	88,083	15.5
5–15 acres	252,799	36.6	191,854	33.6
15–30 acres	79,342	11.5	141,311	24.8
Above 30 acres	48,625	7.0	149,090	26.1

The economic significance of these figures is left for later, and
more detailed, comment. In social terms the figures virtually
speak for themselves. The number of cottiers and small-farmers
had been substantially reduced, through death, disease,
emigration and the workhouse. There had been substantial
consolidation of smaller holdings, the cultivators of which had
been, by one means or another, 'cleared'. A major social change
had been effected.

Statistics, however, give little idea of the terrifying reality of
famine conditions as experienced by its victims, and as reported
by relief workers, newspaper reporters, doctors and clergymen.
Corpses left unburied for days, either because no one knew they
were dead or because neighbours feared the contagion of fever;
unreported deaths and furtive burials, overcrowded workhouses;
the sinking despair as workers on relief schemes felt their strength
ebbing away; the coffins with sliding bottoms to facilitate their
repeated use. It is not necessary to extend further this litany of
misery, except to remark that the winter of 1846–7 was the most
severe in living memory.

The full range of famine sufferings was manifested chiefly in
those areas where most of the elements of dire poverty were
already deeply ingrained. A Cork magistrate has left us this
account of a visit to the neighbourhood of Skibbereen in west
Cork (perhaps the worst afflicted locality in the country) in late
December 1846:

I entered some of the hovels . . . and the scenes that presented themselves were such as no tongue or pen can convey the slightest idea of. In the first six famished and ghastly skeletons, to all appearance dead, were huddled in a corner on some filthy straw, their sole covering what seemed a ragged horse-cloth, and their wretched legs hanging about, naked above the knees. I approached in horror, and found by a low moaning they were alive, they were in fever — four children, a woman and what had once been a man . . .

Even today these words bring a chill to the heart.

RELIEF — PUBLIC AND PRIVATE

This brief attempt to measure, in some way, the social impact of the potato famine, and to convey some sense of its intensity, prompts us to ask many, some of them fundamental, questions. Was the calamity avoidable? Need it have been as bad as it was? How effective were the relief measures? Enough has been said to indicate that, given the structure of Irish society and the nature of the Irish economy, a major failure of the potato crop meant, of necessity, a major crisis. Attention then, may be directed to the more controversial question of the effectiveness of the efforts made to meet this crisis. This is a question which has always generated a great deal of heated argument: the most extreme nationalist view, from Mitchel onwards, has tended to indict government policy as showing clear signs of genocidal intent; government apologists, on the other hand, claim that the famine was a 'natural disaster', could not have been anticipated, and was met by the expenditure of energy and money, which, by the standards of the day, were on an unprecedentedly massive scale. What basis, if any, there may be to either case can only be judged by examining exactly what were the relief efforts made by the government.

The response of Peel's administration to the partial failure of the crop in 1845–6 was prompt, energetic and imaginative. The Irish crisis of autumn 1845 finally convinced Peel that the time had come to remove the tariffs imposed, in the interests of the

British farmers, on grain imported into Britain. This dismantling of the Corn Laws was a policy likely to cause deep political divisions; it certainly would take time to carry it through. Meantime, more immediate action was called for in Ireland. There were early set-backs. A team of experts hastily dispatched to investigate the blight diagnosed its nature incorrectly and suggested the wrong remedies. The practical steps taken to relieve distress were more successful.

Peel, while encouraging the maximum degree of local initiative, nevertheless realised that a strong central body would be necessary to co-ordinate these local efforts, and, when necessary, to compensate for their deficiencies. Accordingly, in November 1845 a special commission was appointed, charged with the co-ordination of relief measures throughout the country. The relief policy itself had two main objectives. The first was the provision of employment, so that labourers might earn the wherewithal for buying food. This had been the linchpin of all previous schemes of relief during times of distress in Ireland. The second objective of policy was to ensure that local traders would not capitalise on the food shortage by raising prices to an exhorbitant level; this, in effect, meant ensuring that a reserve supply of cheap food be made available for use in controlling such profiteering.

To provide employment the government resorted, as usual, to schemes of public works. The relief schemes authorised by the Bills introduced by Peel in early 1846 included improvements to piers and harbours, improved drainage facilities and, above all, road-works. Official policy regarding the financing and operation of these schemes sought maximum efficiency through combining initiative with central control. Encouraged by the government, local relief committees were formed throughout most of the country. These committees, which numbered about 650 by August 1846, raised subscriptions, provided the government with full information on the severity of the blight in their respective localities, made suggestions for relief schemes, and drew up lists of those needing employment.

Relief schemes involving the outlay of public money were of

two kinds. Firstly, in the case of those schemes carried out entirely under the direct control of the Board of Works, half the cost was covered by a grant from the Consolidated Fund, while the other half was to be repaid by the local landowners as county cess over a period of years. Secondly, the government also sanctioned relief schemes which were planned and carried out entirely under the control of local committees. In such schemes the government met the entire cost with a loan, all of which was repayable. The cost to the exchequer of all these activities was considerable; the Board of Works schemes alone ate up some £475,000, half of which was in grants. This heavy outlay brought results; through all the various agencies an estimated 140,000 found employment on relief schemes in the season 1845–6.

Peel also acted swiftly to counter the more immediate hazards of the potato failure, namely, price inflation on food supplies, and actual starvation. As early as November 1845 Peel had authorised the purchase of £100,000 worth of Indian meal. By January 1846 these supplies were secretly stored in the country, and between March and June special food depots began operations in Munster, Leinster and Connaught. The government saw the food depots as a last line of defence against starvation, and as a guarantee against excessive price rises by food monopolists. They were not meant to replace or even to compete with existing retail agents.

These assumptions of policy were reflected in the detailed regulations drafted for the depots by treasury officials ever vigilant of the perils of State interference with private enterprise. Private traders were forbidden to purchase food at the special depots; local committees were only to purchase when prices in their areas were rising; relief committees were instructed to sell the food purchased at the depots at cost price and were permitted to distribute it gratuitously only to the unemployable, and only when the local workhouse was already full. In the event, the task of meeting distress as it occurred in different areas did not allow for strict adherence to this manual of instructions. Despite persistent treasury nagging, committees in many areas were allowed considerable latitude in operating their schemes of food relief. It is possible that the government's willingness to allow such latitude was not unconnected with the fact that its chief executive had cut his administrative teeth in Ireland, dealing at first hand with just such rural distress.

Moreover, the Administration's response to the reality of Irish conditions was not confined to a simple, passive, official acceptance of a limited amount of bending and breaking of treasury directives. In the more remote areas of the south and west where local relief committees either did not exist or were too poor to be effective, and where in any case the retail distribution network could not be relied upon to ensure a supply of food, the government authorised the establishment of special sub-depots, manned by the police and coastguards, who were permitted to sell meal directly to the people in need. During the summer of 1846 over 100 of these sub-depots came into operation. In all, the government spent some £185,000 on food supplies (chiefly Indian meal) in the 1845–6 season; but about three-quarters of this was recovered in sales.

Finally, the enterprise of committees in collecting subscriptions for local relief activities was rewarded by government grants which in many cases equalled the sums contributed locally.

Historians have tended to echo the praise which contemporaries bestowed on Peel for his handling of the distress of 1845–6; praise, on the whole, well deserved. True, some of the relief measures caused problems. Some labourers preferred working for the Board of Works for a money wage to working for some farmer in order to pay off rent arrears or to gain access to a patch of diseased potatoes. Yet for all that, Peel's measures met the immediate crisis. No one died from actual starvation in the season of 1845–6. However, it must be remembered that the potato failure in this season, for all its severity, was only partial, not total; nearly half the country escaped the blight. A total failure was quite a different matter; and when 1846 brought such a failure Russell was Prime Minster and Peel was the deposed leader of a shattered party.

The advent of the Whigs to office in the summer of 1846 heralded a major change in government policy towards Irish distress. The new men at the helm were deeply committed to the doctrines of free trade and private enterprise; Russell had little of Peel's independence of judgment, and none of his Irish administrative experience. Most important of all, perhaps, the new Chancellor of the Exchequer, Sir Charles Wood, held similar views to Trevelyan, the doctrinaire permanent secretary at the Treasury, as to the proper role of the State in economic affairs. Very soon a dominant set of views emerged on what the government ought to do about future Irish distress, and formed the basis from which the cabinet approached the problem of Irish distress. The following is a not unfair summary of these prevailing Whig views: the State role in alleviating Irish distress ought to be confined to providing employment on public works which, ideally, ought to be of a non-productive nature; the provision of food ought to be left to private enterprise, except in isolated areas where a very limited degree of State intervention seemed unavoidable; the cost of relieving Irish distress should, in the final analysis, fall on Irish shoulders. The tragic pressure of events caused many of these beliefs to be modified or abandoned sooner or later. But too often withdrawal from doctrinal trenches was too grudging and too late to avert the suffering which rigid adherence to mistaken policies had done much to aggravate.

There were three distinct phases in the Whig handling of the Irish famine. During the first phase, covering roughly the second half of 1846, the government placed almost total reliance on an extensive public works programme, with but a limited and reluctantly accepted involvement in the supply of food. At first glance certain similarities with Peel's 'relief package' are obvious. But whereas Peel had had to deal with a partial potato failure which struck late in the season, the failure of 1846–7 was total. Moreover, Trevelyan's obsession with economy and efficiency was now dominating implementation of policy. The wasteful expenditure which, it was believed, had occurred during the previous season was not to be repeated. After Peel's Special Commission wound up its operations in the summer of 1846 the task of acting as 'vigilantes for economy' fell in many cases to a corps of commissariat officers of the army, under the direction of

Sir Randolph Routh. Officers were engaged in the zonal supervision of the activities of relief committees throughout the country. New rules of membership and conduct were drawn up for these committees.

The inadequacy of the retail network dictated that, however disagreeable, the purchase of a limited quantity of Indian meal by the government was unavoidable. But it was decided to limit the operation of food depots to the western half of the country, and even there only when all other sources of supply had failed. Supplies were to be sold at the prices prevailing in the nearest market town. These conditions were to apply even in the exceptional sub-depots on the west coast which were now under the control of commissariat officers. The results of this policy were calamitous. The government was slow in purchasing supplies for the depots and compliance with its litany of conditions meant that it was near Christmas before many of the food depots began to operate effectively. By this time many had already starved in the west, and countless others had contracted fever as the country experienced the worst winter on record.

However, the top priority in the Whig relief programme of 1846 was the provision of employment, not food. Here the new measures differed markedly from Peel's. At Trevelyan's suggestion it was decided to place all public works under the control of a completely reorganised Board of Works. The cost of the schemes was to fall on property owners in the distressed districts. It was assumed that central control would mean greater efficiency, and that local financial responsibility would induce relief committees to limit the numbers they listed as needing employment. These assumptions were soon proved wrong. Proposed schemes now needed the sanction of ratepayers in session, of Board of Works experts and of treasury officials. There were long delays; it was late autumn before the schemes became operative, and they were heavily criticised from the outset. Wages were often not paid on time or in full, works were left unfinished; landholders complained that the land was being neglected as labourers and cottiers flocked to the works in search of money-wage employment. Complaints about the unproductive nature of the works brought minor concessions, allowing for limited activity in fishing and drainage. But the ultimate failure of the public works policy was not a question of this or that detail, but rather that, in a crisis greater than anybody in authority had anticipated the machinery simply could not cope with the numbers needing relief. From 250,000 in October 1846 the total employed on public works climbed to a massive 720,000 in the spring of 1847. The Board of Works chiefs felt equipped to manage about 100,000 at a maximum; but not even the Herculean efforts of their 12,000 strong establishment could supervise effectively the employment of three-quarters of a million people. The government had no option but to alter its policy. It was decided at the end of 1846 to wind up the relief works and to resort to an emergency scheme of direct outdoor relief. This reversal could not become effective overnight, and it was only in the second quarter of 1847 that the phasing out of the relief works became effective.

The model chosen for the direct relief programme was the soup kitchen. This method had already been used in the relief efforts of the Society of Friends and other voluntary relief organisations during the winter of 1846. A special commission was set up to supervise the new scheme. The unit of administration adopted was the poor law union, since poor rates were to supply part of the cost of the new scheme. But unrealistic criteria for deciding who was entitled to relief, unenforceable conditions regarding the actual distribution of food, unforgivable delays in making supplies of meal available at the kitchens; all produced a predictable harvest of deception, recrimination, and hardship. Yet for all that the soup kitchens were operating in virtually every poor law union in the country in the summer of 1847. In August an incredible 3,000,000 people were receiving rations at the soup kitchens daily, the vast majority of them free gratis. To this must be added the numbers receiving relief through the continued charity of individual benefactors and of such societies as the Society of Friends and the British Relief Association.

By the summer of 1847, then, the government had deployed its full resources to ensure that nobody should die of starvation. However, the delay in implementing the new scheme, allied with the severe winter of 1846–7, had resulted in a widespread outbreak of famine, disease and fever. The commendable government plans for dealing with this latter problem were vitiated, as usual, by delays in putting them into operation and by an excess of irritating official directives. A special Board of Health, mistakenly allowed to lapse in August 1846, was reconstructed in early 1847, and its officers were soon co-operating with local committees in establishing temporary fever hospitals. By September 1847 some 26,000 patients were being treated in these hospitals. If this figure seems small compared with the death total from famine disease, it ought to be remembered that the officers of the Board of Health were not to blame for the overcrowding in jails and workhouses, nor could they prevent the mobility or congregation of lice-carrying fever victims in search of work or food. Within its limited competence the Board of Health spared no effort in combating disease.

The soup kitchen scheme was never meant to be more than a temporary emergency operation. On its termination the government decided that the best way of dealing with Irish poverty was by improving the existing poor law machinery. Accordingly, in June 1847 a Poor Law Amendment Act was passed. A separate poor law commission was established for Ireland; the boundaries of the unions were revised and their members increased from 130 to 163, and a paid inspectorate was instituted. The Act contained the key provision that under certain conditions the boards of guardians could grant relief outside the workhouse. This applied not only to the old and disabled, but also to the able-bodied poor, and by mid-1848 over half the unions were providing some 800,000 persons (chiefly engaged in breaking stones) with relief, in the form of food rations, outside the workhouse enclosure. Within the workhouses themselves as many as 930,000 persons received relief at one time or another during 1849.

Figures, however, tell little of the misery endured in the last phase of the Whig famine policy. Penal discipline, overcrowding and bad diet produced appalling conditions in the workhouses. The basic government assumption was that Irish property should pay for Irish poverty. The workhouse system was to milk in rates from the Irish landowners (whom the British public as well as the government saw as the chief villains of the tragedy) the kind of aid to the poor which they would not undertake voluntarily by providing employment or charity. This policy could not be maintained. Some unions were simply too poor to pay for their relief programme; the government was forced to intervene, first by direct loans and later by levying a special rate-in-aid on all rateable property in Ireland to clear the debts of the poorer unions. Many boards of guardians sought in every way to effect economies; after all, they represented the interests of ratepayers, indeed were themselves usually substantial ratepayers. But economies were often achieved at considerable cost in human suffering. Moreover, the liability of landlords for the entire rates on holdings below £4 valuation made them anxious to rid their estates of such expensive holdings. This meant evicting smallholders and demolishing cabins. A further agent of eviction and misery was the infamous 'Gregory Clause' in the 1847 Act, by which anybody with a holding of more than a quarter acre was excluded from relief. Not surprisingly, these measures provoked sporadic rural disorder as landlords, large farmers, rent and rate collectors were intimidated, or worse, by a desperate peasantry. Finally corruption and incompetence characterised the operations in many unions, so that by 1850 the boards of guardians in about a quarter of them had been suspended and their functions transferred to paid officials.

By this time the worst of the famine was over. In 1850 the maximum number receiving poor relief outside the workhouses had fallen to 148,000, less than a fifth of the previous year's total, and this trend was to continue in succeeding years. The debts which the famine left in its wake were considerable. State loans had been advanced at every phase of the relief schemes. The original intention was to recover much of this money in rates of various sorts over a period of years. This hope was soon abandoned, and in the 1853 budget Gladstone, while extending income tax and spirit duties in Ireland, completely remitted the famine debts.

One final word on the enormous amount of relief work undertaken voluntarily. We have already mentioned the exertions of the Society of Friends and of the British Relief Association. Both of these bodies maintained a high level of activity throughout the full duration of the famine, often directing their efforts to those areas where official relief schemes were either slow in starting or defective in operation. Other charitable societies engaged in similar activities, though on a smaller scale. The many serious sins of which the landlord class, taken as a whole, was guilty in the famine period should not obscure the generous exertions of many individual resident landlords, whether as active members of relief committees or as independent dispensers of charity from their own pockets. Clergymen of all denominations were also active in assisting the poor. Unfortunately, a small minority of clergymen, mainly of the Established Church, attempted to make 'religious conversion' a condition in the distribution of food. This distasteful proselytism left a legacy of ill will which lasted long after the event. However, it would be wrong if the excesses of this minority were to prevent the generous sacrifices of the majority of their colleagues from receiving due acknowledgment.

CONCLUSION

Enough has been said to show that to describe official policies during the famine as being genocidal in intention is simply incompatible with the evidence. Admittedly certain treasury reflections do sound disturbingly callous when considered against the background of human misery in which they found expression. Yet Trevelyan's expressed belief that the role of the famine in solving the problem of over-population in Ireland reflected the wishes of 'an all-wise Providence' did not prevent him and his colleagues from working long hours in planning and administering relief measures. The real case against the ministers is not that they acted with evil intent but that they based their policies on false assumptions and that they committed some crucial errors of judgment. The full extent of the potato crop failure of 1846 was seriously under-estimated in official circles.

The long delay in importing emergency food supplies in the
winter of 1846 meant that, in the absence of price control or an
embargo on grain exports, local monopolists and money lenders
were able to hoard supplies and charge extortionate prices. The
exploiters of misery were quick to seize their opportunity. Again,
the 'sacred' dictum that Irish property owners should support
Irish paupers not only ignored the fact that many Irish estates
were already too heavily encumbered with debt to discharge this
duty, but also accepted, by default, the suffering which would
inevitably result from the attempts of ratepayers to keep down
the poor rates.

Finally, the unproductive nature of much of the relief
programme was inexcusable. Had the poor rate been devoted to
schemes aimed at improving the productivity of the land the
land-owners would not perhaps have been quite so
parsimonious. In the same way, when the government did decide
to advance emergency loans the pity was that the capital wasn't
utilised on a productive project, such as railway construction (as
Lord George Bentinck vainly proposed). Instead, the limited
number of productive schemes sanctioned by the government
were so tightly bound by red tape as to severely impair their
effectiveness.

Sheer stupidity has its place in explaining some of these policy
mistakes. But basically they derived from the very process of
decision-making. There were the purely political factors. Russell's
position was difficult; he was a Prime Minister whose party did
not have a majority in Parliament; his advent to office was the
result of a major rupture in the Conservative ranks. Even had
Russell been more decisive by temperament than was the case, he
was unlikely to have been anxious to cause further political
confusion by adopting controversial policies for the relief of Irish
distress. In the event he generally bowed to the conventional
wisdom of the treasury.

It is here, in talking of the prevailing conventional wisdom, that
we come closest to an understanding of the underlying causes of
what seem in retrospect almost inexplicable decisions in policy.
The educated classes of early Victorian Britain shared a solid

body of opinions on what constituted the optimum conditions for economic activity and the proper role of the State in this sphere. By 1846 private enterprise, the inviolability of property rights, free trade, and the laws of supply and demand, had become the dominant economic orthodoxies among the governing classes. There were dissenting voices, but they failed to make an impression where it mattered most — in the corridors of power. The disciples of *laissez faire* ruled the roost. This ideological universe inhabited by the governing classes of early Victorian Britain simply did not contain answers to the problems posed by the Irish potato famine.

Geography was a complicating factor. Whitehall was a long way from Mayo, and the delays involved in getting the bureaucracy of the one to understand and respond to the misery of the other was part of the frustration experienced by administrators at all levels in Ireland. Nor was distance the only problem of communication. Words such as 'farmer' and 'small-holder' simply did not mean the same thing in an Irish context as in Britain. Unfortunately, officials and politicians in London were not always capable of making the necessary conceptual adjustments. Failure of comprehension, however, was not confined to the ministers and Whitehall. Consider some of the alternatives suggested by critics of the government policy. The Repealers, among others, frequently demanded an embargo on food exports. This was understandable; the sight of ships leaving port with grain exports aboard while at home people died of starvation and disease, could not have done other than provoke deep anger. And yet apart from a crucial period in the winter of 1846–7 when imports of Indian meal were slow in arriving, there was no absolute shortage of food in Ireland at any time during the famine. Indeed, during the period 1 September 1846 to 1 July 1847 Ireland imported five times as much grain as she exported. Clearly the problem was not one of food shortage, but of ensuring that those in need had access to existing supplies, or, as Lord Lansdowne's agent put it, 'bringing the food and the people together'.

Achieving this objective proved a difficult, at times impossible, task. Under existing conditions in Ireland, it was the payment of *rents* which separated people from food in the first place. In the absence of a suspension of rents (an unthinkable infraction of property rights) the avoidance, or at least the containment of famine conditions demanded a highly synchronised State intervention in such areas as price control, retail distribution, and the provision of purchase power for the destitute. Even in our own day such synchronised intervention would be difficult to achieve. There can be no denying the stupidity and bureaucratic insensitivity which caused many aspects of the famine policy to fail. But, ultimately, the task of coping with the emergency created by the total failure of the potato crop in the Ireland of 1846 called for resources, as much intellectual as physical, which the Victorian State had simply not yet developed. The real tragedy was, in a sense, more a failure of comprehension than a lack of compassion.

EPILOGUE

The famine has been described as a watershed in Irish political and social history. The society which emerged from behind its dark shadow was, in certain key respects, structurally different from what it had previously been. The society whose dangerous tensions — e.g. the growing numerical imbalance between rich and poor — had been noted by Arthur Young as early as 1776, and which had survived several crises since Waterloo, was shaken to its foundations by the horrors of 1845–50. That grim visitation effected many changes, but none more important than the changes relating to population. A population which had been rising continuously for almost a century fell by over two million in a half-decade. This decline was to continue over the following hundred years. Chronic emigration was one factor in this decline, and it was accompanied on the home front by low marriage and birth rates. Ease of access to subdivided plots had facilitated early marriages in the pre-famine era; but after the clearances and consolidation of 1846–51 landlords and farmers alike were intent on keeping holdings intact. This resulted in the inheriting son's having to postpone his marriage until a late age, or indefinitely. Thus, a major reversal of socio-economic trends was effected within a very short time.

The economic consequences of the famine were quite complex. Clearly the reduction of a country's population by some twenty per cent in a decade had a profound impact on the size and distribution of the labour force and on the potential market for consumer goods. The main casualties of the famine were the labourers and smaller farmers. As the number of larger farms increased livestock farming began to play an increasingly important role in the agricultural economy. From 1,863,116 in 1841 numbers jumped to 2,967,461 a decade later. Livestock exports increased, encouraged by attractive prices in Britain and by reduced transport time (due to the railways). The increase in livestock numbers was largely on farms over fifteen acres in size. 'The very small tillage farm', as Dr Green has written, 'was already ceasing to be typical'; the bigger family farm, concentrating more on cattle, was becoming more common.

The aftermath of the famine brought changes of ownership as well as structure in Irish agriculture. The crippling burden of poor rates finally broke the backs of many already heavily-encumbered landlords. Even had they been willing, these bankrupts were incapable of making the much-needed investments in Irish land. The Government was aware of this situation, but, being unwilling to take steps to encourage investment 'from below' (by conceding some form of tenant-right), it had no option but to facilitate a change of ownership. Accordingly, by an act of 1849, an 'encumbered estates' court was established to facilitate the transfer of debt-ridden estates from bankrupt to solvent owners. The court had powers to pay creditors out of the purchase price, and to guarantee an indefeasible title to the new owner. By thus creating 'free trade' in the sale of land the Government hoped that English and Scots capitalists would buy Irish estates, become improving landlords, and invest in Irish agriculture. This did not happen; and although the court disposed of over 3,000 estates in ten years, the new owners were, for the most part, totally uninterested in becoming 'improving landlords'. They were largely native gombeen men out to make high profits. The famine itself, combined with the unloading on to the market of a large number of estates at one time, caused a downward movement in land prices. The speculators moved in, snapped up the estates, and thereafter their chief concern was with maximising rents. The new men adopted the old vices, and made them worse.

'Landlordism' was not the only element of the pre-famine rural economy to survive. Indeed, for all the new emphasis on livestock, tillage showed considerable resilience in the early 1850s and it was not until the poor harvests of the early sixties that the increasingly diminishing importance of tillage relative to grazing became a marked feature of Irish agriculture. Furthermore, in certain areas along the west coast the old pattern of subsistence farming on uneconomic small-holdings persisted long after the famine. The causes of chronic poverty survived here; only the numbers of the poor declined. The problems of these areas were to challenge the ingenuity of Balfour's 'congested districts board' in the 1890s; many of them still await solutions.

It is rather more difficult to measure the impact of the famine on some of the other social and economic developments which took place in the decades after 1850. It is true that the famine contributed to changing popular attitudes to diet; and that remittances from emigrants were an important factor in consumer demands. But the famine relief schemes were mostly short-term and unproductive; the few exceptions to this were limited in scope and their direct impact on the economy as a whole of minor significance. In fact it was the railway, almost entirely an affair of private enterprise, which was probably the main agent of change in the decades after 1850. By reducing transport time and costs, absorbing hitherto remote areas into a single market economy, providing much-coveted jobs in construction and administration, the railway brought significant changes to the patterns of Irish life. As the railway penetrated the countryside, bringing with it a wide range of consumer goods, fashions in diet and dress soon altered. Less fortunately, perhaps, the extension of the railway network caused the final collapse of many local industries before the invasion of cheaper imported or Dublin-made goods. The famine years were boom years in railway construction in Ireland. But, despite certain points of interaction (e.g. land prices), the relation between the two events was coincidental, not one of cause and effect. The extension of the railway was very much an independent determinant of social change in post-famine Ireland.

One further feature of the pre-famine economy which the famine did little to alter was the growth of a distinctive regional economy, firmly rooted in a strong industrial base, in Belfast and its hinterland. As we have seen, the potato crop was not as vital to the economy of this area as it was in other parts of the country. Accordingly, its failure in the 1840s did not produce an economic crisis in the north-east. This is not to suggest that the area was unaffected by the famine. Disease-ridden migrants from the hardest-hit areas of the province crowded into Belfast, where congested living conditions helped the spread of disease. But this was essentially a public health emergency, not an economic crisis. Given time, medical aid, and administrative effort, a public health emergency could be brought under control; and it was. But the crucial economic fact was the continued expansion of manufacturing industry in the Belfast area. It was this fact which ensured that the Belfast region, unlike most of the country, did not have a problem of chronic unemployment. It was due to this expansion that the north-east entered the second half of the century an expanding industrialised enclave in a country with an otherwise underdeveloped economy. The rise of the great ship-building industry was yet some years in the future, but already by the mid-century the Belfast region had a distinctive economic identity all its own.

Finally, let us consider the psychological impact of the famine on the Irish people; on the way they looked at life in general, and at politics in particular. The harrowing events of the famine years left those who survived them with memories which haunted them for the rest of their lives. The decimation of entire communities was such a traumatic experience that the surviving communities carried its psychological scars for generations. Many old customs and pastimes of the countryside died virtually overnight, and a state of almost chronic melancholia settled on the surviving fragments of many shattered communities. This mood of depression was intensified by the pattern of steady emigration which continued to drain Irish society of many of its most enterprising members for many decades after the famine. Indeed the change in popular attitudes to emigration was one of the most significant legacies of the famine. It is true, of course, that in the decades after Waterloo the idea of large-scale emigration was often advanced as the panacea for Ireland's economic problems, and these years (particularly the eighteen-thirties) did witness an increase in the numbers leaving the country. But it is difficult to quarrel with Professor McDonagh's verdict that 'the potato blights of 1845–9 caused a *volte face* in the general attitude to emigration'. Reluctant parting from home was transformed by the famine into an exodus of mass panic from a stricken land. After the crisis had passed, emigration had become an accepted fact of life in Ireland. The letter home contained glowing accounts of the opportunities in Boston or Philadelphia; it also contained the fare which would enable the next member of the family 'to try and seek his fortune in far Amerikay'. A pattern had been established which was to endure for a very long time.

It would scarcely be possible to exaggerate the influence of the famine on the political history of modern Ireland. By 1848 the Repeal movement of O'Connell was as dead as its leader; its last echoes drowned in the cries of a starving peasantry. The Young Irelanders had made their separatist gesture; but it had been no more than that. In the Ireland of 1846–9 political activity for a strictly constitutional objective, however radical, seemed somehow irrelevant. The entire social system was in the grip of a crisis, and it was inevitable that social questions should push their way to the centre of the political stage. Lalor produced his new analysis. Yet few of his contemporaries were listening, and it was left to Davitt in a later generation to take his message to heart. A more immediate consequence of this new emphasis on the social question was the growth in the late forties and early fifties of a movement demanding legal recognition for some form of tenant-right. The politics of the eighteen-fifties, however, did not bring tenant-right; instead the cumulative effects of sectarianism, political opportunism and blatant corruption reduced popular respect for constitutional politics to an all-time low by the end of the decade. The time was then ripe for the emergence of an idealistic nationalist movement, austerely dedicated to the independence of Ireland. And in the secret revolutionary movement which assumed this role in the early sixties the deep political consequences of the famine at last became fully apparent. The memory of the famine was a main source of that hatred of English rule which was a canon of the Fenian faith. Mitchel's view of the famine, as a crime committed by the British Government against the Irish people, was shared by thousands who had never read a line of his works. For these, the abiding memory was of food leaving the country while people starved; and they placed the guilt for this on the Government which had allowed it to happen — a British Government. Most important of all, thousands who held this view were now settled on the far side of the Atlantic. Patterns of settlement, and the anti-Irish prejudices encountered on arrival, ensured the survival of group-consciousness and national sentiment among these immigrants. The scenes of desolation from which they had fled and the sufferings endured on the dangerous voyage, combined to leave them with a deep-seated hatred of that which they identified as the root of all Irish misfortunes — British misrule in Ireland. To play their part in ending this misrule became the burning political passion of many of these exiles. In all future phases of the struggle for independence the support, mainly financial and propagandist, of the Irish in America was of crucial importance to those involved on the home front. The struggle was destined to be a protracted and, at times, frustrating one. But the sons and grandsons of the famine exiles were determined to see it through to the end. Only then would Tone's mission, to break the connection with England, be finally accomplished. Only then could the accusing ghost of 'black '47' be finally laid.

REVISED BIBLIOGRAPHY (1990)

This highly selective reading list is intended as no more than an indication of the principal works in which the reader may expect to find a more detailed and extensive consideration of the themes and issues raised in this volume. We have tried, in particular, to give a fair sample of the extraordinarily rich body of historical writing on the pre-Famine period which has been published during the past twenty years or so. While we adhere to the convention of relating titles to chapters we begin with a note on general surveys of Irish history and of Irish historiography which relate to the pre-Famine period. Unless otherwise stated, the place of publication is London.

— In the Royal Irish Academy's *New History of Ireland* project, volume IV (*Eighteenth Century Ireland 1691–1800*, edited by T.W. Moody and W.E. Vaughan) and volume V (*Ireland under the Union, 1: 1801–70*, edited by W.E. Vaughan) are now available (Oxford 1986 and 1989) and offer a detailed narrative and a valuable work of reference. Ancillary volumes in the NHI project containing invaluable data are W.E. Vaughan and A.J. Fitzpatrick (eds), *Irish Historical Statistics: Population 1821–1971* (Dublin 1978), and B.M. Walker (ed.), *Parliamentary Election Results in Ireland, 1801–1922* (Dublin 1978). Among general surveys, R.F. Foster's *Modern Ireland 1600–1972* (1988) is unfailingly stimulating, while K.T. Hoppen's more concise *Ireland Since 1800: Conflict and Conformity* (1989) is especially strong on changing social and economic conditions. Liam de Paor, *The Peoples of Ireland* (1986) is stylish, lucid and perceptive. Donal McCartney's *The Dawning of Democracy: Ireland 1800–1870* (Dublin 1987) is sensible and balanced, and R.B. McDowell's *Public Opinion and Government Policy in Ireland, 1801–1846* (1952), though dated, remains useful and eminently readable. Works offering original but different interpretations of the modern period of Irish history are Oliver MacDonagh, *Ireland: The Union and its Aftermath* (1977) and *States of Mind: A Study of Anglo-Irish Conflict 1780–1980* (1983), and Patrick O'Farrell, *Ireland's English Question: Anglo-Irish Relations 1534–1970* (1971) and *England and Ireland Since 1800* (1975). Several works of quality examine different aspects of Irish political culture over long periods: Tom Garvin, *The Evolution of Irish Nationalist Politics* (Dublin

1981); D.G. Boyce, *Nationalism in Ireland* (1982); and J. Prager, *Building Democracy in Ireland: Political Order and Cultural Integration in a Newly Independent Nation* (Cambridge 1986).

— T.W. Moody (ed.), *Irish Historiography 1936–70* (Dublin 1971) and J. Lee (ed.), *Irish Historiography 1970–79* (Cork 1981) may be supplemented by the annual bibliographies published by relevant Irish scholarly journals.

Chapter 1

— On the later eighteenth century see R.B. McDowell's rather lengthy *Ireland in the Age of Imperialism and Revolution 1760–1801* (Oxford 1979) and the concluding sections of David Dickson's *New Beginnings: Irish History 1660–1800* (Dublin 1987). Edith M. Johnston, *Great Britain and Ireland, 1760–1800: A study in political administration* (Edinburgh 1963) and the more general *Ireland in the Eighteenth Century* (Dublin 1974) are strong on formal political and administrative history. M.R. O'Connell's *Irish Politics and Social Conflict in the Age of the American Revolution* (Philadelphia 1965) remains useful, but see also Gerard O'Brien, *Anglo-Irish Politics in the Age of Grattan and Pitt* (Dublin 1987). David N. Doyle, *Ireland, Irishmen and Revolutionary America, 1760–1820* (Dublin 1981) and Owen Dudley Edwards, 'The Impact of the American Revolution in Ireland' in R.R. Palmer (ed.), *The Impact of the American Revolution Abroad* (Washington 1976) are both excellent in their different ways. There are essays of outstanding quality in T. Bartlett and D. Hayton (eds), *Penal Era and Golden Age: Essays in Irish History 1690–1800* (Antrim 1979). The interplay between socio-economic change, political ideas, sectarian tension, political movements and popular protest has been a growth area in recent years, and this is reflected in such collections as S. Clark and J. Donnelly, Jr (eds), *Irish Peasants: Violence and Political Unrest 1780–1914* (Manchester 1983); P.J. Corish (ed.), *Radicals, Rebels and Establishments: Historical Studies xv* (Belfast 1985); and C.H.E. Philpin (ed.), *Nationalism and Popular Protest in Ireland* (Cambridge 1987), all of which include detailed references for further reading. Writings on the convulsion of the 1790s are surveyed by J.S. Donnelly, Jr, in *Irish Economic and Social History* xi (1984), while a conventional study of Orangeism is provided by H. Senior, *Orangeism in Ireland and Britain, 1795–1836* (1966). Marianne Elliott's two major works, *Partners in Revolution: The United Irishmen and France* (New Haven 1982) and *Wolfe Tone* (New Haven 1989) are now the essential starting points for the study of the United Irishmen in the context of their times; but see, also, Nancy J. Curtin, 'The Transformation of the Society of United Irishmen into a Mass-Based Revolutionary

Organisation 1794–96', in *Irish Historical Studies*, vol. xxiv. F. Pakenham, *The Year of Liberty, The Great Irish Rebellion of 1798* (1969) is an absorbing narrative. G.C. Bolton, *The Passing of the Irish Act of Union* (Oxford 1966) is the standard account, but A.P.W. Malcomson, *John Foster: The Politics of the Anglo-Irish Ascendancy* (Oxford 1978) is much more than a classic political biography. A.T.Q. Stewart's *The Narrow Ground: Aspects of Ulster 1609–1969* (1977) is sensitive and sympathetic, as is his essay 'A Stable, Unseen, Power: Dr William Drennan and the Origins of the United Irishmen' in John Bossy (ed.), *Essays Presented to Michael Roberts* (Belfast 1976).

— On economic developments, L.M. Cullen's *An Economic History of Ireland since 1660* (1972), *Anglo-Irish Trade 1660–1800* (Manchester 1968), and (edited) *Formation of the Irish Economy* (Cork 1969) provide the background to the pre-Famine economy. The growth in research in this area is illustrated by distinguished essays in the following collections: L.M. Cullen and T.C. Smout (eds), *Comparative Aspects of Irish and Scottish Social and Economic History, 1600–1900* (Edinburgh 1977); L.M. Cullen and F. Furet (eds), *Ireland and France, 11th–20th Centuries* (Paris 1980); L.M. Cullen and P. Butel, *Negoce et Industrie en France et en Irlande aux xviii^e et xix^e Siecles.* T.M. Devine and David Dickson (eds), *Ireland and Scotland, 1600–1850* (Edinburgh 1983); R. Mitchison and P. Roebuck (eds), *Economy and Society in Scotland and Ireland, 1500–1939* (Edinburgh 1987); J.M. Goldstrom and L.A. Clarkson (eds), *Irish Population, Economy and Society: Essays in Honour of the late K.H. Connell* (Oxford 1981). K.H. Connell, *The Population of Ireland 1750–1845* (1950) was the pioneering work, but it has been greatly modified by more recent research, notably, L.M. Cullen, 'Irish History without the Potato' in *Past and Present*, 40 (1968); J. Mokyr, 'Irish History with the Potato' in *Irish Economic and Social History*, viii (1981); S. Daultrey, D. Dickson and C. Ó Gráda, 'Hearth Tax, Household Size and Irish Population Change 1672–1821' in *Proceedings of the Royal Irish Academy*, vol. lxxxii (1982); J. Mokyr and C. Ó Gráda, 'New Developments in Irish Population History, 1700–1850' in *Economic History Review*, xxxvii (1984).

Chapter 2

— Two major projects are now completed on Daniel O'Connell: R.M. O'Connell (ed.), *The Correspondence of Daniel O'Connell*, 8 vols. (Dublin 1972–80), and Oliver MacDonagh's two-volume biography, *The Hereditary Bondsman 1775–1829* (1988) and *The Emancipationist: Daniel O'Connell 1830–47* (1989). A variety of perspectives are to be found in

K.B. Nowlan and M.R. O'Connell (eds), *Daniel O'Connell: Portrait of a Radical* (Belfast 1984) and Donal McCartney (ed.), *The World of Daniel O'Connell* (Dublin 1980), while Seán Ó Faoláin, *King of the Beggars* (Dublin 1970 edition) will always engage the historical imagination in a specially rewarding way. On O'Connell in folklore see Ríonach Uí Ógáin, *An Rí gan Choróin* (B.Á.C. 1984). On the Emancipation campaign, Fergus O'Ferrall, *Catholic Emancipation: Daniel O'Connell and the Birth of Irish Democracy 1820–30* (Dublin 1985) is the standard work, though J.A. Reynolds, *The Catholic Emancipation Crisis in Ireland, 1823–29* (New Haven 1954) is still worth reading. For the British context see G.I.T. Machin, *The Catholic Question in English Politics, 1820–30* (Oxford 1964), while an important facet of the politics of Emancipation is covered in Oliver MacDonagh, 'The Politicization of the Irish Catholic Bishops, 1800–1850' in *Historical Journal*, xviii (1975). The politicisation of sections of the Protestant community is considered by Ian D'Alton, *Protestant Society and Politics in Cork, 1812–1844* (Cork 1980) and by J. Hill, 'Popery and Protestantism, Civil and Religious Liberty: The Disputed Lessons of Irish History 1690–1812', *Past and Present*, no. 118 (1988). See also Peter Jupp, 'Irish Parliamentary Elections and the Influence of the Catholic Vote, 1801–20', *Historical Journal*, x (1967). On ecclesiastical history and religious culture in general, there has been a bountiful crop of significant studies in recent decades; see, in particular P. J. Corish, *The Irish Catholic Experience: A Historical Survey* (Dublin 1985); Seán J. Connolly, *Priests and People in pre-Famine Ireland 1780–1845* (Dublin 1982) and 'Catholicism in Ulster, 1800–1850' in P. Roebuck (ed.), *Plantation to Partition: Essays in Ulster History in Honour of J.L. McCraken* (Belfast 1981); Kevin Whelan, The Regional Impact of Irish Catholicism 1700–1850', in William J. Smyth and Kevin Whelan (eds), *Common Ground: Essays presented to T. Jones Hughes* (Cork 1988); D.H. Akenson *The Church of Ireland: Ecclesiastical Reform and Revolution 1800–1885* (New Haven 1971); Desmond Bowen, *The Protestant Crusade in Ireland 1800–70* (Dublin 1978); D.N. Hempton, 'The Methodist Crusade in Ireland 1795–1845', *Irish Historical Studies*, xxii (1980), and 'Methodism in Irish Society, 1770–1830', *Transactions of the Royal Historical Society*, 5th series, xxxvi (1986); Peter Brooke, *Ulster Presbyterianism: The Historical Perspective 1610–1970* (Dublin 1987); R.F. Holmes, *Henry Cooke* (Belfast 1981) and 'Ulster Presbyterianism and Irish Nationalism' in S. Mews (ed.), *Religion and National Identity: Studies in Church History* (Oxford 1982); David Miller, 'Presbyterianism and "Modernization" in Ulster', *Past and Present*, no. 80 (1978).

Chapter 3

— R.B. McDowell, *The Irish Administration 1801–1914* (1964) is the basic
  work of reference. A close-up of the post-Union administration in
  action is provided by Norman Gash, *Mr Secretary Peel* (1961); see also
  Oliver MacDonagh, *The Inspector General: Sir Jeremiah Fitzpatrick and
  Social Reform, 1783–1802* (1981). R. Barry O'Brien, *Thomas Drummond,
  Under-Secretary in Ireland 1835–40: Life and Work* (1889) and M.A.G. Ó
  Tuathaigh, *Thomas Drummond and the Government of Ireland 1835–41*
  (Dublin 1977) examine the career of the most able and popular of the
  pre-Famine Castle officials. The influence of economic theorists on
  state activity in Ireland is well treated in R.D.C. Black, *Economic
  Thought and the Irish Question 1817–70* (Cambridge 1960) and in Antoin
  E. Murphy (ed.), *Economists and the Irish Economy* (Dublin 1984). See
  also D.H. Akenson, *A Protestant in Purgatory: Richard Whately:
  Archbishop of Dublin* (Hamden, Connecticut 1981). Gerard O'Brien has
  examined the establishment of the Irish Poor Law in 'The New Poor
  Law in Pre-Famine Ireland: A Case History', *Irish Economic and Social
  History*, XII (1985); and for the general problems of poverty, see
  Timothy P. O'Neill, 'Poverty in Ireland 1815–45', *Folklife*, XI (1973). On
  law and order, see G. Broeker, *Rural Disorder and Police Reform in
  Ireland 1812–36* (1970), and Stanley H. Palmer, *Police and Protest in
  England and Ireland 1780–1850* (Cambridge 1988).

— A delightful study in intellectual as well as administrative history is J.H.
  Andrews, *A Paper Landscape: The Ordnance Survey in Nineteenth-
  Century Ireland* (Oxford 1975).

— On education developments, see D.H. Akenson. *The Irish Education
  Experiment* (1969); Patrick J. Corish (ed.) *A History of Irish Catholicism*,
  vol. v, no. 6 (Dublin 1971), and Mary E. Daly, 'The Development of the
  National School System, 1831–40', in A. Cosgrove and D. McCartney
  (eds), *Studies in Irish History presented to R. Dudley Edwards* (Dublin
  1979).

Chapter 4

— In addition to the works on economic history already cited under
  chapter 1, Mary E. Daly's *Social and Economic History of Ireland since
  1800* (Dublin 1981) is an admirable survey, to be complemented by the
  relevant chapters in L. Kennedy and P. Ollerenshaw (eds), *An Economic
  History of Ulster, 1820–1940* (Manchester 1985). Cormac Ó Gráda, *Éire
  Roimh an nGorta* (B.Á.C. 1985) is concise and perceptive, and Joel
  Mokyr, *Why Ireland Starved: A Quantitative and Analytical History of
  the Irish Economy 1800–1850* (1983) is methodologically innovative.
  E.R.R. Green, *The Lagan Valley 1800–1850* (1949) remains useful and so

does P. Lynch and J. Vaizey, *Guinness's Brewery in the Irish Economy, 1759–1876* (1960) — but see J. Lee, The Dual Economy in Ireland 1800–1850' in T.D. Williams (ed.), *Historical Studies*, VIII (1971).

— There has been an explosion of high-quality work on agricultural history and pre-Famine rural society. Raymond Crotty, *Irish Agricultural Production: Its Volume and Structure* (Cork 1966) still deserves recognition for its originality, though J. Lee's review of it in *The Agricultural History Review* vol. 17 (1969) should also be read. American scholars have made a major contribution to this field — see, for example, James S. Donnelly, Jr, *The Land and People of Nineteenth-Century Cork* (1975) and Kevin O'Neill, *Family and Farm in pre-Famine Ireland: The Parish of Killashandra* (Madison, Wisconsin 1984). An excellent study of a landed estate is W.A. Maguire's *The Downshire Estates in Ireland 1801–1845* (Oxford 1972); see also L. Proudfoot, 'The Management of a Great Estate: Patronage, Income and Expenditure on the Duke of Devonshire's Irish Property c. 1816 to 1891', *Irish Economic and Social History*, XIII (1986); and William Greig, *General Report on the Gosford Estates in County Armagh 1821* (*PRONI*, Belfast 1976). On urban development see D. Harkness and Mary O'Dowd (eds), *The Town in Ireland* (Belfast 1981); R.A. Butlin (ed.), *The Development of the Irish Town* (1977); J.C. Beckett and R.E. Glasscock (eds), *Belfast: The Origin and Growth of an Industrial City* (1967); M. Craig, *Dublin 1660–1860* (Dublin 1969); Patrick J. O'Connor, *Exploring Limerick's Past: An Historical Geography of Urban Development in County and City* (Newcastle West 1987). G.L. Barrow, *The Emergence of the Irish Banking System 1820–45* (Dublin 1975) is solid institutional history. K.B. Nowlan (ed.), *Travel and Transport in Ireland* (Dublin 1973); R.B. McDowell (ed.) *Social Life in Ireland, 1800–45* (Dublin 1957); and two series of essays entitled *Ulster Since 1800* edited by T.W. Moody and J.C. Beckett (1955, 1957) all contain essays of interest, but David Thomson (ed.) with Moyra McGusty, *The Irish Journals of Elizabeth Smith 1840–50* (Oxford 1980) provides an absorbing personal perspective.

— T.W. Freeman, *Pre-Famine Ireland: A study in historical geography* (1957) was a pioneering work, and the significant contribution of historical geographers in recent decades to the study of the Irish past is well advertised in the following works: William Nolan, *Fassadinin: Land Settlement and Society in Southeast Ireland 1600–1850*; William J. Smyth and Kevin Whelan, *Common Ground: Essays on the Historical Geography of Ireland* (Cork 1988); W. Nolan and T.G. McGrath, *Tipperary: History and Society* (Dublin 1985); K. Whelan and W. Nolan (eds), *Wexford: History and Society* (Dublin 1987); and Patrick O'Flanagan, Paul

Ferguson and Kevin Whelan (eds), *Rural Ireland 1600–1900: Modernisation and Change* (Cork 1987).

— On language change and literacy, see B. Ó Cuív (ed.), *A View of the Irish Language* (Dublin 1969); Victor C. Durkacz, *The Decline of the Celtic Languages* (Edinburgh 1983) and the relevant chapters in L.M. Cullen, *The Emergence of Modern Ireland, 1600–1900* (1981).

— The social history of leisure awaits systematic research, but Liam Ó Caithnia, *Scéal na hlomána* and *Báirí Cos in Éirinn* (Baile Átha Cliath 1980, 1984) have been unjustly neglected.

— Women's history for this period remains an untilled field, but see Donnchadh Ó Corráin and Margaret MacCurtain (eds), *Women in Irish Society: The Historical Dimension* (Dublin 1978). Emigration has been a major growth area of recent scholarship. The earlier works of W.F. Adams, *Ireland and Irish Emigration to the New World from 1815 to the Famine* (New Haven 1932) and J.E. Handley, *The Irish in Scotland, 1790–1845* (Cork 1943) now stand alongside a major corpus of recent publications: Kerby A. Miller, *Emigrants and Exiles* (Oxford 1985); Roger Swift and Sheridan Gilley (eds), *The Irish in the Victorian City* (1985); Patrick O'Farrell, *The Irish in Australia* (New South Wales 1987); David Noel Doyle and Owen Dudley Edwards (eds), *America and Ireland 1776–1976* (Westport, Connecticut 1980); Donald A. Akenson, *The Irish in Ontario* (Montreal 1984); C. Ó Gráda, 'Across the Briny Ocean: Some Thoughts on Irish Emigration to America, 1800–1850' in Devine and Dickson (eds), *Ireland and Scotland 1600–1850* (Edinburgh 1983).

— David Fitzpatrick, *Irish Emigration 1801–1921* (Dundalk 1984) is a lively pamphlet containing a useful bibliography, while David Noel Doyle, 'The Regional Bibliography of Irish America 1800–1930' in *Irish Historical Studies*, XXIII (1983), and 'The Irish in Australia and the United States: Some Comparisons, 1800–1939', *Irish Economic and Social History*, XVI (1989) are both wide-ranging and discursive.

Chapter 5

— We have already cited several studies of O'Connell (see under chapter 2). The best study of O'Connell the political tactician and of the context in which he operated is A. Mac Intyre, *The Liberator: Daniel O'Connell and the Irish Party, 1830–47* (1965); but O. MacDonagh's essay in Brian Farrell (ed.), *The Irish Parliamentary Tradition* (Dublin 1973) is an admirably concise and assured assessment. K.B. Nowlan, *The Politics of Repeal* (1965) remains the standard work on the subject, but Donal Kerr, *Peel, Priests and Politics: Sir Robert Peel's Administration and the Roman Catholic Church in Ireland, 1841–1846* (Oxford 1982) is also required reading on Peel's Irish policy. J.F. Broderick's *The Holy See and the Irish*

Movement for the Repeal of the Union with England 1829–49 (Rome 1951) remains useful, while Michael Hurst, *Maria Edgeworth and the Public Scene* (1969) is a provocative study of 'liberal-colonial' ascendancy attitudes during the turmoil of O'Connellite popular politics. On the context of parliamentary politics K.T. Hoppen, *Elections, Politics, and Society in Ireland 1832–1885* (Oxford 1984) is the definitive work.

— On the Young Irelanders, R. Davis, *The Young Ireland Movement* (Dublin 1987) is the most recent synthesis, though Boyce's *Nationalism in Ireland* (1982) has much to offer on political ideas. For opposition to Repeal, see Jacqueline Hill, 'The Protestant Response to Repeal: The Case of the Dublin Working Class', in F.S.L. Lyons and R.A.J. Hawkins (eds), *Ireland under the Union: Varieties of Tension: Essays in Honour of T.W. Moody* (Oxford 1980). Older works which remain essential reading include Charles Gavan Duffy, *Young Ireland: a fragment of Irish history, 1840–45*, 2 vols (revised edition 1896); T.W. Moody, *Thomas Davis 1814–45* (Dublin 1945); L. Fogarty (ed.), *James Fintan Lalor: patriot and political essayist* (Dublin 1947).

Chapter 6

— The definitive work on the Famine remains T.D. Williams and R.D. Edwards (eds), *The Great Famine* (Dublin 1956); but Mary Daly's *The Famine in Ireland* (Dublin 1986) offers a concise over-view of more recent scholarship. Specific aspects of the Famine and its impact are discussed in: J.M. Goldstrom, 'Irish Agriculture and the Great Famine' in the volume of essays edited by J.M. Golstrom *et al* in honour of K.H. Connell (see under chapter 1); K.H. Connell, *Irish Peasant Society: Four Historical Essays* (Oxford 1968); D.W. Miller, 'Irish Catholicism and the Great Famine', *Journal of Social History*, IX (1975). Joel Mokyr, *Why Ireland Starved* (see under chapter 4) raises fundamental questions on the Famine itself, but *Irish Economic and Social History*, XI (1984) contains important reviews of Mokyr's work by Peter Solar and Liam Kennedy. The wider significance of the Famine for the more long-term developments of the Irish economy is discussed with characteristic originality by Cormac Ó Gráda in his richly rewarding *Ireland before and after the Famine: Explorations in Economic History 1800–1925* (Manchester 1988).

— Finally, academic interest has been growing in recent decades in different aspect of mentality, in popular attitudes towards politics and other aspects of life, and in the rich but problematic value of 'literary' texts as historical sources. The following works may serve to whet the appetite of the interested reader:

G.D. Zimmermann, *Irish Political Street Ballads and Rebel Songs,*

1780–1900 (Geneva 1966); O. MacDonagh, *The Nineteenth-Century Novel and Irish Social History: Some Aspects* (Dublin 1970); Tom Dunne, *Maria Edgeworth and the Colonial Mind* (Dublin 1984); W.J. McCormack, *Ascendancy and Tradition in Anglo-Irish literary History from 1789 to 1939* (Oxford 1985); Seamus Deane, *Celtic Revivals: Essays in Modern Irish Literature 1780–1980* (1985); Tom Dunne, 'The Morbid Anatomy of Anglo-Ireland: New Approaches in Literary History', *Irish Economic and Social History*, xiv (1987); J.R.R. Adams, *The Printed Word and the Common Man: Popular Culture in Ulster 1700–1900* (Belfast 1987); D.H. Akenson and W.H. Crawford (eds) *Local Poets and Social History: James Orr, Bard of Ballycarry* (Belfast 1977); Breandán Ó Buachalla, *I mBéal Feirste Cois Cuain* (Baile Átha Cliath 1968); Breandán Ó Madagáin, *An Dialann Dúlra* (Baile Átha Cliath 1978); Breandán Ó Conchuir, *Scríobhaithe Chorcaí 1700–1850* (Baile Átha Cliath 1982).

GLOSSARY

béaloideas	oral tradition, folklore
poitín	illegally-distilled Irish whiskey
rinnce-fada	the long dance, often danced at cross-roads
seanchas	traditional lore
fáistiní	prophecies
tithe	in simple terms, meant one-tenth of the yearly increase in produce, and therefore in the profits, of the land

TRANSLATIONS OF VERSE EXTRACTS

1. But our mayor didn't come to us at the break of day;
   And we ourselves were not properly organised;
   But, rather, like a herd of cattle without a drover,
   On the sunny slopes of Sliabh na mBan.

2. I exhort everybody, don't leave yourselves open to insult,
   I will sing your praises always, if you but pay the Catholic
      rent;
   Sure, a farthing a week doesn't amount to much in a month,
   And let ye not run the risk of shame or scandal.

3. Even though many people who do not fear justice,
   Believe that there is no help or protection available to them;
   Still, the leader will come from France without delay,
   And he'll take the English down a peg or two — that's Bony.

4. 'Tis but a fraction of the rent, and it will free the land;
   There wont be any demands made on you for tithes, as
      heretofore;
   You will have right and just law throughout the land,
   There's no fear of us from now on, so long as O'Connell is
      alive.

INDEX